Premodern Faith in a Postmodern Culture

Premodern Faith in a Postmodern Culture

A Contemporary Theology of the Trinity

Peter Drilling

ROWMAN & LITTLEFIELD PUBLISHERS, INC.
Lanham • Boulder • New York • Toronto • Oxford

ROWMAN & LITTLEFIELD PUBLISHERS, INC.

Published in the United States of America
by Rowman & Littlefield Publishers, Inc.
A wholly owned subsidiary of The Rowman & Littlefield Publishing Group, Inc.
4501 Forbes Boulevard, Suite 200, Lanham, Maryland 20706
www.rowmanlittlefield.com

PO Box 317, Oxford
OX2 9RU, UK

British Library Cataloguing in Publication Information Available

Library of Congress Cataloging-in-Publication Data

Drilling, Peter, 1942–
  Premodern faith in a postmodern culture : a contemporary theology of the
Trinity / Peter Drilling.
    p. cm.
  Includes bibliographical references and index.
  ISBN-13: 978-0-7425-5152-7 (cloth : alk. paper)
  ISBN-10: 0-7425-5152-0 (cloth : alk. paper)
  ISBN-13: 978-0-7425-5153-4 (pbk. : alk. paper)
  ISBN-10: 0-7425-5153-9 (pbk. : alk. paper)
  1. Trinity—History of doctrines. 2. God—History of doctrines. I. Title.
BT111.3.D75 2006
231'.044—dc22   2006005767

Printed in the United States of America

♾™ The paper used in this publication meets the minimum requirements of
American National Standard for Information Sciences—Permanence of Paper
for Printed Library Materials, ANSI/NISO Z39.48-1992.

Contents

Preface

In the foreword to the English-language edition of Jean-Luc Marion's *God without Being*, David Tracy contrasts the theological strategy which attempts in various ways to correlate "reason" and "revelation" with the strategy which rejects the possibility of such correlation.[1] The latter strategy is thought by some to be exemplified by St. Paul, who claims that God has "made foolish the wisdom of the world" (I Cor 1:20).[2] But Paul and his Lord can be invoked in favor of the former strategy, too, since both used their minds to reflect upon the divine self-communication within the world in which they found themselves. Thus, Paul claims in his Letter to the Romans that God can be known from a careful observation of nature (Rom 1:20).

The present work is an effort to demonstrate how the divine self-communication is received in the minds and hearts of Christians who believe that God is the Three-in-One. To this extent the theological strategy correlates reason and revelation. It is a strategy which arises from religious faith that God is self-revelatory and that this self-revelation is an utterly gracious gift of the One who absolutely transcends the human capacity to know and love, but who chooses to communicate the divine self with human beings. Within the acceptance of revelation, however, is the acknowledgment of creation, including creation of human reason, as a gift of the transcendent God. The ability of human persons to think about God and to love the divine Persons, while enabled by the gift of divine grace, is not divorced from humans' ability to think about and to love other realities. God communicates with the whole human person. God invites the whole person to respond to divine self-revelation. Thus, religious faith invites the use of reason.

I owe my confident conviction about the possible correlation of faith and reason to Bernard Lonergan's studies on human intentionality and theological method. Throughout the pages that follow I often direct the reader to Lonergan's books and essays. Beyond specific references, however, his influence upon both the structure of this effort and many of the particular positions proposed appears over and over again. With gratitude, I acknowledge Bernard Lonergan as my mentor. How he would evaluate my efforts in the pages that follow is another matter entirely.

Thinking about God has its peculiarities, but it is still human thinking. One way to sort out the distinction is in terms of models based upon different applications of human consciousness. In his *Method in Theology*, Lonergan distinguishes various ways in which the process of human thinking operates.[3] Thinking in the manner of prayer and theology differs in several respects from the way one thinks when operating out of common sense, or investigating in an area of natural science, or formulating a philosophical theory. It behooves one to take the difference into account to avoid unnecessary and unfortunate confusion.

From the perspective of the differentiation of consciousness noted by Lonergan, it is evident that, over the centuries, the tension between reason and revelation has been misconceived. Creation and redemption are both gracious initiatives of the triune God. Believers who seek to be faithful disciples of Jesus have nothing to fear from a study of the psychological genesis of their faith in God or of its development (and aberrations) under the influence of quite particular cultural contexts, some influenced by common sense, some by philosophical theory, some by cognitional psychology, some by hard science, some by artistic sensitivity, and so on. It is an activity of reason to examine the series of human acts by which one comes to faith and articulates that faith in beliefs and understanding. It is an activity of reason to probe why one's convictions of faith make sense as authentic human positions about truth and value in the way that we make sense of human behavior by means of anthropology, sociology, psychology, political science, and other disciplines. It is an activity of reason to critically examine positions of faith developed in various cultures.

None of this intellectual probing nullifies or even diminishes the acceptance of revelation as an utterly transcendent gift of the God of love. Rather, it does the service of assuring believers that their religious faith is consistent with carefully maintained positions on other matters of importance for human living. It demonstrates that the human spirit need not be dichotomous. If we are willing to make the effort in collaboration with many others who seek to understand, the human spirit can function with integrity.

Human faith and reason, of course, are not active in some sort of otherworldly atmosphere far from influence by the vagaries of human history. Both human processes function within and with reference to quite particular historical circumstances. The origin and development of Christianity took place within what today can be named the premodern period, which is to say, the span of history in the West up to the fourteenth century of the Common Era. But much of the world's population conducts both its individual and social lives to a greater or lesser extent under the influence of modernity and now, increasingly, postmodernity.

The first chapter of the present study considers these three periods of Western intellectual history and how they have shaped the question of God. This is not to claim that Western history has moved neatly from one period to the next. In fact, in the lived order, apart from theoretical abstraction, the three intellectual approaches overlap—which contributes a good deal to the complexity of the present situation.

Despite the difficulty entailed in interpreting just where Christian faith in God stands in the contemporary context, there is no need for despair, although weariness is understandable. There is no need for despair because the method articulated by Bernard Lonergan assists greatly in naming, interpreting, assessing, and relating the components that lead Christians to faith in God as Father, Son, and Holy Spirit. But weariness is understandable because the method itself is complex, since human consciousness is complex, and the method is not a recipe for unassailable and undeniably certain analysis. Lonergan is not Descartes, who proposed a method to discover what is sure and certain. Lonergan is quite comfortable living with the human mind's finitude and its ongoing need for self-correction. Chapter 2 presents an outline of Lonergan's method of the cumulative and normative operations of human consciousness.

Chapter 3 takes up the first operation of consciousness, each person's self-experience. Experience opens the door to every area of human meaning and truth and value. Chapter 3 studies particular types of experience that can be named religious because they open the door to a dimension of meaning, truth, and value that transcends natural and human reality. Such experience intimates to some persons that the evidently human person of Jesus is more than human. For those who put faith in him, Jesus leads them into divine reality.

Historical and theological development of faith in Jesus from the unitary monotheism of Judaism to the trinitarian monotheism of Christian faith is the topic of chapters 4 and 5. Chapter 4 studies the beginnings of trinitarian faith in the New Testament and on through the first and second centuries up to Irenaeus, the bishop of Lyons, who attempted a clear articulation of the rule or norm of faith. Chapter 5 picks up with the early third-century theologian, Tertullian, and continues on to the creedal profession of faith in the triune God. In terms of Lonergan's articulation of the cumulative and normative operations of consciousness, these chapters demonstrate how the Christian church came to make a judgment about the truth of God expressed in a statement of belief.

Once the faith can be expressed in the communally accepted language of the Creed of Nicea, expanded by the Creed of Constantinople, a new task is set. For the operations of consciousness now push on toward efforts to understand the meaning and value of this faith for those who profess it. Chapters 6 and 8 are concerned almost exclusively with meaning. Chapter 6 proposes analogies that may help believers who are interested in such things to come to some understanding of how the one and only God can yet be Father, Son, and Holy Spirit. Chapter 8 asks more philosophical questions that vex some contemporary believers. Without specific reference to the revelation of the New Testament and Christian tradition, how can faith in God be demonstrated to be reasonable, especially in an age driven by neo-Darwinian theories of evolution and mechanistic views of natural process?

Chapters 7 and 9 ask about the value of faith in the triune God. What difference does this faith make to human beings whose task is to create a socially livable world? Chapter 7 suggests that the divine communion of three persons in one God means that human beings who are believed to be created in the divine image will only find true, if partial, happiness in this world when community, communal well-being, is the motivation and goal. Such a purpose for society does not entail the diminishment, let alone the destruction, of individual rights, but it recognizes that a balance must be sought between the equal dignity of every human being, the diverse needs and interests of the world's individuals, and the mutual self-gift of human beings, one to another. This is a project within the Christian community of the church and within the larger human society, even worldwide.

Chapter 9 turns to one important area in which human community can be fostered. It takes up the issue of interreligious dialogue. So often religion divides humanity. Trinitarian faith as it is now understood by many Christians— this chapter offers a Roman Catholic perspective—ought rather to be a catalyst for human community rather than human separation and intolerance. Dialogue is a value promoted by genuine trinitarian faith. Chapter 9 examines how dialogue about the divine can move forward.

Chapter 7 follows from chapter 6, reflecting as it does upon values expressive of the divine, triune communion, which is understood slightly by the analogies presented in chapter 6. Chapter 9 follows upon chapters 6 and 7 as a value of communion, but also upon chapter 8, which reflects upon the universal human demand for one God, the creator and goal of human being.

The book ends with a sequel to chapter 9. Chapter 10 continues the theme of interreligious dialogue. Recognizing that some Christian thinkers have concluded that genuine interreligious dialogue leads to significant compromise in the ancient Christian faith in the divinity of Jesus and in his role as savior, it is necessary to indicate that such compromise is neither required nor desirable.

The present volume is one of many contributions to trinitarian theology that are appearing in print in the last several years. No contribution provides the last word on such weighty and profound issues. My hope is that the present volume add to the discussion. Let the conversation continue.

NOTES

1. Jean-Luc Marion, *God without Being: Hors Texte*, trans. Thomas A. Carlson (Chicago: University of Chicago Press, 1991; original French edition, 1982).

2. All quotations of the Bible throughout the text are from the New Revised Standard Version.

3. Bernard Lonergan, *Method in Theology* (New York: Herder, 1972), 286–87.

1

Premodernity, Modernity, Postmodernity

Before such a need was greatly mitigated by the rise of the natural sciences and of the technology which is their product, women and men regularly turned to the gods or to God in order to have a loved one cured of an illness, to assure fertile soil for crops, to enable the firewood to hold out for the long winter. Now most people count on medicines, fertilizers, and the oil cartel to meet such needs. Nevertheless, God continues to be a topic that generates considerable interest, whether to affirm or to deny divine existence, whether to affirm or to deny the possibility of understanding something of God and of God's involvement in daily living once divine existence is affirmed.

The present book joins the discussion of God on the assumption of Christian faith. I do not seek to demonstrate the existence of God, but to express faith in the triune God of Christian doctrine in such a way that Christians who are presently subject to the influence of modernity and postmodernity can continue in their faith as an enterprise that does not contradict but even enhances faith's reasonability. The intention is to offer a theological reflection on several dimensions of Christian faith in God that presuppose faith but that become more intelligible when submitted to inquiry. The question is asked with regard to each topic that is introduced: Just what does this mean?

What is the problem of faith for sincere Christian believers today? While there are many expressions of the problem, my sense is that the inquirers among Christians who gather for worship on Sundays, and among the women and men who enroll in programs of Christian theology, believe that the Christian religion is indeed a divine revelation, but at some level, more or less explicitly, they wonder just what it means that God enters into dialogue with humanity by means of the eternal Word who became incarnate in history in Jesus of Nazareth, and in and through the church that supposedly mediates the risen Jesus through its scriptures, doctrines, sacraments, moral code, ministries, and social structures. These are committed Christians who believe, but they are puzzled by the historical character of Jesus and/or by much of what is taken to mediate his reconciling ministry throughout subsequent history. Do not the many cultures, languages, symbols, and claims of truth that prevail in contemporary society seriously hamper, if not destroy, the possibility of meanings, truths, and values that can be accepted across cultures and generations and languages? Does not the inevitable mix of understanding and misunderstanding, truth and falsehood, good and evil in every human person, along with the particular cultural differences, undermine the credibility of every human authority, whether it be scripture, doctrine, symbol, or church leader? All these are quite historical, culturally conditioned mediations of God and of God-language. How adequate are they for such a lofty objective?

SITUATING THE PROBLEM

To deal with a problem it is helpful to know what prompted its emergence. How did this quite contemporary problem of God arise for people of religious faith? An attempt to answer this question leads to a distinction of what can be recognized as three periods of Christian history: the premodern, the modern, and the postmodern. Beyond the distinction, an appreciation of the impact upon religious faith of the three periods requires that the philosophical roots of each be highlighted. Why? Because the historical periods embrace not just religion but the entirety of human being in the world, and because philosophy studies the basic human worldview. As Bernard Lonergan has written: Philosophy is "the basic and total science."[1]

More needs to be said about philosophy's role in responding to the problem of the meaningfulness of faith, especially since there are those, and they are not a few, who find philosophy to be less and less relevant to life in this present age, and there are some who want it thrown out of the sciences and disciplines accepted by reasonable adults. Michael McCarthy assists us in saying something about the significance of philosophy today. In his book, *The Crisis of Philosophy*, McCarthy, professor of philosophy at Vassar College, writes: "Philosophy's permanent theoretical function is the distinction and critical unification of the existing modes of human knowledge."[2] At another place McCarthy claims: "Philosophy exists to meet the native human demand for the integration of knowledge." He goes on to caution: "Serious doubts now exist whether that need can be met, whether philosophy or any human activity can order and unify the extraordinary pluralism of our time."[3] Such doubts are clearly postmodern in their origin and expression, for the extraordinary pluralism of our time, connected as it is with a sense of human historicity and the relativity of an increasingly vast array of human creations, is a product of modernity moving beyond itself. Allowing the remarks of Lonergan and McCarthy to provide a working hypothesis, even as we keep in mind the current skepticism about philosophy's possible role in contemporary culture, I attempt to describe briefly the three periods within which Christian doctrine and theology have taken shape and to distinguish the philosophical roots of each period.

PREMODERN CULTURE

The philosophical foundations of premodern civilization originate especially in the dialogues of Plato and the subsequent wide-ranging corpus of works of Aristotle. Eventually, Greek philosophy, most notably the works of Aristotle, was transported via Islam into the Latin West. Premodern civilization reached its high point in the West in the thirteenth century with the able assistance of thinkers such as Thomas Aquinas and Bonaventure. But it also began to wane already in the thirteenth century when, as Bernard Lonergan has written, a decadent scholasticism started to take hold.[4]

The philosophy which informs the premodern period holds that reality is orderly, indeed hierarchically orderly, and appears in its true form to inquiring minds. Moreover, the ordered quality of reality has its origins in the order of the divine mind. God and all reality can be grasped in an orderly relationship. And God, or the divine, governs the realm of being.

This may be called an ontotheological view of reality, to use a term coined by Immanuel Kant. It considers God as the ordering principle of all possible being.[5] The laws of nature, of humanly created society (*polis*, as the Greeks say), of the mind that thinks and knows: All these run parallel to each other. And fundamentally they all participate in an orderly cosmos that is directed by the divine in some way.

Christian thinkers debated with their contemporaries about how the divine invests the cosmos with order. For example, they argued against Plato's view of the eternity of matter, insisting, because of the Book of Genesis, that God creates everything, even matter, out of nothing. Part of the reinforcement arose as Christianity not only inherited the ontotheological perspective of reality, but developed it further, recognizing the rule of God in every dimension of nature, human and otherwise.

In this premodern cultural context Christianity was formed:

- doctrines were developed on Christ, the Trinity, creation, sin, grace, sacraments;
- the foundations of Christian interpretation of the moral law were laid— not only the biblical statements of the Decalogue and the two great

commandments highlighted by Jesus, but interpretation of these through natural law and divine positive law and human law, along with the meaning and role of conscience;

- church structures were established—the role of the ordained, the place of the baptized, the jurisdiction of diocese and parish, papal primacy;
- Christian liturgy was developed, so that it is said that the Roman liturgy had reached a "magnificent completeness" in the centuries immediately subsequent to Pope Gregory the Great (540–604 c.e.).[6]

The Christian worldview came to be remarkably ordered in nearly all its details during the thirteenth century in the *summae theologiae* of several theologians, but especially of Thomas Aquinas (1225–1274 c.e.). Aquinas developed the view that all things created come forth from God and are ordered toward a return to God.

I conclude this brief exposition of the premodern period of Western culture, in its Christian context, with a summary of its philosophical foundation as formulated by Thomas Aquinas. For Aquinas, God has endowed human reason with the possibility of coming to know reality, as it is, in two moments. In a first moment, the inquirer asks about the nature of things, seeking to grasp the inner essence or form by an act of understanding. The basic question asked is: What is the inner nature or form of whatever it is that I happen to be inquiring about? Something is presented to the intellect by means of the five senses. (Aquinas names this sensible presentation a phantasm.) This sensible unity prompts the question about its underlying form. So, an inquirer might conclude from various sensible presentations that the species "cat" is a member of the genus "mammal." And the same inquirer might conclude from a different set of sensible presentations that the species "unicorn" is a member of the genus "mammal."

In a second moment of intellectual reflection the inquirer seeks to affirm or deny the actuality of objects whose essence or form has been grasped by an act of understanding. If the form that the inquirer has grasped is embodied in the small, four-legged, whiskered, sensate animal that is meowing at the back door, then the form "cat" can be affirmed actually to exist in particular beings. On the other hand, the only place that one can find the form of pony-like creatures with a single horn, "unicorn," is in literature. Thus, in the second moment of intellectual reflection, the actual existence of unicorns is denied. They are affirmed to be products of the imagination.

The examples offered here are elementary. However, the two-step process remains the same for every object of inquiry, no matter how elementary or complex. In every instance of coming to understand and to know, the objective order of being is achieved in its truth and its goodness. What is more, every instance of coming to know being, the true, and the good is an approach to the eternal mind, a step on the way to God.[7] Aquinas thus formulated a correspondence theory of knowledge: What one truly knows corresponds with what actually exists. Often with great effort, but nevertheless with surety, the mind is able to affirm what is true and to deny what is false.

MODERNITY

In his book on the subject, *Passage to Modernity*, philosopher of religion at Yale University Louis Dupré claims that premodern Western civilization began to metamorphose into modernity early in the fourteenth century.[8] Dupré bases his thesis on two things that happened at that time.

First, the emergence of humanism generated a notion of human creativity that attributed powers to the human imagination that had, of course, always been part of being human and had always been used, but had never been acknowledged in quite this way. Partly this was a recovery of creativity as it had been valued in classical Greece, but partly it was new, namely, an invitation to discover new modes of human expression: artistic, political, philosophical. Thus, the emergence of the Renaissance.

Second, nominalist theology with its skepticism about the inherent meaningfulness of things began to break up the Thomist synthesis. Now creation was interpreted as an act of an arbitrary God, not of the supreme intelligence who endows all created reality with intelligible essences, a participation in the divine Logos, as premodern philosophy claimed. Now the dominant viewpoint became: God can do as God wills. There is no inherent meaning in things.

Since there is no inherent connection between the intelligence of God and the intelligibility of things, reality is only what God decides to make. Thus, names do not denote the inner meaning of things. They are mere terms that human minds impose on things that in their particularity may be far more different from one another than they are similar, thus nominalism. In a sense, the concepts formulated to interpret them create the meaning of things. According to nominalist theories of knowledge, the human mind can only know particular cats and cannot assume that the individuals share anything in essence with other cats. The same is true for humans and even imaginary unicorns.

Nominalism became a powerful force in the formation of the early modern period. Together with the new humanism, it created a sense of focusing all reality in the creativity of human minds in the present moment. Louis Dupré explains the impact this way: "Only when the early humanist notion of human creativity came to form a combustive mixture with the negative conclusions of nominalist theology did it cause the cultural explosion that we refer to as modernity."[9]

No doubt many individual events catalyzed the full bloom of modernity.[10] Here I gather them together into two moments. The first was the scientific revolution of the seventeenth century. During this period, the experimental method became the vehicle of a remarkable new moment of human creativity. Suddenly human beings could take control of nature as never before. They could direct it to their own ends.[11]

The second moment was the Enlightenment of the eighteenth century. During this period the newfound and powerful experimental method became adopted as an agenda for all dimensions of life: the economy, politics, religion, ethics. Human beings were challenged to take charge of life for themselves.[12] Promoters of the Enlightenment encouraged that control does not need to be just in the hands of civil and religious authorities, who claim, after all falsely and therefore unjustly, to speak on behalf of the eternal, divine order.

In the beginning of the modern age, regimes of church and state were totally outside the area of extraordinary power being exercised by means of the new knowledge of the new natural sciences. In state and church, it was the age of absolutism. But as the new appreciation of the human individual began to be applied to the construction of human society, people felt increasingly adept at determining their own destiny. Individual freedom and personal autonomy became the order of the day, along with a determination to go about things on the basis of certitude and clear and distinct ideas.[13]

The rationalism of René Descartes, which was constructed during the period of the scientific revolution, became in the eighteenth century the philosophical basis for judgments and decisions about reality that was almost universally adopted by theorists of all sorts. On the opposite side, the control of authorities of church and state was criticized for its basis in obscure mysteries of faith or in what passes for them, but this basis was determined to be only a front used by the authorities for control. Furthermore, the devastation of the Thirty Years' War (1618–1648), which was readily attributable in great part to the post-Reformation divisions within the Christian church and to the close ties of each church with various absolute monarchs, left European intellectuals disgusted with church and state. Thus, the political revolutions of the eighteenth and nineteenth centuries led to a quest for democracy as the political order of choice, wresting control from aristocratic and theocratic elites.

The philosophies of René Descartes and Immanuel Kant sum up the philosophical roots of modernity. The moderns turned from the premodern assumption that the mind could know and linguistically express a world of beings that participated in the order of Being to the conviction that the human person is a subject whose mind posits reality. Reality is what the mind conceives it to be. For Descartes, science is achieved in "clear and distinct ideas." The world to be affirmed is the world that the mind can conceive clearly and distinctly.[14] But to achieve this goal, the mind must activate a procedure of doubt. Methodical doubt is just that, a method employed "with the purpose of reaching absolutely certain truths, 'so that after we have discovered that they are true we cannot doubt any longer.'"[15]

This analysis of mind seemed to fit neatly with the methods of the new natural sciences. The new scientists tried to assume nothing, a sort of doubt. Then they sought to be precise about the inner workings of things by means of carefully constructed empirical experiments conducted upon particular existents. Rather than proceeding from what is presumed to be known universally about all things within a general category and from the universal drawing conclusions about individuals (the deductive method), now individuals are studied and the conclusions may be more generally applied or may not be, depending upon particular circumstances (inductive method).

Immanuel Kant takes this line of reasoning a step further. For Kant, the human person as subject of thought is the very foundation of humanly accessible reality. The ego of the subject transcends all experience and orders it by the a priori categories of understanding. Scientific knowledge deals with objects that subjects intuit with their spatial and temporal qualities. "But," to quote Michael McCarthy, "space and time, though empirically real, (that is, verifiable features of perceptual experience), are understood by Kant to be transcendentally ideal, since they are pure forms of human sensibility and not mind-independent properties of things in themselves."[16] Moreover, the mind achieves the truth of things by means of synthetic a priori judgments. Ideas and judgments posit reality, rather than formulate insight into and affirmation of reality. The process that began when the late medieval, humanist notion of creativity became joined to theological nominalism eventually developed into Kantian idealism.

The rationalism of Descartes and the idealism of Kant were not philosophies created out of nothing. They were articulations of the spirit of the times. They fit right in with the new discoveries of the natural sciences and with the new assessments of humanity of the intellectual elites.

Much of what Descartes and Kant and their fellow intellectuals were attempting to articulate philosophically is laudable. The freedom of the human subject, the importance of the subject in knowing, the magnificence of human creativity, a political order respectful of the intelligence and responsibility of its citizens—these are worthy constitutive factors of modernity. What the moderns failed to appreciate was the dark side of their philosophy, that their version of the turn to subjectivity tended toward the breakdown of all sense of common truths and values, that is, of the common good, and with that loss a consequent fragmentation of human social order.[17]

On 4 July 1994, the president of the Czech Republic, Vaclav Havel, world-renowned playwright and anti-Communist dissident, gave a speech in Philadelphia to celebrate American Independence Day.[18] He spoke glowingly

of the successes of the modern era.[19] The technologies of the modern world
in nearly every area of life have opened opportunities that people never even
dreamed of in the premodern age: instant global communication through cy-
berspace, the comforts and conveniences of modern households, air transport that allows people to travel across the world in hours, and so on. Moreover, Havel noted, the product of Enlightenment autonomy that is political
democracy is now increasingly being achieved after the collapse of the com-
munist states of Eastern Europe.

Despite his words of praise, the main purpose of Havel's speech was not
to celebrate modernity's success, but to announce its wane. Havel contends
that for all our enthusiastic welcome of modernity's contributions, it is time
to recognize its limitations. Technology easily leads to technocracy without
much attention paid to the quality of human life. Moreover, while appreciation of and respect for individual rights is enormously important, nevertheless, if attention to individual rights is not balanced by care for the common
good, society can fragment into thousands of self-interest groups. Self-
destruction is not far behind. Thus Vaclav Havel.

When we take up the question of God, we can recognize the contribution
of modernity as well. For, as I hope to demonstrate when I offer a route toward a solution to the problems contemporary people of religious faith confront, modernity's discovery of the central role of the human subject in every
instance of knowledge opens the way to precisely the grounding of faith that
was lacking in the premodern period. But since modern philosophy has not
worked out the turn to the subject in several of its ramifications, religious
faith, at least faith in revealed religion, is often banished from socially acceptable discourse of the important issues of the day. It is thought to be too
arbitrary to be included among the eminently successful human pursuits,
such as natural science and technology, and human sciences such as anthropology, psychology, and sociology. Nevertheless, modernity is willing to
consider religion, as long as religious reflection is concerned with the God
of reason and with natural religion. But religious faith is hardly taken for
granted as it mainly was in the premodern era.

Besides the questionableness of religious faith as a mode of knowledge,
human projects themselves no longer need God for their success or even
their maintenance. The great accomplishments of the modern period in the
areas of natural science and technology, political democracy, education, and
art are all the products of human ingenuity. Moderns are welcome to maintain a belief in God as creator and sustainer of the universe if they wish, but
belief in God is of little practical value in moving the human enterprise forward. So, why bother with such a belief? Moreover, if one has learned to be
wary about the value of belief in God as the ever-engaged sustainer of life
and order, which had been a staple of religious commitment, one might do
well to be wary of maintaining other beliefs about God as well, for example,

a divine goal of the universe, divine redemption of humanity from sinfulness, divine love of humankind.

THE POSTMODERN

If the modern age is still very much dominant, how are we to imagine and deal with the postmodern period, which, presumably, overlaps the modern? Anthony Thiselton offers a powerful description of this present age by contrast with its predecessor: "Postmodernism implies a shattering of innocent confidence in the capacity of the self to control its own destiny."[20] That innocent confidence can be summarized in the four presumptions of modernity: "the 'turn to the subject,' universal reason, historical progress, and androcentrism."[21] Another read on postmodernity is offered by Vaclav Havel in his Philadelphia speech. He suggests that if we are going to preserve our world for the future, then we need to bring to an end the hegemony of that sort of political democracy that focuses so much on individual rights that it neglects the common good. Moreover, even as we embrace the genuine contributions of technology, we do not want to be controlled by a technological economy that is insensitive to sharing the goods of the world in a more equitable way than is happening at present. If we act on Havel's wisdom, then we are moving away from certain aspects of modernity into some sort of postmodern age, but including a retrieval of certain premodern values.

Calls to get beyond modernity were already being issued in the nineteenth century by the great demythologizers of modernity. Karl Marx had derided Enlightenment idealism, especially Hegel's type, which glorifies human reason in a kind of completion of Descartes and Kant. Marx proposed the necessity of turning idealism on its philosophical head to show up the social order for what it was, a crass play for power over the proletariat by the elites of the world.[22] Although this proposal is remarkably reminiscent of Enlightenment criticism of the authoritarian rule of the church-state alliance, Marx was sounding what is a chief theme of the postmodern: Don't get so enamored of your present perception of things; there is an entirely other way of looking at things that challenges your perception of reality.

Sigmund Freud echoed Marx's concern for the other in a different area of human life. He wasn't concerned about economic order but about the illusions by which we human beings imagine order within ourselves.[23] He sought to show that underneath our waking consciousness, there is an other, a very different dimension of ourselves, which is the unconscious. This unconscious exerts more control over our feelings and our images, and therefore over our behavior, than what we are consciously thinking.

Finally, a third great exponent of the other is Friedrich Nietzsche.[24] To read Nietzsche is to read outrageous, but often well-placed, criticism of society.

Nietzsche looked at what passed as morality by the people of his day, all the behavioral customs, including religion (and especially the moral teachings of Jesus and of Christianity), and he pronounced it a sham. Mostly, human behavior is a matter of self-preservation; or, as Nietzsche's Zarathustra would claim, virtuous living is a human creation whose purpose is to help one sleep well at night, without being disturbed by a guilty conscience.[25] As for God, Nietzsche declared that the new culture of modernity had killed God, and the churches were actually tombs of the dead God.[26]

By the end of the nineteenth century it was simply a matter of acknowledging the criticisms against religious faith of the three famous critics of modernity. Marx and Freud, for their own reasons, agreed with Nietzsche about the need to proclaim the illusory character of faith in God.[27] One needed to look to the other, the opposite of illusory religion. One would then choose against religious faith altogether.

However, there was another avenue pursued in the first half of the twentieth century, one which sought to remove the question of God from philosophical consideration so that it could be retrieved within its own field of theology. This was the effort of Martin Heidegger. Heidegger's rejection of philosophical thinking about God was intended to save religion. Heidegger argued that the God of the philosophers is an improper reduction of the God of revelation to a philosophical need or, put biblically, to human "foolishness" (à la St. Paul).[28] Expressed another way, Heidegger claims that the philosophical conception of God is *causa sui*, the uncaused cause of Being. But humans "can neither pray nor sacrifice to this God."[29] Christian theology, in Heidegger's view, needs to find its way to God on its own terms, namely, by means of love, trust, relationship.[30] By rejecting philosophical attempts to create a theologically oriented metaphysics, an ontotheology, religious faith would actually be saved.

But Heidegger could not ward off further challenges to religious faith, and not simply because his own approach suffers from its limitations. In the move to the postmodern, modern philosophy has been left behind with its too-facile assurance of a brave new world. The philosophical roots of premodernity were largely abandoned in the move to modernity: the conviction that the human mind has the capacity to know, to grasp the inherent intelligibility of, divinely grounded cosmic reality.[31] The philosophical crisis in the postmodern context may be phrased in the form of Michael McCarthy's question: "What is the theoretical contribution of philosophy to be once the autonomous and historically developing sciences abandon the quest for certainty?"[32] Now we are into the age of the postmodern skeptics, who abandon the modern philosophical roots, now considered naïve, of the possibility of achieving certainty based upon clear and distinct ideas confirmed by the methods of the natural sciences.[33] When humanity finds itself in the situation of continually discovering the Other (some postmodern authors prefer to highlight this sense of opposition between dominant and marginalized perceptions by capitalizing "Other") that contrasts with what we had previously assumed meaning, truth, and value to be, then plurality, relativity, historicity become the coins of the realm. Science, in Thomas Kuhn's famous description, becomes the most probable explanation for the evidence at hand.[34] Sooner or later new data and new explanations are anticipated, as Kuhn's theory of paradigm shifts in science implies. No one expects cognitive invariance, but rather a continual correction of the ideas and judgments one currently holds.

With such a narrowly circumscribed possibility of knowing and understanding realities which are more readily accessible, how stable can religious belief be, the objectives of which are less accessible? Christians have always claimed that our belief in God is largely a matter not of unaided human investigation but of revelation. But how secure are Christian convictions about revelation when certainty is so elusive? How devotedly can one commit oneself to a specific religious faith when one's manner of questioning and formulating answers is profoundly influenced by the particularities of one's place and time, when other people in other places and times have formed quite different religious faiths?

These are some of the challenges of postmodernity, which can be summarized as Roger Haight does in his recent effort to formulate a relevant contemporary Christology. Claiming that the present human context is "increasingly postmodern," Haight highlights four themes that press his point: (1) "a radical historical consciousness" or "the sheer contingency of history"; (2) a pessimistic "critical social consciousness" that views society to be "driven by little more than the interests of power, or class, or gender, or greed," so that the human subject is no longer accepted as "a transcendental clearing house of truth"; (3) an utterly "pluralist consciousness"; and (4) "a cosmic consciousness" that rings the death knell for "naïve anthropocentrism."[35] An even more terse summary of the core position of postmodernity is expressed by postmodernist John Caputo, paraphrasing another postmodernist, Jacques Derrida: "[T]he truth is that there is no truth, and she, being herself a creature of fiction, device, art, artifice, illusion, and ornamentation, cannot be fooled at her own game, fooled into believing that she herself has an essence and truth."[36]

Just as the challenges of modernity led some to abandon Christian faith as no longer tenable once the premises of modernity had been accepted, so, understandably, there are those who find that the challenges of the postmodern premises overwhelm a Christian faith that came to its original fruition under premodern conditions. How can the Christian worldview expressed in doctrines, liturgy, and moral practice survive postmodern ambiguity, truth as power, fragmentation, and pluralism? These characteristics can be profoundly unsettling to a church member who takes them seriously.

And yet, avowedly postmodern thinkers have come to find that the same characteristics of postmodernity that some find so off-putting actually invite a fresh articulation of Christian faith, perhaps one more faithful to its meaning. Here I mention just three.

Michel de Certeau seeks to balance two dimensions of a living Christian faith. On the one hand, Christianity, in order to continue to be Christianity, must maintain a transcendental dimension: a relationship to the event of Jesus Christ. Anyone who is genuinely Christian wants "to be *faithful* to the inaugural event."[37] On the other hand, de Certeau wants Christians not to be afraid of the radical historical consciousness that is one of the characteristics of postmodernity. Indeed, he claims, in order to be faithful to the Christian event in the changing circumstances of human being from place to place and from time to time, the "intellectual and social forms" of Christianity need to be "*different*" from Christianity's beginnings.

De Certeau's claim is that "the life, words, death, and resurrection of Jesus left traces on the organization of the early Christian communities or writings. But the map of these traces is not a 'proof' nor the 'truth,' but only an effect."[38] The Jesus-event makes possible opportunities for believers to create something new for humanity in their own cultural context: new opportunities of meaning in terms of faith and charity, of solidarity with others, and even new opportunities to deal with "one's own limit and death."[39]

Is all this risky? Indeed it is, but for de Certeau "[t]he Christian faith has no security other than the *living* God discovered by communities which are alive and which undergo the experience of *losing* objective securities. In the last analysis, Christianity is thinkable only if it is alive. And there is no life without new risks in our actual situation."[40] De Certeau maintains that faith is not for the faint of heart.

Our second author, Jean-Luc Marion, accepts, at least for the sake of argument, the postmodern contention that metaphysics is bankrupt, including the metaphysical position on God as the Being that is the ultimate ground of all being, the "last Reason," the uncaused cause.[41] Marion suggests another way to God, the way of phenomenology. He flags the givenness of being and then, moving from philosophy to divine revelation, claims that God is "being-as-given *par excellence*."[42] And since, in I John 4:8 and 4:16, God is revealed to be love, God can be said to be given in love, to be "the lover in the strict sense."[43]

Marion offers a concrete instance of this givenness of transcendent love when he turns his attention to the Eucharist. Once again the reflection is a-metaphysical (but not anti-metaphysical): Metaphysics deals with the presence of the being that is common to all beings, including Being. But the Eucharist functions in the tension between the very particular past of the events of Jesus' suffering and death and the future of the Lord's coming in glory. The Eucharist mediates the mystery of divine love. Marion puts it this way:

[T]he Son took on the body of humanity only in order to play humanly the trinitarian game of love; for this reason also, he loved "to the end" (John 13:1), that is, to the Cross; in order that the irrefutable demonstration of the death and resurrection not cease to provoke us, he gives himelf with insistence in a body and a blood that persist in each day that time imparts to us. . . . The consecrated bread and wine become the ultimate aspect in which charity delivers itself body and soul.[44]

Here the human subject must cease to focus on itself and instead become centered in the Other who is love.

Finally, we turn to René Girard. Like the previous two thinkers, Girard reflects upon the Christian Gospel. One characteristic of postmodernity that drives his thought is its crucial social consciousness. For Girard, God identifies with history's victims. Christ himself is a victim of political and religious machinations that result in his condemnation and cruel execution. But Girard is incensed that so much Christian theology of the passion and death of Jesus attributes the violence perpetrated against him chiefly to his Father, to God himself.

Theories inspired by Anselm of Canterbury (c.1033–1109 c.e.) that the innocent God-man must suffer a cruel death in order to satisfy the honor of God that has been offended by human rejection of God in sin miss the point, in Girard's view. So, too, does any form of the theory that humanity needs to be punished for its defiant disobedience of sin, and the only person big enough to accept the punishment for the whole human race is the sinless Jesus.

Jesus suffers as he does because, like so many other victims in history, he is scapegoated. And all humanity is to blame—not just Jews, although to some extent the Jews are the representatives of humanity in this instance.[45] Why does God allow his Son to endure this suffering, which is at once cruel and unjust? For Girard, the answer is clear. In his own words:

The teaching of Jesus and the Passion in the Gospels constitute the strict development of a paradoxical logic. Jesus wants nothing to do with all that makes someone divine in the eyes of men: the power to seduce or constrain, the ability to make oneself indispensable.

He would seem to want the very opposite. In reality, it is not that he desires failure but that he will not avoid it if that is the only way he may remain true to the Logos of the God of victims. He is not secretly motivated by a taste for failure, but rather by the logic of the God of victims that unerringly leads him to death.[46]

These brief vignettes of three thinkers whose writings have a postmodern tone reveal some of the salutary ways in which postmodernity's jaundiced view of premodernity and, especially, of modernity can jolt contemporary Christians out of complacent and/or facile and/or inadequate assumptions about the meaning of the Christ-event and of Christian doctrines and practices. Fresh theological reflection is called for.

Still, if each of the three eras of Christian history has something to offer, and if, nevertheless, each can be criticized as inadequate, is there a way to go forward that can accommodate the contributions of all three eras and also be appropriately critical of the limitations of each? That is the question to be addressed in the next chapter.

NOTES

1. Bernard Lonergan, "Questionnaire on Philosophy," composed in 1976, published in *Method: Journal of Lonergan Studies* 2 (1984): 7.

2. Michael McCarthy, *The Crisis of Philosophy* (Albany: State University of New York Press, 1990), xvi.

3. McCarthy, *Crisis of Philosophy*, 227.

4. Bernard Lonergan, *Method in Theology*, 80.

5. See, e.g., Immanuel Kant, *Lectures on Philosophical Theology*, trans. Allen W. Wood and Gertrude M. Clark, with intro. and notes by Allen W. Wood (Ithaca: Cornell University Press, 1978), 31. According to "transcendental theology," a metaphysics of God as expounded by Kant in his lectures, God is the original being and the most real being (*ens realissimum*) (80).

6. Joseph A. Jungmann, S.J., *The Mass of the Roman Rite: Its Origins and Development*, trans. Francis A. Brunner, C.SS.R. (New York: Benziger Brothers, 1959), 55–56.

7. Bernard Lonergan analyzes Aquinas's theory of the two moments of knowledge at length in the first two chapters of *Verbum: Word and Idea in Aquinas*, 2nd ed., edited by Frederick E. Crowe and Robert M. Doran (Toronto: University of Toronto Press, 1997).

8. Louis Dupré, *Passage to Modernity: An Essay in the Hermeneutics of Nature and Culture* (New Haven: Yale University Press, 1993). See also Louis Dupré, "The Modern Idea of Culture: Its Opposition to Its Classical and Christian Origins," in *Modernity and Religion*, ed. Ralph McInerny (Notre Dame: University of Notre Dame Press, 1994).

9. Dupré, *Passage to Modernity*, 3.

10. See Graham Ward's list of several such events in his introduction to Graham Ward, ed., *The Postmodern God: A Theological Reader* (Oxford: Blackwell, 1997). "Spatiality, temporality, and corporeality" become reorganized (xvii–xx); here arose a "shift toward the autonomy of human reasoning" (xxiii).

11. On the monumental significance of the scientific revolution of the seventeenth century, see Herbert Butterfield, *The Origins of Modern Science: 1300–1800* (New York: Free Press, 1957).

12. In a well-known essay, dated 30 September 1784, Immanuel Kant offered a definition of the Enlightenment as it was blossoming at the time: "Enlightenment is the release of people from their refusal to come of age" (my rather free translation). Later in the essay Kant assesses the Enlightenment relative to religion: "As things now stand, much is lacking which prevents men from being, or easily becoming, capable

of using their own reason in religious matters correctly, with assurance and free from outside direction. But, on the other hand, we have clear indications that the field has now been opened wherein men may deal with these things and that the obstacles to general enlightenment or the release from self-imposed tutelage [i.e., the refusal to come of age] are gradually being reduced" (Immanuel Kant, "What is Enlightenment?" in *Kant Selections*, trans. and ed. Lewis White Beck [New York: Macmillan, 1988], 465–66).

13. The autonomy of the individual is a fundamental element of modernity. The modern notion of freedom is compared with the Christian notion of freedom by Walter Kasper in the 1988 Père Marquette Lecture in *Theology, the Christian Understanding of Freedom and the History of Freedom in the Modern Era: The Meeting and Confrontation between Christianity and the Modern Era in a Postmodern Situation* (Milwaukee, WI: Marquette University Press, 1988).

14. Arthur Wollaston's introduction to *Descartes: Discourse on Method and Other Writings*, which Wollaston also translates, provides a useful summary of Cartesian philosophy (Baltimore: Penguin, 1960).

15. Alicia Villar Ezcurra, "Descartes: la pasión por la verdad," *Razón y Fe*, 234 (1996): 415–26, at 419.

16. McCarthy, *Crisis of Philosophy*, 20.

17. See Michael McCarthy, "Liberty, History, and the Common Good: An Exercise in Critical Retrieval" in *Lonergan Workshop*, ed. Fred Lawrence, vol. 12 (Chestnut Hill, MA: Boston College, 1996), 111–45. McCarthy opens his essay by noting that Thomas Hobbes and John Locke, the founders of modern political philosophy, explicitly rejected both "the classical republican tradition of public liberty and the Aristotelian tradition of the common good."

18. Vaclav Havel, "The New Measure of Man," *New York Times*, 8 July 1994, A27.

19. Walter Kasper does the same in his Père Marquette lecture, *Theology, the Christian Understanding of Freedom and the History of Freedom in the Modern Era*, 15.

20. Anthony C. Thiselton, *Interpreting God and the Postmodern Self: On Meaning, Manipulation and Promise* (Grand Rapids, MI: Eerdmans, 1995), 11.

21. Thus, Michael Scanlon, O.S.A., "The Postmodern Debate," in *The Twentieth Century: A Theological Overview*, ed. Gregory Baum (Maryknoll, NY: Orbis, 1999), 228.

22. Early in his career, Marx comments: "The philosophers have only interpreted the world in different ways; the point is to change it" ("Theses 'On Feuerbach'" of 1845, in *Marx: Early Political Writings*, trans. Joseph O'Malley with Richard Davis [Cambridge: Cambridge University Press, 1994], 118). In the same volume, see "The German Ideology," 145f.

23. For Freud, illusions are not necessarily erroneous in themselves, but they are products of human wishes that disregard the relation of the wishes to reality. There is no thought of verification. See Sigmund Freud, *The Future of an Illusion*, trans. W. D. Robson-Scott (Garden City, NY: Doubleday/Anchor, 1964), 48–49.

24. On the other hand, Leo Strauss understands Nietzsche as introducing, not postmodernity, but the third wave of modernity. See his "The Three Waves of Modernity," in *An Introduction to Political Philosophy: Ten Essays* by Leo Strauss, ed. Hilail Gildin (Detroit: Wayne State University Press, 1989), 94–98. In the analysis I offer, Nietzsche is more a prophet of the postmodern.

25. See Walter Kaufmann, translator and editor, *The Portable Nietzsche* (New York: The Viking Press, 1954), 43–44, 140–42.

26. See *The Gay Science* in *The Portable Nietzsche*, 95–96, and *Thus Spake Zarathustra*, 197–200. Leo Strauss claims that Nietzsche well knew the danger of unmasking the relativity of every human custom, for unmasking "would destroy the protecting atmosphere within which life or culture or action is alone possible" ("Natural Right and the Historical Approach," in *An Introduction to Political Philosophy*, 116).

27. In Marx's case, God is not so much the topic of discussion as religion. For Marx, "[t]he religious world is but the reflex of the real world" (*Capital: A Critique of Political Economy*, trans. Samuel Moore and Edward Aveling [New York: International Publishers, 1967], 79). And to what real world does Marx refer? A world in which the human person "has either not yet found himself or has already lost himself again" ("Contribution to the Critique of Hegel's Philosophy of Right," in K. Marx and F. Engels, *On Religion* [Moscow: Foreign Languages Publishing House, 1955], 41). For Freud, God is a creation of humanity's wish to make its "helplessness tolerable" (*Future of an Illusion*, 25–27). It is not difficult to recognize in these postmodern criticisms a further step in modernity's promotion of the autonomous individual and of the human subject's creation of its self.

28. Martin Heidegger, "The Way Back into the Ground of Metaphysics," in *Existentialism: From Dostoevsky to Sartre*, ed. Walter Kaufmann (New York: World Publishing, 1956), 218.

29. Martin Heidegger, "The Onto-theo-logical Constitution of Metaphysics," in *Identity and Difference*, trans. and intro. Joan Stambaugh (New York: Harper & Row, 1969), 72.

30. Merold Westphal, "Overcoming Onto-theology," in *God, the Gift, and Postmodernism*, ed. John D. Caputo and Michael J. Scanlon (Bloomington: Indiana University Press, 1999), 163.

31. Making precisely this point, Paul Hazard begins a chapter on the Enlightenment in these words: "In the eyes of the religiously minded, reason was a divine spark, a particle of truth vouchsafed to mortals until the time should come when, having passed through the gates of the tomb, they would see God face to face. But in the eyes of the newest school of thinkers all such ideas were the vain imaginings of a day that was over and done with." See *European Thought in the Eighteenth Century: From Montesquieu to Lessing*, trans. J. Lewis May (Cleveland: Meridian, 1963; originally published 1946), 26.

32. McCarthy, *Crisis of Philosophy*, 11.

33. For a resume of twentieth-century postmodern thinkers, see Martin Henry, "God in Postmodernity," *Irish Theological Quarterly* 63 (1998): 3–21, and Martin Henry, *On Not Understanding God* (Dublin: Columba Press, 1997), 261–82.

34. Thomas S. Kuhn, *The Structure of Scientific Revolutions*, 2nd ed., enlarged (Chicago: University of Chicago Press, 1970), 145.

35. Roger Haight, *Jesus: Symbol of God* (Maryknoll, NY: Orbis, 1999), 330–34.

36. John D. Caputo, *Radical Hermeneutics: Repetition, Deconstruction, and the Hermeneutic Project* (Bloomington: Indiana University Press, 1987), 156.

37. Michel de Certeau, "How Is Christianity Thinkable Today?" in Ward, ed., *The Postmodern God*, 142.

38. de Certeau, "How Is Christianity Thinkable," 144.

39. de Certeau, "How Is Christianity Thinkable," 149.

40. de Certeau, "How Is Christianity Thinkable," 155.

41. Jean-Luc Marion, "Metaphysics and Theology: A Summary for Theologians," in Ward, ed., *The Postmodern God*, 288.

42. Marion, "Metaphysics and Theology," 291.

43. Marion, "Metaphysics and Theology," 293.

44. Marion, *God without Being: Hors-Texte*, 177–78.

45. Gerard Loughlin, "René Girard (b.1923): Introduction," in Ward, ed., *The Postmodern God*, 100. Loughlin writes: "Jesus is portrayed by his persecutors as the cause of people's misery, as the one who endangers their security; his impieties tempting divine wrath."

46. René Girard, "The God of Victims," in Ward, ed., *The Postmodern God*, 108.

2

A Way Forward: Keeping the Faith

Whereas the previous chapter indicated some major clashes among the three eras of Western culture, the present chapter proposes that centrally important characteristics of each of the three can be retained as we move into the future. Even more, I suggest that elements of each era need to be maintained in order for individuals and the church to be faithful to the demands of life in the human world.

In short, the ontotheology of premodernity is salvageable. God is the ordering principle of all being. Only now, under the influence of postmodernity, God's existence cannot simply be assumed as it so often was in premodernity. Rather, God can be recognized to overtake human persons by the revelatory gift of mysterious, loving difference. One commentator names this achievement "ontotheology to excess," a postmodern project indeed.[1]

The new ontotheology has the added advantage of being quite clear that the human subject is self-consciously involved in the process of knowing where and how God is self-revelatory. God is self-revelatory in the state of consciousness in which transcendent love transforms a person. In this sense, modernity's centrally important turn to the subject is acknowledged and endorsed. From there, statements of belief and of understanding may unfold.

As it stands, this summary of how to retain important characteristics of the three eras of Western culture is too akin to slogans. What is needed is a method that critically elaborates just how the process of integrating the three eras can be implemented, preserving what can be preserved and eliminating what cannot or should not be preserved. Moreover, the method must be capable of demonstrating the reasonableness of ontotheology to excess. No less, it must be a method capable of guiding the emergence and formation

19

of religious beliefs and understandings. In short, the method must demonstrate convincingly that faith and belief in God are reasonable.

Fortunately, such a method is at hand. It is a method that acknowledges the possibility for human persons to discover meaning, truth, and value. It is available in an implementation of the operations of human consciousness patterned to attain insight, "the grasp of immanent explanatory intelligibility verifiable in empirical instances."[2] The method is articulated in Bernard Lonergan's analysis of human intentionality. Moreover, Lonergan's analysis shows that religious faith is one of the specifications of the pattern.[3]

On the basis of Lonergan's philosophical-theological analysis I am confident that we can affirm the philosophical conviction of the premoderns, who found in their discoveries of the true and the good something of the truth and goodness of God. I am confident that we can affirm the philosophical conviction of the moderns that there is a method by which human subjects can achieve meaning, truth, and value with some assurance that they are on a correct course. I am confident that the postmodern emphasis upon plurality, relativity, and historicity as characteristics of human activity can enrich, rather than debilitate, that quest of human subjects for meaning, truth, and value.[4]

Before offering a summary of Lonergan's intentionality analysis that will be serviceable for an understanding of the chapters which follow, I return briefly to Vaclav Havel's Independence Day speech, referred to in the previous chapter. In his effort to move contemporary culture beyond the modern, Havel invites a recovery of the Other that is the transcendent, the sacred. For, he claims, we will lose our humanity unless we can achieve such a recovery. Here is how Havel expresses this:

> Politicians at international forums may reiterate a thousand times that the basis of the new world order must be universal respect for human rights, but it will mean nothing as long as this imperative does not derive from the respect of the miracle of being, the miracle of the universe, the miracle of nature, the miracle of our own existence.
>
> Transcendence [is] the only real alternative to extinction.[5]

INTENTIONALITY ANALYSIS AND TRANSFORMATIVE PRAXIS[6]

Bernard Lonergan's proposals, formed during a writing and teaching career of over fifty years, deal with the issues of human knowledge and choice in a way that solves the modern problem of whether humans know and relate to a world solely of their own device, or whether they not only bring about reality in the myriad ways of human expression, but also conform to a world which exists both before and beyond the human enterprise.

Lonergan's answer, in brief, agrees with the premoderns that there is a divinely created and ordered reality, including the world of human beings, which it is possible gradually to know and understand, and which human persons are invited to love as a creation of the loving God, even as we seek to overcome the aberrations that distort God's intelligible and lovable creation. Lonergan also endorses the modern project that highlights the role of the human subject, insofar as only through human acts of experiencing, understanding, knowing, and evaluating can human beings relate to the world as it is and constitute the world that ought to be, that is, a humanly formed world that conforms, by the free and responsible choice of human persons individually and communally, to the divine ordering of creation. And Lonergan acknowledges, with the postmoderns, that the historical conditioning of every human being assures some degree of relativity to every expression (language, proposition, project, including religious faith). Thus, it will always be possible, and needful, for human persons to be surprised and jolted out of complacency by the "Other" in its various forms, to recognize the "difference" that had previously been overlooked or rejected,[7] and to recognize the Other that is transcendent mystery.[8]

Intentionality Analysis

Lonergan's analysis of human intentionality is the reason that he is able to gather up what at first appear to be quite diverse elements from the three periods of Western and Christian history. On the one hand, every human person, of every time and place, relates to her or his environment out of the conditioned subjectivity which he or she has acquired. In other words, there is no such thing as a presuppositionless approach to understanding, truth, and values. At the same time, by intending whatever makes up the environment, the human person reaches or can reach beyond self to a wider world than herself or himself alone. An elementary example illustrates this twofold point. Long experience has taught residents of northern countries that in January one should expect cold weather and dress appropriately. A visitor to the North from a tropical region may be subjectively quite unprepared for a northern winter, but a simple step outside the door of the airport terminal will lead the visitor to feel and know (i.e., to intend quite objectively) cold weather. In the case of both the northerner and the southerner there is a subjective dimension, a preformation already informing the person (including images of a cold, northern winter, feelings about it, expectations of how to react, etc.) and a dimension of intending something quite real that exists apart from the person.

By studying the procedures of the natural sciences, mathematics, psychiatry, and common-sense practicality, as well as by reading in the philosophical and theological tradition, Bernard Lonergan has sorted out four chief operations of human consciousness: experience, understanding, judgment, and decision. Each represents a distinct level of consciousness. Several comparable activities of the subject cluster at each level of consciousness. These activities spontaneously pattern themselves in an orderly progression from experience to understanding to judging to deciding. By all these activities each human person relates both to the objects of the environment and to self.

Activities indicated by the umbrella term *experience* are the sensations of touch and taste, hearing, seeing, and smelling by which persons are impacted by their environment. Simultaneously, feelings are activated: pleasure or pain, fear or complacency, anger or goodwill, and so on, along with the sights and sounds and smells. What focuses the sensations and feelings are the interests and questions of the subject of the experiences.[9] A botanist looking at a mushroom senses in a different way from a chef looking at the same mushroom. Same sight, but different seers, same taste, but different tasters, with different concerns and so distinct experiences.

Indeed, the questions with which a person may or may not approach any set of experiences leads to the next set of activities, those clustering around the term *understanding*. People without questions relevant to particular experiences of touch or taste or sight may pay no heed. But people with questions probe and organize their experiences. They imagine what this or that set of experiences might mean. Insights into the meaning of the experiences pop into their heads. The questioner may devise some experiments to generate more insights cognate to those that are "out of the blue." Investigators may develop theories, sometimes very elaborate theories.

But insights and theories need to be tested. Can the experiences, sometimes ordered in various ways by means of experiments, and the possible meanings be demonstrated to coincide, to fall together? Does the understanding really explain the confluence of experiences? Do the experiences support the supposed understanding? If the answer to both questions is "yes," a *judgment* can be made that, yes, indeed, one's questions have been satisfactorily answered. The degree of satisfaction may vary from certainty to probability to a reasonable conclusion—barring further data to the contrary.

Often judgments of what is so, or not so, complete the dynamic process. If one is wondering whether a hurricane is brewing in the Atlantic Ocean in August or whether monarch butterflies migrate south to Mexico, a satisfactory judgment of fact can bring the matter to a close. But very often the judgment is of a moral good or evil, of a course of action to be pursued or avoided. Then another and further level of activities cluster around the term *decision*. A person or a group of persons evaluate together in order to decide whether to act or to avoid action. Should I pursue an intimate relationship with this person? Is this an honest way to make some money? Collectively, the political leaders of a nation might ask not only whether they would vanquish a foe if they entered into combat, but if it is a genuine good to invade the territory of a neighboring nation.

Evaluation includes making a judgment of the value of an action. Included in the judgment is the determination of moral/ethical good. Is something good just for me and just for now? Will the choice of this course of action harm me or others or the environment? An affective component enters into the process of making such a judgment because feelings inevitably come into play. Hope and fear, longing and revulsion, love and hate, and so many other feelings affect judgments of value. Lonergan describes feelings in this sense as intentional responses to value, and to make them "moral" such feelings have to be "cultivated, enlightened, strengthened, refined, criticized and pruned of oddities."[10] Finally, in an act of responsibility a decision is taken. Thus, the dynamic human process of seeking meaning, truth, and value has fully unfolded.[11]

In summary, the inquirer begins with the presentations of experience and then moves on to an effort to understand all the data that has been presented. After achieving some understanding, or perhaps various possible understandings, of the data, the inquirer tests the understandings against the presentations and may be able to achieve an affirmation of the truth. Finally, especially if the affirmations are judgments of value, the inquirer searches for the right course of action or, to put it another way, for the good way to proceed, and makes a responsible decision.

This pattern of the operations of consciousness is the way of investigation in the natural sciences and the humanities:

- observation, gathering, and arrangement of data;
- inquiry into the meaning of the data that leads to insights and, perhaps, theories;
- the adequacy of the insights and theories is determined by testing them over against the data;
- if the adequate insights or theories have implications for action, then questions are asked to determine what action is responsible.

Another route to the world beyond the self begins with feeling. By studying the knowledge imparted by feelings, especially by the paramount feeling of interpersonal love and the specialized feelings of religious experience, Lonergan has further differentiated a second organization of the chief operations of human consciousness, in this case moving from affective intentionality and decisions to beliefs and values, and from there to efforts to understand and share achieved beliefs and values on the level of experience, where they have the most profound effect upon persons. The operations of consciousness remain the same, but the process begins with affective experience leading to decisions, rather than ending up there. One implementation of this latter route through feeling is the way of religious consciousness.[12]

It is the same four operations of consciousness—experience, understanding, judging, and deciding—but now the dynamic movement takes its start from the experience of evaluative feelings that urge a person to make a *decision* to love because one feels oneself to be loved, to repent because one feels ashamed, to rejoice because one feels euphoria, to reject something because one feels hatred. In other words, the inquirer begins with decision, rather than ending up there. From there, the inquirer must let another feeling also have its influence, namely, desire or longing for the truth, in order to determine that what seems to be lovable really is a lovable person, that what has made one feel shame is actually shameful, that what is causing euphoria is worth the joy, that what one wants to reject is truly despicable (e.g., never a person, but an act such as murder or racial prejudice). In almost all instances one's grasp of the true situation is not a matter of evidence confirmed by the senses and related experiments that motivate the judgments of natural science. Instead, it is more a matter of *judgments* of belief. One believes because a witness has been shown to be eminently trustworthy. Sometimes the witness is the sincerity of one's feelings and the corroboration of one's own reflective reason; sometimes it is another person upon whom we confidently rely. In such instances, it makes more sense to believe than it does not to believe.

Many who begin with evaluative feelings and proceed to belief judgments stop there. But the dynamism of human consciousness pushes further toward some systematic *understanding* of related beliefs, whether in the political or the social or the religious order. Connections become important. How do these beliefs relate to beliefs and other sorts of judgments and understandings in other areas of human concern and endeavor? It is a question of the meaning of it all, sometimes reaching toward a worldview. Finally, as one comes to some greater or lesser understanding one is back again in the world of sights and sounds, of a sense of oneself, of *experience*. Only now it is a world transformed by feelings and beliefs and the understandings brought to bear upon them. One is worshipful and ethical and neighborly and domestic, forming communities accordingly, because of the dynamic operations of consciousness proceeding from evaluative experience through decisions and beliefs and understandings to enriched day-to-day living.[13]

In summary, this pattern of the operations of consciousness is the way of human community, including religious faith communities:

- inner experience of feelings leads to commitments to a course of action, often including a decision to believe;
- formulations of beliefs follow;
- there is a search for what these beliefs mean for the rest of human living;

- one is back in the everyday world, but now the world of daily living is invested with the implications of the beliefs that have been affirmed.

While it is not difficult to appreciate how one's world is transformed when the acts of consciousness operate from evaluation down, it is also true that one's world can be transformed by observing the operations of consciousness from experience to understanding to judgment and decision. When the process operates in this way one carries on in everyday life with the changes wrought by the development of sophisticated medicines and Internet access and air travel and globalization of the economy, and many other ways served by the natural sciences and the resultant technology. These all change the world too, and they influence the existential stance of those who live in it.

The interrelationship among the four levels of consciousness is normatively patterned. That is to say that one cannot understand or make a judgment or decision if there are no data upon which to focus. Experience of data precedes the other operations. Likewise, some understanding of what "cold" means, at least appreciation of how to use the word, is required before one could judge, on the basis of one's experience, "It is cold outside." Moreover, no matter how facilely one has judged a possible action to be the right thing to do or the wrong, some such judgment has to precede one's decision to choose between alternatives. So, Lonergan maintains that there is a way in which, in a wide range of instances, decision requires prior judgment, and judgment requires some sort of understanding, and all three could not operate at all without some experience of data. In another range of instances, affectively influential decisions precede judgments of belief, which in turn precede acts of understanding, which discern the intelligibility of sights and sounds, taste and touch. Fidelity to the process, in either direction, is what makes the difference between authenticity and unauthenticity.

The Vagaries of Human Individuals

While maintaining the normative pattern of the operations of consciousness, we do not want to dehumanize the relationships. At whatever point in their life's journey adult human persons reflect upon themselves as experiencing, understanding, judging, and deciding in a pattern, they bring with them the accumulation of their lifetime of experiences, understandings, judgments, and decisions. How they came to some of their understandings and judgments they can recall quite clearly. How they came to many is hidden in the subliminal consciousness, and, indeed, may have been attained on that level.

So, one child, living in one household, experiences data similar to a child living next door. But each learns particular meanings of family relationships, judgments of the character of neighbors, evaluations of the worth of human activities under the strong influence of the home environment. Thus, people not part of the culture find it difficult to understand why Protestants and Catholics in Northern Ireland should harbor such antipathy toward one another. In fact, increasing numbers of citizens of Northern Ireland are changing their social and political judgments and thus making decisions for acceptance of the other. But many in Northern Ireland, relying on generations of accepted understanding of the other as enemy and continuing to read the data as evidence of untrustworthiness, judge and decide accordingly. The example illustrates that prior understandings, judgments (including beliefs), and decisions create an interpretive framework within which one will experience data. To repeat a previous statement, there is never any presuppositionless experiencing, questioning, reflecting, and deliberating.

Still, once we recognize that we are influenced by our history and by our language, we can become alert to our biases, to what we may be overlooking, and respectfully learn to heed others whose understandings, judgments, and decisions differ from ours.[14] This is not to suggest an unevaluative tolerance of every viewpoint and position, but a healthy appreciation on the part of each person of the relativity of her or his perspective.

It is for this reason that conversation must be so much a part of the implementation of the operations of consciousness.[15] It is not a matter of solitary individuals going about the business of experiencing, understanding, judging, and deciding in neat and orderly patterns of activity. It is a matter of conversation partners entering into dialogue with each other, and this includes, of course, our ancestors down through history, as well as contemporaries who tend to be left out of the conversation. And while chance (or luck, good fortune, fate, grace) plays a significant role in the possibility of the many, many human conversations taking place at any given time yielding genuine meaning (the product of understanding), truth (the product of judgment), and value (the product of decision), still the chances are improved if all the partners try to be attentive to all the data, bar none of the questions for understanding, take seriously all the evidence, and accept full responsibility for their decisions.

What the Operations of Consciousness Can Achieve

Such is something of the significance of the phrase *intentionality analysis*. Now let us turn our attention to its counterpart, the phrase *transformative praxis*. It is a phrase which here expresses the valuable outcome of putting intentionality analysis into practice. It is a phrase which recognizes that the relationship of human persons to their world has three moments: receptive (corresponding to the operation of experience), interpretive (corresponding to the operations of understanding and judgment), and constitutive (corresponding to the operation of deliberation). In the receptive moment, subjects are immediately present to themselves as experiencing. But the receptive moment extends further than the immediacy of the person's experience of self. It is also a reception of our environment as given, whether the sights and sounds of the street, the acrid smells in the chemist's laboratory or near a fire, the marks of print on a page of paper or a computer screen, or feelings of elation, dejection, calm, agitation, and so on. Of course, as noted above, we never simply "receive" data. From the start, we wear an interpretive lens. But when we no longer simply "interpret" unwittingly, but seek to be attentive and carefully raise questions for understanding and judgment, then we mediate meaning (i.e., genuine understandings) and truth (i.e., things as they actually are—reality). Finally, when our understanding and judgments have to do not with what is, but with what might be and even what ought to be, we are moving into the constitutive moment of the human relationship to the world, which reaches its fulfillment in decisions to do things and in the implementation of decisions.

But how can any individual person or group of persons be assured that they have genuinely achieved meaning, truth, and value? For Lonergan it goes back to questions. When a person raises questions, he or she may be too quick to come to an answer. Then the effort to understand misses the meaning or the effort to judge misses the truth or the effort to decide misses the good. To be genuine a person must ask all the relevant questions for understanding and judging and deciding. And since alone we humans are prone to make mistakes, conversation is also a must. Not least, we should listen to those who disagree with us, as well as to those who would confirm our conclusions. Respectful, thoughtful conversation is part of authentic intentionality.

The implementation of human intentionality leads to practice, namely, practice to effect something, whether within ourselves or in our society or in nature. But "transformative" refers primarily to the way in which commitment to intentionality analysis can lead to a person's transformation of herself or himself, and in intimately profound ways. We become persons who transcend ourselves by being in a world that exists beyond ourselves. In such cases, "practice" becomes "praxis."

The "beyond" toward which we reach can be surprisingly transcendent, quite beyond any expectations.

- As we become alert to the data, and allow ourselves to be alert to the data as far as they take us, we may note, among the data, feelings of wonder, awe, longing, love which invite us beyond ourselves and beyond what is immanent in the world of the senses to a transcending world. Our subjectivity becomes transformed.
- Or, on the level of the operations of decision, when we are deliberating or evaluating, it can happen that the inner, personal demand to be

responsible is so forceful that we cannot but affirm and choose values that we must adopt, no matter how inconvenient to ourselves and our life style.

- Or the experience of love for the other is so intense that we cannot but affirm, "I love you," and then seek to understand the subject, object, and predicate of the judgment in all their complexity. We become transformed; our lives become transformed by love.

- On the level of the operation of understanding, which is always closely linked with its related operation of judging, the questions for meaning and truth can be so dominant that our conscience refuses to allow us to accept shortcuts, quick answers, the easy way. We find ourselves compelled to seek the whole truth and nothing but the truth, and to understand the truth as best our human resources enable us to do. We become transformed by our implementation of the operations of understanding and judging; by our search for meaning and truth. Thus, fully cognizant, faithful implementation of human intentionality as disclosed through intentionality analysis becomes a human action (praxis) transformative of ourselves as persons.

REALITY, DIVINE REALITY, RELIGIOUS FAITH

This section begins with a summary of the normal course of how persons come to know what is there to be known. From there the reflection moves to the relationship between religious faith and knowledge of reality that is beyond the possibility of human comprehension, namely, religious reality. How does religious faith work? Is it trustworthy as a reliable mode of human knowledge? How far can we go with it?

To Know Reality

The operations of consciousness provide the way that we humans interact with the world, a world which includes ourselves as well as a vast array of beings other than ourselves. When we experience data we are potentially in contact with something. The data may be simply products of ourselves, perhaps induced by a fever or a dream. In such a case, of course, the data put us in immediate contact with some dimension of ourselves. To determine which dimension they put us in touch with requires that we mediate our experience by questions for understanding and then for judgment. Conversation with physicians, including the application of various medical tests and treatments, can be of great help in the interpretation of data induced by fever, and conversation with psychologists can be of help in the interpretation of data induced by dreams.

Because the persons reading this text have all implemented the operations of consciousness over a period of some years, it will not come as a surprise to add that very frequently, when persons experience data, they have come into immediate contact with realities other than themselves. The identification and nature of the reality encountered has to be determined by asking some questions about the accuracy of each individual's understandings. Those understandings are themselves the result of questions that probe the meaning of the data. To the extent that inquirers are able honestly to acknowledge that they have attended to all the data that are there to be observed, and asked all the relevant questions that have posed themselves, and carefully related the understandings with the data through whatever process of sifting and weighing seems necessary, to that extent persons can confidently claim that they know and understand something of the world that is there to be known. Needless to say, in countless areas of human inquiry, the process of coming to know can take years and require huge numbers of investigators.

True enough, we humans need to be modest about how extensive our knowledge is and how comprehensive our understanding. There is always the possibility that overlooked data will be discovered later and that previous understandings and judgments will later be shown to have been shortsighted. Time and again later inquirers have demonstrated that earlier inquirers had overstepped what the insight grasped and what the evidence warranted. Precipitously, sometimes rashly, possibilities have been raised to the status of probabilities, and probabilities to the status of certainties. In any case, mistakes, even egregious ones, are easy for any inquirer to make.[16] One need not be embarrassed to have taken on a major question and to have essayed an answer only to learn subsequently that one must revise the earlier conclusions. The quest for understanding and knowledge is a self-correcting process of learning.

However, although we make mistakes, and plenty of them, we do not need to take the route of the timid or the skeptical in the direction of denying altogether the possibility that inquiry is worthwhile and promises to yield genuine understanding and truth.[17] We only need to persevere. Openness to a universe that is accessible to engagement by human subjects is a fundamental attitude connected with the program of intentionality analysis.

Transcendent Mystery and Religious Faith

Religious faith is one area in which openness to the universe functions profitably. It is true that data do not put us in immediate contact with a transcendent realm. They are the data of discernible feelings that uncannily urge us on toward something more, something beyond. Or they are the data of sight and sound, taste, touch, and smell that awaken our inner reach beyond human grasp. Because this is the case, religious faith is an instance of human intentionality that differs in significant ways from the natural sciences, the humanities, and the determination of many everyday, practical understandings, judgments, and decisions. Nevertheless, religious faith is a dimension of human being to which intentionality analysis is applicable and which certainly is an instance of transformative praxis. I would argue that it is the most significant instance.[18]

Religious faith is the product of attentiveness to the data at hand. In this sense it takes its start in the manner of every branch of inquiry. But, in religious faith, when affirmations of truth are made they acknowledge reality that is transcendent. Moreover, the evidence compelling affirmation is very much tied in with the feelings of the person of faith.[19] A person is so moved by wonder in the face of some human event or natural phenomenon that he is led to affirm by belief a realm of transcendence. Or someone is so caught up in love which she knows to be personal and yet not attached to anyone at hand, indeed, beyond this-worldly love in uncanny ways, that she is led to affirm by belief the existence of a transcendent person.

Understandings of religious beliefs, when they occur, are admittedly quite feeble, simply glimpses into the religious reality which do not ultimately satisfy one's desire to understand but which are sufficient to enable a more sophisticated attachment to the object of faith. There is a healthy and close relationship between a faith which does not speak in the presence of transcendence and a faith which does speak, however incipiently.[20]

How does divine revelation fit into all this? German theologian Walter Kasper has proposed that human freedom is the door that opens onto divine revelation. In the face of death, the human being has the choice to "surrender self in order to gain self."[21] In this freedom the subject can believe in God as the fulfillment of human freedom, and subjects who so believe are basically claiming that it makes more sense to believe than not to believe. Belief from this perspective is not mindless. It is not a voluntaristic leap of faith. It is a matter of responsible choice leading to affirmation.

Kasper's placement of both the origin and the reasonableness of religious faith in human freedom is, to some extent, comparable to Lonergan's analysis of the openness of intentionality. While much modern philosophy specifically rules out the possibility of religious faith on a par with, for example, natural science, Lonergan demonstrates that human intentionality is open to whatever is knowable and lovable, including God. But, of course, the infinite God can only become accessible to finite humans if, and to the extent that, God chooses to reveal Godself. In the case of divine revelation, it is possible for theology, in conjunction with philosophy of religion, to articulate how and why human subjects are able reasonably and responsibly to choose a religious faith that names God, and to come to some determination about action consonant with the name of God. That is the purpose of this book.

I am writing as a Christian believer, reflecting as a theologian out of the long heritage of Christian faith in God as triune. My purpose is not to offer a philosophy of religion without any presupposition of faith, but to ask from within Christian faith and from within the church which professes it, how this faith takes shape and how it makes sense in the contemporary context of postmodernity—thus, the use of the philosophical meanings of intentionality analysis and transformative praxis. Because Christian faith is in God as triune, the chapters that follow are cast in explicitly trinitarian terms. Throughout I reflect upon the one God whom Christians confess to be at once three and distinct and personal. My reflection employs intentionality analysis to assist the formulation of a theology of religious faith that claims divine revelation as its source.

The Project Ahead

For the sake of clarity, without, I trust, oversimplifying the matter, I shall devote the next several chapters to each of three operations of consciousness: evaluative experience, judgment, and understanding.[22] Chapter 3 will ask the question of God on the level of evaluative experience. On this level we reflect upon subjects in their experience of inner data, namely, feelings, but as these experiences prompt a decision of faith. How does religious experience lead one into transcendent reality such that the person feels urged toward religious faith, hope, and love? What are the particular evaluative experiences that attract some to find that Jesus of Nazareth evokes religious faith in themselves?

Chapters 4 and 5 ask the question of God on the level of operations which lead to judgment. When compelling religious experience joins with reflection upon specific data related to faith in Jesus, affirmations gradually follow and accumulate, namely, belief statements about Jesus and Jesus' relation to God. Originally, these take shape in short, doxological or confessional utterances, often imaginative. So, the early Christians profess, "Jesus is Lord" (I Cor 12: 3) or "Jesus Christ is the same yesterday, today and forever" (Heb 13:8), or they pray, "Amen. Come, Lord Jesus!" (Rev 22:20).[23] Eventually, because the doxological utterances are open to interpretations that groups of Christian believers feel or sense to be contrary to their evaluative experiences, or to convictions they bring with them to their meeting with the Christian word, there is conflict and a process of sorting out acceptable meanings. The defining trinitarian and christological church councils of the fourth and fifth centuries result. Chapters 4 and 5 will study this process as a move toward judgments of truth. They will also include a discussion of the reasonableness of such doctrinal formulations for Christian believers today.

As Christian doctrine on God accumulated, theologians sought to understand more explicitly and in greater detail what the doctrine on the triune

God might mean. Beyond images, which could be ambiguous, there is the hope that faith in Christ might not only be professed but also understood in some small way. The best theologians always have understood that doctrine expresses something about God who infinitely surpasses the human potential for getting to the heart of the matter. Nevertheless, it is of great value to understand what can be understood. The quest to understand the doctrine of God which Christians profess is the project of the sixth, seventh and eighth chapters. Often understanding is sought for its own sake. Often it is sought specifically for practical purposes. Even in the former quest, however, transformative effects upon the inquirer(s) can follow, as well as implications for the church's structures and mission. Such understanding learns from the past but needs also to be judged adequate within the contemporary context.

The interreligious dialogue which has been taking place over the last several decades raises important questions that are profitably addressed in the light of the first part of this book. Chapter 9 takes note how the global interaction of people of different religions invites dialogue, a genuine conversation, between Christians and non-Christian people of religious faith. While interreligious dialogue is pertinent to all dimensions of faith, the discussion in chapter 9 deals with the question of God. Finally, chapter 10 probes how interreligious dialogue affects the Christian affirmation of Jesus as the unique, explicitly personal manifestation of God in human history and, as such, the unique savior of humankind. The discussion in chapter 10 is important for trinitarian faith and theology since faith in Jesus as the Word become incarnate is the catalyst for the doctrine of the Trinity in the first place.

NOTES

1. Anthony J. Godzieba, "Ontotheology to Excess: Imagining God without Being," *Theological Studies* 56 (1995): 12, 19. One of Godzieba's dialogue partners is Jean-Luc Marion, especially in his book, *God without Being: Hors-Texte.*

2. McCarthy, *Crisis of Philosophy,* 276.

3. The two major works of Lonergan which articulate his views are *Insight: A Study of Human Understanding* (Toronto: University of Toronto Press, 1992; originally published 1957) and *Method in Theology* (Toronto: University of Toronto Press; originally published 1972). On religious faith, see esp. chapter 20 of *Insight,* and chapters 4 and 11 of *Method in Theology.*

4. In taking up the challenge to employ Lonergan's philosophy of intentionality analysis and transformative praxis as the best available way to value much of postmodern concern for relativity and historicity without becoming relativist and historicist, I also refer the reader to Fred Lawrence, "The Fragility of Consciousness: Lonergan and the Postmodern Concern for the Other," *Theological Studies* 54 (1993): 55–94. Similarly, Robert Doran expresses his confidence in Lonergan's achievement

in *Theology and the Dialectics of History*. Doran writes: "On the basis of Lonergan's resolution of the modern turn to the subject, and in an effort to increase the probability of survival of this already emergent achievement, we must turn to the negotiation of Marx, Freud, and Nietzsche, and of their contemporary disciples. A turn to the subject, brought to completion, will be able to incorporate, while transforming, the masters of suspicion in an understanding and constitution of historical process in terms of the dialectics of community (Marx), the subject (Freud), and culture (Nietzsche)" (Toronto: University of Toronto Press, 1989), 158.

5. Vaclav Havel, "The New Measure of Man."

6. Throughout his writings, Bernard Lonergan discusses these two themes. For a sampling, I suggest three articles by Lonergan: "Cognitional Structure" and "The Dimensions of Meaning," in *Collection*, vol. 4 of *Collected Works of Bernard Lonergan*, ed. Frederick E. Crowe and Robert M. Doran (Toronto: University of Toronto Press, 1988) and "Healing and Creating in History," in *A Third Collection*, ed. Frederick E. Crowe, S.J. (Mahwah, NJ: Paulist Press, 1985).

7. If I understand Heidegger correctly, this is what he is urging when he labors over the "difference" between Being and beings. We must let beings show themselves in their differences, and not bypass their differences in our search for what they share in common as Being. See, e.g., "The Onto-theo-logical Constitution of Metaphysics," 50–51.

8. In *Method in Theology*, Lonergan remarks that "transcendent mystery" is "the primary and fundamental meaning of the name, God" (341).

9. Lonergan writes of different configurations or patterns of experience determined by a person's "direction, striving, effort." He lists such patterns as biological, aesthetic, intellectual, and dramatic in *Insight*, 204ff. In *Method in Theology*, Lonergan adds reference to another pattern of experience, the mystical or religious (29).

10. *Method in Theology*, 30–34, 38.

11. On the dynamic structure of human knowing, involving the first three operations of consciousness, see Lonergan's "Cognitional Structure." A text that includes the fourth level of consciousness is *Method in Theology*, 6–13.

12. Besides chapter 4 of Lonergan's *Method in Theology*, which traces the route from religious experience to religious faith and then to religious belief, see also Lonergan's "Philosophy of God, and Theology: The Relationship between Philosophy of God and the Functional Specialty, Systematics" in *Philosophical and Theological Papers 1965–1980*, vol. 17 of *Collected Works of Bernard Lonergan* (Toronto: University of Toronto Press, 2004). See, e.g., 179–91.

13. See Lonergan, "Healing and Creating in History," 106. See also *Method in Theology* on "another kind of knowledge" than that of "factual knowledge" (115). For yet another way to express the two routes to meaning, truth, and value, see Frederick E. Crowe, S.J., *Lonergan* (Collegeville, MN: Liturgical Press, 1992), 109–10.

14. Because human beings are easily biased, intellectual, moral, and religious conversion are imperative. See *Method in Theology* on intellectual (238–40), moral (240), and religious (240–41) conversion. On bias, see *Method in Theology*, 53.

15. James L. Marsh writes of the need of "rational, evidential communicative praxis" in "Ambiguity, Language, and Communicative Praxis: A Critical Modernist Articulation," in *Modernity and Its Discontents*, ed. James L. Marsh, John D. Caputo, and Merold Westphal (New York: Fordham University Press, 1992), 96. David Tracy

writes that "[c]onversation in its primary form is an exploration of possibilities in the search for the truth," in *Plurality and Ambiguity: Hermeneutics, Religion, Hope* (San Francisco: Harper & Row, 1987), 20.

16. Thomas Kuhn, in *The Structure of the Scientific Revolution*, states in question form what is universally accepted as frequently the outcome of scientific investigation: "Is it really any wonder that the price of significant scientific advance is a commitment that runs the risk of being wrong?" (101).

17. James L. Marsh, in the section "Postmodernism/Critical Modernism," in *Modernity and Its Discontents*, drives home the importance of this point when he criticizes the statement of John D. Caputo quoted in chapter 1: "The truth is that there is no truth." Marsh points out that such a statement is not "self-referentially consistent." By his statement Caputo is claiming that his account of the state of affairs is "truer, more adequate, more comprehensive" (18). Thus, Caputo implicitly acknowledges the dynamism of the operations of consciousness toward meaning and truth. See also James L. Marsh, "Ambiguity, Language, and Communicative Praxis: A Critical Modernist Approach," in the same volume, 90.

18. See Lonergan, *Method in Theology*, 19 n. 5.

19. See Lonergan, *Method in Theology*, 115f.

20. Dietrich Bonhoeffer remarks on the presence of this quality of Christian faith in *Letters and Papers from Prison* (London: Fontana Books, 1959), 50: "It is only when one knows the ineffability of the Name of God that one can utter the name of Jesus Christ."

21. Walter Kasper, *The God of Jesus Christ*, trans. Matthew J. O'Connell (New York: Crossroad, 1999; originally published 1982), 104–9. At p. 106 I have altered the text slightly in service of gender inclusivity.

22. These are specific implementations of Lonergan's functional specialties, foundations, doctrines, and systematics as formulated in *Method in Theology*, chapters 11, 12, and 13.

23. Anthony Kelly, CSSR, distinguishes further modes of expressing trinitarian awareness in *The Trinity of Love: A Theology of the Christian God* (Wilmington, DE: Glazier, 1987), 30–48.

3

Drawn into Mystery

At least while awake, humans are constantly experiencing. This is true when we consider experience in the sense of seeing, hearing, touching, tasting, smelling. It is also true in the sense of consciousness, persons' experience of themselves not only seeing, hearing, touching, tasting, smelling, but also their experience of themselves asking questions and understanding, judging, and deciding. It is true, too, in the sense of persons' experience of themselves feeling various affections: wonder and awe or their opposite, ennui; attraction and longing or their opposite, repulsion; joy or sorrow; enthusiastic welcoming or fear; trust or distrust; love or hate; and others. Sometimes we seem to be assaulted by sensory data and the data of our consciousness, especially conflicting feelings, to the point of being overwhelmed. Sometimes the context of our experience is more tranquil, even orderly; we are at peace with our world and ourselves. Either by our insights and affirmations we have sorted things out, or we don't feel a need to have sorted things out. Sometimes we long for stimulation. As often as not, the faster or slower pace of experience is due as much to our moods as to events in our environment.

RELIGIOUS EXPERIENCE

Among descriptions of experience is the designation "religious." People speak of religious experience. What constitutes an experience that makes it religious? W. Norris Clarke, emeritus professor of philosophy at Fordham University, offers the following description: "any direct existential awareness of the presence or activity of an ultimate, absolute, transcendent dimension of reality, especially the more intense forms of unitive awareness of this Transcendent which have traditionally been called 'mystical experience.'"[1]

If we focus on sensory data, we could single out what various people might take to be religious experiences: the sound of Gregorian chant or a Bach chorale or a native American hymn to a rain god; the sight and smell of incense or of the blood of a sacrificed animal; the touch of prayer beads; the taste of flesh at a burnt offering or of eucharistic bread and wine. Such experiences, however, are not religious in themselves. The sound of Gregorian chant may signal a nonreligious New Wave event; the smell of incense may simply be a cover-up for a drug party; prayer beads may serve as quaint jewelry; a congregant may taste communion mindlessly. To invest sensory data with religious meaning a pattern of understandings and judgments and evaluations needs to be functioning. True as this is, any one of these experiences of sensory data, and many others besides, could be a catalyst or an expression of what is more properly named religious experience.

More primal than sensory data are the feelings in which human beings experience themselves being tugged at and pulled into a world beyond that with which they are familiar. We find ourselves at some point in our lives secure, perhaps very secure, in our world of meanings, truths, and values. But then an event can intrude into our secure world and prompt feelings that draw us beyond: a life-threatening illness, a blossoming friendship, job loss, a view of natural beauty and power. Such events can engender feelings that knock persons off their balance. Suddenly, a person becomes caught up in wonder, consumed with longing, beset by fear, overwhelmed by sorrow, gathered up in trust, filled with love.

There are other times, when life is going along quite smoothly, that the same sort of feelings can demand attention of a person more quietly, subtly, unobtrusively. The feelings start at the edges of one's world and gradually work their way toward the center, drawing the person increasingly into attentiveness to the feelings. Persons find themselves distracted while at other tasks. They find themselves taking time to stay with the feelings, allow their force to hold sway, accept their lead beyond the world in which they have been comfortable.

What can be happening to persons who acknowledge and become engaged by such experiences is that affective feelings are drawing them into self-transcending reflection. Upon questioning the meaning of the feelings, persons find that nothing in the world they currently inhabit is up to being the cause of the feeling or its goal. The feeling is apparently "otherworldly" in its source and objective. Just what this other world might be remains unknown. One is in the realm of mystery.

At this point an example might be helpful. In the late 1970s, as I was going about my daily living, motivated by religious faith and regularly taking time for personal prayer, I began to feel fear. It was a recurrent feeling, often arising unexpectedly, often lingering at the edges of my prayer. Why was I feeling fear? My life was moving along quite well at the time. I lived in a pleasant neighborhood. Work was satisfying. Social relationships were friendly. Religious faith and prayer were personally enriching. There was no physical or personal threat, no economic or other job-related threat. At the same time, I felt psychologically healthy, even content. Nevertheless, the sense of fear persisted, reaching quite obviously beyond me or my environment.

Gradually by eliminating possible sources of the fear, I came to understand that the fear was associated with my feeling of the embrace of total love and its demands. I began to realize how such total love, magnificent as it is, was increasingly requiring total commitment of me and would, if I followed through, eventually require total self-giving in some form. I was feeling a transcending fear associated with a transcending love that inevitably would shake all my this-worldly security and comfort. A fearsome prospect.

When we allow our feelings to draw us into the realm of mystery, comfort in and control of our world of meanings and values has to be exchanged for readiness to submit to the power of mystery. This is no easy commitment to make. It is a risk. For one thing, what if there is no meaning or value in the realm of mystery? What if it is nothing, illusory?

Second, even if there is something quite real about the realm of mystery, and even if the something is someone who is infinitely loving and lovable, the world to which we have become accustomed, in which we have become comfortable, now no longer holds. One must let go in order to embrace mystery. One can feel herself or himself to be in a free fall. Then what?

Despite the risks, the overwhelming power of the affections begins to rearrange what is important to the subject of the experience such that the person becomes increasingly transformed by mystery. Experiences which are so characterized by transcendence and have such power over the person who experiences can be named religious experience. From a theological perspective, we would say that experiences of this sort are a gift of God's grace drawing the recipient into communion with the loving God.

In the paragraphs which follow, I examine some feelings that can take on the quality of religious experience. Nine are singled out for consideration: wonder, awe, longing, love, fear, trust, guilt and shame, sorrow, and joy. Following the exposition of the feelings, I speak to the intentionality of the feelings, their objective, the goal toward which they head. In other words, what do we mean in the present context when we speak of the realm of mystery? Finally, I address, on the level of experience, the issue of the particularity of Christian faith, namely, attraction to the person of Jesus.

Wonder

Wonder and knowledge are closely related. In his second book of *Metaphysics*, Aristotle writes that everyone wonders why things are as they are. I trust that the reader can recall instances of wonder. Wonder expresses itself in questions. Very young children wonder about a seemingly endless array of things that their adult caretakers take for granted. Adults wonder regularly about the reason for events and they are mystified by the behavior some people demonstrate. Scientists wonder about the universe in its details. Clearly, wonder is an intentional feeling that is important in the practical world of everyday living as well as in the world of scientific investigation. It keeps the process toward understanding and knowledge on the move. Without wonder, human beings might be quite satisfied with the world at hand at any given point in time. Wonder keeps emerging anew to move us on.

Much experience of wonder is not religious. Its objective, once determined, can be tested by appeal to sensory data or at least by appeal to human feelings and imaginative constructs. Sometimes, however, wonder does not terminate in the world of immanent knowledge and understanding. The person moved by wonder examines possible objects of her or his inquiring spirit, testing whether they might not be evoking the feeling of wonder. But when the testing is completed with no object sufficient to satisfy the wonder, and with the wonder drawing the inquirer into a transcendent realm, one is led to conclude that the wonder is evoked by and heading into mystery.

Scientists can be moved by wonder as religious experience toward affirmations of mystery.[2] Then they find that unlocking the meanings of the universe not only does not dissipate their wonder about the transcendent but excites it. The same can be true for other areas of human meaning. The more life unfolds and we face the certainty of death, we can wonder about the finality of our human existence and be drawn into a world transcending this world. Encounter with the senselessness of evil, both the horror of its enormity and its pervasive intrusion into life, while it can engender rejection of any possibility of transcendent goodness, can just as much engender wonder about a meaning that might transcend and, perhaps, transform evil. It is possible.

What, then, is wonder when it can be qualified as religious experience? It is a longing to understand and to know that rejoices in every instance of understanding and knowledge, but remains an energizing force in those persons who cannot rest until they understand in its ultimate dimensions whatever is to be understood. Anyone who has lived for long will entertain no expectation of arriving at such a comprehensive understanding. But it might be possible to achieve some hint of such an objective. Moreover, recalling that this study is theological, going forward on the assumption of religious faith, we can recall an aphorism of Blaise Pascal to the effect that one does not usually seek God unless God has already somehow revealed the divine self to the seeker.[3] From this perspective, wonder has a transcendent object.

Awe

Wonder and awe complement one another. Whereas wonder draws a person into the realm of mystery, awe can be characterized as the experience awakened when mystery erupts within the world of immanent reality. Thus, wonder is an affection of striving for closer contact with the unknown; awe is an affection of shocked reverence when a person realizes that the unknown, in its surpassing grandeur, is very much present to her. One becomes surprised by intimations of meaning that seem to be communicating themselves within a situation in which one was expecting nothing out of the ordinary. Suddenly one finds oneself in the realm of mystery.

Entering one of the great medieval cathedrals, both a first-time visitor and a daily communicant might be awestruck. The experience may be confined within determinable aesthetic limits, or it may break out of this-worldly limits and intimate mystery. Being present at the delivery of a baby can be awe-inspiring as much for the delivering physician as for the first-time witness. The awe may be evoked by the magnificence of human life regenerating itself, or it may be amazement at the irruption of transcendent mystery in the very act of regeneration. To offer a third example, a person may have been puzzling for months in an effort to solve a persistent problem. Suddenly, the inquirer adverts to a clue that generates a convincing solution to the problem. The experience of the insight is so freeing for the subject that she is caught up in awe. As she becomes accustomed to her solution to the long-troublesome problem, she may simply remember the awe as a momentary reaction to the freeing power of her insight. Or the awe may remain subliminally within the inquirer's consciousness, returning to memory now and then as an intimation of how marvelously mysterious a reality the human mind and its knowing are.

Each of these examples indicates an experience of awe which may be limited to the event at hand. It is astonishment at the grandeur of reality. But the awe may be endowed with a further quality, an intimation that the grandeur participates in a transcendent meaning. In that case, the experience may be religious experience.

Longing

Also related to wonder is longing. Both reach into the realm of mystery. Wonder leads one into the unknown. Its objective is whatever is to be known. Longing is a yearning for the interpersonal. It is less related to knowledge, and more related to love. Thus, at least as here understood, longing is associated with companionship. Physical absence can be the catalyst of longing. Having had to move to a distant city because of a job opportunity, or living away at university to study, or simply out of town on a business meeting, we long to be back home again with our loved ones. More spiritual sorts of absence, or the threat of such absence, can also catalyze longing. For example, we long to share healthy companionship with a spouse who is terminally ill. We long to share tension-free companionship with a friend with whom we have had a falling-out. We long for a loving response from someone who seems not to care for us in the devoted way that we care for them. In all these instances, persons readily know the objects of their longing. They long to be with a family member or friend.

Longing can also happen, however, when human companionship does not resolve the longing. One is surrounded by loving friends and family. One is content in this love. Yet, the longing persists. There is an ache for intimacy that reaches beyond the persons we love and who love us. Upon reflection, a person realizes that no one in this world could bring the contentment for which she longs. This longing is an ache reaching into the infinite, into the realm of mystery. St. Augustine has captured the meaning of this religious experience in his renowned statement in the opening paragraph of his *Confessions*: "Our hearts are restless until they rest, O God, in you."

Love

Bernard Lonergan describes the chief feeling associated with religious experience as "being in love in an unrestricted fashion."[4] It includes self-surrender that is "without limits or qualifications or conditions or reservations." Lonergan relates the experience of love to the experience of wonder and the questioning which follows wonder: "Just as unrestricted questioning is our capacity for self-transcendence, so being in love in an unrestricted fashion is the proper fulfillment of that capacity."

As with wonder, awe, and longing, a person does not initiate transcendent love. It simply overtakes one. One has the sense that one is loved by and in love with someone. There is the feeling of elation, sometimes quiet and understated, sometimes enthusiastic and excited, which comes with a sense that we are centrally significant to another person. There is the strength to face every adversity which comes with the assurance that we rest in our beloved and that nothing can take our beloved from us nor us from our beloved. The unrestricted character of this love alerts those who experience it that they have, in some way, encountered ultimate meaning.

Subjects of religious experience may not think through the meaning of their love. As Lonergan puts it, "Ordinarily the experience of the mystery of love and awe is not objectified. It remains within subjectivity as a vector, an undertow, a fateful call to a dreaded holiness."[5] But the sense of love recurs. One adverts to it, at least occasionally, when one prays. Sometimes, and in any sort of situation, love is unexpectedly present. One cannot plan for it.

This is a further indication that unrestricted love is not of the person's own making; rather, it happens to him.

Even when the subject in love in a transcendent way feels the all-embracing quality of love, he is not without a sense that the beloved is also absent. There is a sense of longing for the absent beloved in every experience of presence. Moreover, the embrace of such love is not simply pleasurable; equally present, as the above quotation from Lonergan indicates, is the feeling of dread or fear.

Fear

Wonder and longing strive for mystery. Awe is reverent recognition of the presence of mystery. Fear, when functioning in the realm of the transcendent, shrinks from mystery, as in my example at the start of this chapter. Sometimes religious fear has taken shape in the face of deities conceived to be capricious or avenging in their dealings with mortals. Sometimes fear is existential dread of a perceived enormous threat. Edvard Munch's paintings, *The Scream* and *Anxiety*, express such fear.[6] But when subjects of religious experience advert to the fact that the realm of mystery is characterized by unrestricted love, not capriciousness or vengeance, their fear in the face of mystery has a different meaning. Fear seems to belong to religious experience especially in those moments when they sense their limitations in the face of the infinity of unrestricted love.

First, one feels oneself being drawn into a love so powerful that it seems to be giving itself in an unrestricted, unlimited way. Such self-giving is so far beyond human love that it may strike terror into the heart of the person undergoing the experience. Lonergan refers to this terrifying character of God vis-à-vis humanity in *Method in Theology*: "God's thoughts and God's ways are very different from man's and by that difference God is terrifying."[7] St. John of the Cross may have in mind the same sort of fear when he refers to the "terrors that keep watch by night" in the twenty-ninth stanza of the *Spiritual Canticle*. The recipient of divine love, he writes, feels a terror that comes "from God, when He desires to grant such persons certain favors, . . . and is wont to bring fear and affright to their spirit, and likewise a shrinking to their flesh and senses."[8]

Besides the feeling of fear because of the terrifying character of the source of transcendent love, there is the fear attending the response. Who is going to let himself or herself submit to total, all-embracing love with unhesitating abandon, at least in the early stages of one's response? No one could wish to embrace the terror that can be a part of religious experience. One must give up seeking security in human relationships, material goods, success, prestige, power, physical and mental health, and the other usual places in which human beings seek security. Accompanying one's surrender of this-worldly security, there can be fear that is unlike the fear that one feels in the face of a capricious or vengeful deity. It is the fear experienced when one knows one must risk one's whole self and all the props that make for this-worldly security and let oneself be led into the realm of mystery.[9]

Trust

Even while persons of religious faith may well feel fear as they come to realize ever more fully that the embrace of transcendent love leads them to eschew a sense of security which could be drawn from any ordinary source, they may, nevertheless, gradually feel, even more strongly, an otherworldly trust that we humans live in an ultimately friendly universe. An abiding feeling of trust readily accompanies the feeling of being embraced by unrestricted love. The feeling of trust remains even in the midst of life's many and often powerful ups and downs.

When one is grasped by ultimate concern, those concerns that are less than ultimate may have to go relatively untended. Submitting in trust to the power of mystery, such a person may lack attention to detail and may not be much bothered by it. This can result in confusion in one's everyday living and aggravation to those with whom they live. Alternatively, persons who feel trust engendered by unrestricted love may be quite attentive to the details of daily living, but without worrying much about the outcome. If things work out, fine; if they don't, no matter, for we still live in a friendly universe. Trust in the realm of mystery can show itself in the tranquility with which one faces adversity.

Trust, however, does not lead to indifference toward the sufferings of others. In fact, the trusting person may be more motivated than others to practical care for those in need precisely because all-embracing love and trust in the ultimate friendliness of the universe gives them reason to share this goodness and to dedicate themselves to the task without concern for themselves or even for the practicality of the effort. I am reminded in this regard of two women in India who, against insurmountable odds, have peacefully gone about their efforts to ameliorate the conditions of the lowest caste of humans. One is the famous Mother Teresa, who provided simple but loving care for some of the huge number of beggars left to die in the streets of Calcutta. The other, Vijaya Lavate, has established an ashram in Pune to provide a stable upbringing for a few of the many ill-tended and maligned children of prostitutes.[10] Mother Teresa's Sisters can offer a dignified death to only a few of thousands, and Vijaya Lavate can offer a home to just a few children. It would not be surprising if they were to be overtaken by feelings of discouragement or despair. But they go forward in their efforts with a sense of confidence and trust unwarranted by any social-scientific or political assessment of their accomplishments.

Guilt and Shame

Guilt and shame are associated with personal evil acts. Here evil is understood in the strict sense of sin as utterly unintelligible behavior, behavior that simply makes no sense. It makes no sense ultimately because it contravenes the goodness and love, the truth and wisdom of God.[11] But what kind of guilt is a genuine religious experience?

There is false guilt. Every priest who hears confessions knows that penitents can feel guilt for acts which they have assessed to be evil, but when these acts are subjected to careful scrutiny they are shown not to be evil at all. Thus, a battered wife might feel guilt for deserting a husband who beats her. A scrupulous person might feel guilt for an unintended distraction during prayer or for an unelicited sexual impulse. In these cases, the confessor assists the penitent to correct an inaccurate conscience and let go of feelings of guilt and shame.

There is also elemental guilt. In this case, a person feels guilt and shame that are not evocative of the transcendent. Likely, we have all felt guilty when we were youngsters for disobeying a parental injunction. Or we might feel guilty for breaking a civil law, perhaps cross-country skiing on posted property or jaywalking across a city street. Persons feel guilty for eating to excess or drinking themselves into drunkenness, or for inappropriate sexual advances. In all these instances, perpetrators might feel shame on account of being publicly exposed for an infraction that embarrasses and humiliates them.

The guilt and shame, however, that belong to religious experience draw us into the realm of mystery. Guilt arises out of a sense of transcendent responsibility. We feel that we have failed to be faithful, not first to the people around us but in a way that transcends those to whom we are responsible in the here and now. We feel that we have willfully contravened a greater order. This sense of guilt is expressed in vivid theological terms in Psalm 51:4: "Against you, you alone, have I sinned, and done what is evil in your sight, so that you are justified in your sentence and blameless when you pass judgement."

While the feeling of guilt may be more connected with a sense of law and justice, shame, as a religious experience, relates more to love. One feels intense humiliation for having dishonored the privileged embrace of transcendent love. It is not the (frequently) self-serving shame of being publicly exposed to one's peers (whether one actually feels guilt or not); it is the shame of being exposed for having failed to love when one is loved so much. Perhaps this was the shame of Peter after his denial of the Master, when Jesus' glance evoked bitter tears (Lk 22:62).

Sorrow

Sorrow can be a religious experience when it arises in conjunction with transcendent love. Related to guilt and shame, sorrow can arise together with cognizance of some evil that a person has perpetrated. Then it is clearly related to regret. Or the subject feels sorrow because of solidarity in the human race with other human beings who have perpetrated heinous offenses, for example, a racially motivated crime or the Holocaust or the terrorist attacks on the World Trade Center in New York City. One senses that it is not only the other who is caught in the web of evil; one has a sense that he or she is caught in the same web. And one regrets the evil with feelings of sorrow that human beings can be so callous. It is sorrow related to love.

A person can feel sorrow, of course, without a transcendent dimension, for example, because of awareness of one's guilt, because of the affront to the victim, because of the harm caused by the deed. But when it is an experience that is religious, the sorrow is felt because a sense of the betrayal of unlimited love draws the subject into the realm of mystery. It is not a matter of making amends for the crime; that is hardly possible. It is more a feeling of pain, sadness, regret. It comes to those who stand honestly to face evil. It may be intimately connected with feelings of guilt and shame. Were it not for the conjunction of sorrow with love and trust, it could well lead to despair.

Such transfixing pain can accompany the encounter of a human being with any instance whatever of evil. For example, one can feel the pain of a transcending sorrow that is in touch with the mystery of evil, beyond the known motivations of human cruelty or insouciance, when one reflects upon the maltreated children and dying folk to whom Vijaya Lavate and Mother Teresa have ministered in India. However, in a world in which we become accustomed to hatred, cruelty, and violence, artists have the sad but important task to make use of various media in order to touch our imaginations so that the religious experience of sorrow because of evil can be evoked. Thus, a person may feel such sorrow while reading Elie Wiesel's *Night*,[12] or while viewing Francisco Goya's *The Shootings of May Third,* or while listening to the first and third movements of the Fifth Symphony of Dimitri Shostakovich.[13]

Joy

Akin to trust and love is joy. Quiet or exuberant it celebrates even in the midst of great adversities. Delight and laughter are often its accompaniments. Dorothy Day, it is said, experienced this deep-seated joy. Observers note that she was possessed of two types of laughter, both active in the midst of reasons to be glum.

The first laughter is of naiveté, "the soul's purest and most original response to beauty and simplicity. It is a primeval laughter, delighting in Creation itself."[14] The second laughter "stubbornly insists on laughing in spite of all the reasons to despair and weep. . . . [It] reaches through the brokenness of the world to a unity not yet gained."

Living and working in the Bowery section of lower Manhattan, an area famous for its population of "misfits," Day could say: "We would be contribut-
ing to the misery of the world if we failed to rejoice in the sun, moon and the
stars, in the rivers which surround this island on which we live." And: "There
are always fools and conventionals among us in our various Catholic Worker
houses across the country, and, while I sympathize with the conventionals
and know that they are the backbone of the movement, who keep things going, still I rejoice that we have an abundance of fools."

It can indeed simply be a matter of foolishness to become caught up in
such joy before it is reasonably grounded, but it may be that something quite
real, but transcendent, is drawing the joyous person to a more blessed reality beyond life's limitations and setbacks. Certainly those associated with
Dorothy Day's committed service to the marginalized and the outcasts over
decades recognized that she was in contact with the deeper dimensions of
reality and that this was the reason for her joy.

Observant of the transformative praxis discussed in the previous chapter,
which can be expressed in the imperatives "be attentive, be intelligent, be
reasonable, be responsible, be in love," those who experience it will want to
be attentive to such joy and ask about its meaning.[15] It may be that intelligent
and reasonable questioning will lead to the conclusion that wishful, but un-
grounded, hope is what they are caught up in. But it may be that they will
conclude to the truth of a transcendent reality that enables them to welcome
such joy when they discover themselves to be experiencing it.

THE OBJECTIVE OF RELIGIOUS EXPERIENCE

Each of the experiences described above is characterized as religious when
it draws the experiencing subject into the realm of mystery. Recalling that
this study goes forward as a theological reflection, we affirm from the start
that transcendent mystery names a dimension of human activity in which
God is active, and may be discovered because of gracious divine revelation.
Unlike the philosophers we do not ask whether religious experience reveals
God, but how attention to experience reaching toward mystery reveals
God.[16] Going further, we affirm with Bernard Lonergan that "orientation to
transcendent mystery . . . provides the primary and fundamental meaning of
the name, God."[17] Both before and following upon the achievement of doctrines of God and theologies of God, people of faith are called to nourish the
roots of their faith in their religious experience.

Locating religious experience among the four operations of consciousness
discussed in the preface to this study, we would say that it is a subject's self-
awareness (experience) on the level of transformative evaluation (judgments
of value joined to decision). Christian doctrine can make true statements

about the God in whom Christians believe (judgment), and Christian theology may come to some understanding of God from various perspectives (understanding). But the reality of God remains always infinitely greater than what doctrine and theology can express. Religious experience keeps alerting women and men of faith to the greater, to the mystery beyond whatever we know and understand about anything, but especially God. Even more, doctrines and understandings of God develop first out of reflection on religious experience.[18]

One salutary result of this appreciation of religious experience is the sense of continuity, of connection, between their ordinary lives and the realm of mystery with which persons of faith are blessed. Faith has sometimes been described as a leap of will into the dark abyss. But faith need not be any such leap at all as long as the subject of faith remains in touch with those of her feelings that head into the realm of mystery. These are feelings to be trusted. When we human persons come to the existential recognition that "no finite object or achievement can hold us content for long" and that we are being stretched "beyond any limit we encounter," the moment of truth is that such experience is connecting us with God.[19] In other words, because of God's gracious love, the horizon of human questing opens onto the horizon of the transcendent God.

As the individual lives with the transcending character of these experiences he may find himself asking what they reveal. Where is this wonder leading? No answer to limited questions suffices to satisfy the questing, yet the subject remains hopeful.[20] No other human person is the object of the unrestricted love that overtakes one's consciousness in religious experience, so the subject is led to ask: With whom am I in love?[21] What is the object of this aching longing? Why do I feel so secure in this trust which has no this-worldly term of which I am aware? What is the reason for my fearful hesitation, which is, at the same time, joined with a pervasive feeling of attraction? Why am I so sick with a seemingly boundless sorrow? Why, sometimes for no sufficient reason, am I struck with awe? The wonder and awe and longing, the love and trust, the fear and sorrow may be provoked by some person or event at hand, but their transcendent quality indicates that these feelings are being evoked by someone not at hand who is greater by far than any person or event at hand.

Nor does the wonder cease once one has been able to name God as its objective. One's understanding of God is so paltry in its conceptual and verbal expressions that the wonder continues to overtake the honest subject. Nor does the person who names the transcendent lover, God, find that the naming renders less fascinating and fearsome the continuing experience of transcendent love (Rudolf Otto's *mysterium fascinans et tremendum*).[22] Yet, one knows one has reached the object of the self-transcending experience.

There is another salutary result of remaining focused on religious experience. It restrains religious persons from domesticating God. When persons are continually in contact with the mysterious transcendence of their faith, they are more likely to remain mindful that no theological concept is adequate to God. Every concept of the transcendent reaches beyond its grasp. Religious experience indicates the paradox of God-talk. God is at once intimately close to humanity in love, but utterly Other in terms of the possibilities of human understanding. God always exceeds the limits of human powers.

The existential Otherness of God to which religious experience alerts us sounds one of the prevailing postmodern themes: the sense of the Other, the excess of reality. Religious experience's push ever further into the realm of mystery continually points up the limitations of every human proposition and concept that refers to God. There is no possibility of clear and distinct ideas that satisfy every question. Images and concepts of God, even those expressive of divine revelation, share the human incapacity for comprehension of any spiritual reality, least of all divine reality. God remains always beyond.

EXPERIENCING JESUS?

People of Christian faith might well ask whether, among possible religious experiences, there is an experience of Jesus. My first response is "no." But then I shall add a qualified "yes."

Strictly speaking, there is no experience of Jesus. But, actually, there is no experience of anyone or anything, including of people or things that are empirically present. There is only experience of data, sensory data and data of consciousness (i.e., data of self-awareness).[23] Once one understands the meaning of the data and is able to verify one's understanding by checking its compatibility with the data, one is able to affirm the physical presence of someone sitting across from oneself or walking along with oneself. In the case of physical presence, we human beings normally do not need to carry on a long and elaborate process of reflection to come to such affirmations. Our thinking comes to its conclusions very quickly. Observe how fast we judge its presence when a truck bears down upon us while we are crossing the street.

As questions are asked of the data of sense and of consciousness that the inquirer experiences, it is clear that the operations of intelligent and rational consciousness mediate more than objects that are physically present. Very frequently they mediate objects (including persons) which are not physically, but which are psychologically, present. Persons physically absent are mediated by one's knowledge or understanding of them or by one's feelings for them. Thus, they are present in mind and heart.[24] In this case, persons who lived and events that happened in the past can be present. Persons and events contemporaneous with the subject, but not physically present at the moment, can be present. So a physically absent beloved can be present to her lover psychologically. On the other hand, persons physically present can be variously present psychologically: superficially or significantly or intimately. Of greatest importance is the concomitance of psychological presence and physical presence among people spiritually united, as members of a family gathered for a festive dinner, or a religious congregation gathered for prayer, or two friends sharing a conversation. In these cases, psychological presence is an enormous enrichment of physical presence.

Biblical Witness

Jesus of Nazareth is a historical human being who can be mediated into the psychological present in the manner in which other historical persons are mediated. One can examine sensory data that mediate the past. Artifacts in use by Jesus could mediate his presence. However, while the legend of the Holy Grail gave medievals the hope that they might find the chalice used by Jesus at the Last Supper, and while relics of the Holy Cross still abound, and while an Upper Room in Jerusalem is shown to pilgrims, most people conclude that there are no extant artifacts that Jesus handled. He is not likely to be mediated through artifacts. What is extant are the Gospels and other writings of the New Testament, along with what was sacred writ for Jesus, the Hebrew scriptures. These are the data which can be examined and which, insofar as they are understood correctly, mediate the historical Jesus.

The New Testament, however, does not mediate the historical Jesus without remainder. It mediates the convictions of the faith communities of the early church, and of the redactors of the texts that make up the New Testament. When it comes to mediating the person of Jesus to those who would receive their texts, both the remote and the proximate authors of the New Testament intend to communicate what in Jesus led them to place their religious faith in him.

Whatever they saw and heard, whether of Jesus himself or as it was handed on to them through trusted mediators, they must have felt the kinds of religiously significant feelings which have been described in this chapter, or other feelings alerting them to the realm of the transcendent. The First Letter of John announces "what we have heard, what we have seen with our eyes, what we have looked at and touched with our hands" (I John 1), but in themselves these sensory data do not communicate transcendence. Accompanying seeing and hearing and touching must have been feelings of wonder or awe or love or trust, and so on, leading to faith that this man, Jesus, embodies "eternal life."

When the Gospels report feelings of awe at the words of Jesus or gratitude for a miracle such that religious commitment to Jesus follows, what is being mediated is that people who encountered Jesus felt religious experience in and through his presence. What led them to faith in Jesus, however, was not that they had analyzed the meaning of religious experience as I am attempting to do in these pages, but that they could relate their own previous experience of transcendence, for example of Yahweh, to their present experience of Jesus. Or perhaps in the presence of Jesus people for the first time recognized their experiences of transcendence for what they were, invitations to religious faith.

Varied as the religious experiences of the New Testament witnesses are, there is a thread which runs through the entire set of scriptures that make up the New Testament—the conviction of resurrection. Jesus of Nazareth is not mediated simply as a historical figure, no matter how extraordinary, but as the one who lives on beyond his death in the glory of God. If it were not for their conviction of the resurrection, by which they are led to profess that "Jesus is Lord," it is inconceivable that the early Christians would have had such committed faith or such determination to communicate it. But how was conviction of Jesus' resurrection generated?

What seems to have taken place is that the early Christian community and the redactors of the New Testament texts experienced themselves drawn to faith in Jesus' resurrection by transcendent feelings provoked by stories about Jesus' post-death existence (such as the walk to Emmaus in Luke 24, the encounter of Mary Magdalene in John 20, the breakfast on the seashore in John 21), but evoked by a force so powerful that they could only name it the power of God, or the Holy Spirit.[25] They were convinced that the force was neither self-delusion nor any immanent object.[26] Thus, they were led to make a total commitment of themselves.

That faith in Jesus had to be a result of affirmations motivated by transcendent religious experience may be illustrated by instances of lack of faith on the part of those who were unmoved to faith by Jesus' physical presence—think of his fellow townspeople who even "took offense at him" (Mk 6:3), or by his psychological presence—think of Ananias's false faith (Acts 5:1–11). The key to the difference between experience that leads to faith and experience that does not is interpretation of the transcendent dimension of the data of consciousness when a person is in the physical or psychological presence of Jesus, followed by the conviction that there is no this-worldly explanation for one's experience.

Response to Biblical Witness

Why have individuals down the centuries responded to the convictions of the early Christian community and the redactors of the New Testament texts with religious faith? What is there about the Gospel narratives, the epistles, the Acts of the Apostles, the Book of Revelation that moves some people to religious faith in Jesus? I suggest that it is the same transcending experience that moved the people who composed and compiled the scriptures in the first place. The faith-filled reports about Jesus, the ruminations of Paul, the religious history of Acts, the theology of history of Revelation, when read or proclaimed, strikes a chord with some persons: awe in some, trust in some, sorrow in some, ultimately love in all who come to faith.

These feelings, and the others which we name religious experience, can be variously interpreted. One person feeling transcendent wonder may quickly be moved to awe, while another continues for years to question the meaning of the mystery which is overtaking him. The Christian community embraces both sorts of wonderer. One person feeling fear as she contemplates Jesus' crucifixion can sense the weighty justice of God while another, feeling the same fear, senses rather the infinite grandeur of God's love. Over the centuries Christians have offered both interpretations of the religious experience of fear.

My purpose here, however, is not to study the interpretations of religious experiences that are possible, nor to investigate those that are actually proposed in the New Testament itself. My purpose is to highlight the role of religious experience in the process of coming to faith in Jesus. When some people come into contact with the New Testament mediation of the person of Jesus, they feel an attraction toward his person quite similar to the attraction felt by the persons who met Jesus during his earthly sojourn and similar to the first generations of Christian believers who handed on the initial tradition of religious faith in Jesus. When persons feel wonder, awe, longing, love, trust, joy, fear, sorrow, guilt, and shame as they hear and reflect upon the writings of the New Testament, their feelings alert them to the transcendent meaning of Jesus. They feel about Jesus what they do not feel when they read or hear about other admirable historical persons, such as Socrates. The difference is that, in the case of Jesus, these feelings as they arise in some persons lead into the realm of mystery. For those not so moved, Jesus may be a great historical figure, or not interesting at all.

Contemporary Witness to Jesus

While faith in Jesus is inevitably informed by biblical witness, it is probable that the faith of most Christians is not initiated by proclamation or reading of the New Testament, but by the example of family and friends. Those of us whose faith began when we were children learned from our families and religious communities what faith in Jesus means. In fact, children learn faith in the terms in which it is meaningful in their environments. Thus, not only does family custom originally sway one's profession of faith before any emergence of personal conviction, but the interpretation of the meaning of faith is a function of the family and its religious tradition. The force of custom can continue into adulthood and, indeed, through one's entire life. In such cases, conventionality rather than religious experience is the final reason for religious practice.

Still, many whose faith is originally nurtured in the family gradually become alert to their own religious experience along the way, thus professing faith in Jesus increasingly because of personal conviction rather than because of force of habit or family custom. Force of habit may continue, along with the interpretation of faith rendered by one's family and particular denominational upbringing. But mature persons of religious conviction come to evaluate their faith for themselves. They may come to recognize religious experience at the heart of their conviction. Commitment to Jesus in faith becomes personally validated by the touchstone of their own religious experience.

With adults first coming to faith, the initial influence may be mediated by a friend or some other influential adult (as Augustine was influenced by Bishop Ambrose of Milan). It is possible that one may simply observe others from a distance, as when the media communicate stories of heroic deeds motivated by faith (as Mother Teresa has influenced so many in recent years). What begins as a response to the influential persons or their deeds eventually moves beyond to a connection of religious experience with the person of Jesus.

Liturgical celebrations of word and sacrament also nourish personal faith. Apart from the depth of one's schooling in the meaning of baptismal or eucharistic liturgy, presence at such events, especially if it is attentive and open, often evokes religious experience so that the sacramental moment becomes a moment of authentic faith. Those who have been schooled in liturgy, and who believe that liturgical celebrations of word and sacrament are privileged mediations of faith, discover that their religious experience becomes richer, not at every celebration of liturgy, but at many, if they wait expectantly for the revelation of mystery at each celebration in which they participate. Sometimes without any evident difference in the pattern or manner of liturgical practice, a congregant undergoes a religious experience.

Personal Prayer

The exercise of personal prayer renders existential solidity to faith. It binds together mediation of Jesus by other persons, by the Scripture, and by liturgy with those religious feelings that draw us to experience in Jesus the divine mystery. By prayer, persons relate their religious experience to their encounter with the Lord in each area of the operations of consciousness. It is not that faith cannot thrive without prayer, but without personal prayer faith is not likely to permeate one's whole being.[27]

Personal prayer and religious experience reinforce each other. In the prayer of imagination the person of faith recreates biblical scenes, inserting himself into them, thus appropriating existentially the meaning of faith by interaction and conversation with Jesus and other biblical figures. Feelings are an intimate part of the prayer of imagination. For the prayer is not simply an observational videotape of the biblical scene, but an involvement of the individual in the scene. Inevitably, feelings are associated with one's involvement. Gradually, one may be able to move from the scene and simply remain within the feelings that have been evoked. In turn, the feelings, as gifts of the Spirit in prayer, draw the pray-er into the divine mystery. The prayer I have just described is inspired by St. Ignatius Loyola, who directs those practicing his Spiritual Exercises to engage frequently in this sort of prayer.

Another form of prayer that gathers its practitioners into the realm of mystery is centering prayer. In this prayer, one begins with an activity, such as painting or reading poetry or reciting a line from Scripture, but very often one simply chooses a word to focus one's attention. Gradually one's activity becomes background for one's presence to the mystery of God, who is beyond every mental or affective activity. Carefully executed breathing can enhance centering prayer. Sitting before the Blessed Sacrament and recitation of the rosary can foster centering prayer. But as one enters more deeply into the realm of mystery on the fourth level of consciousness, contemplative or unitive prayer is achieved.[28]

Meditation or, more commonly, *lectio divina* (reading in communion with God), is a style of prayer that engages the pray-er's thinking, even as it ideally evokes and enhances religious experience. This form of prayer begins with a passage of Scripture, which one reads on one's own or to which one listens in choir, as when one is living the conventual life in a monastery. After one or two or three readings of the passage, a word or phrase or sentence may be especially striking to the person at prayer. She mulls over it. The passage may assume existential meaning for her. Feelings leading into the realm of mystery accompany or even replace thought. Again, contemplation is achieved.[29]

Prayer, like good conversation, is peculiar to the shape and style of the person's relationship with Jesus and, through Jesus, with the Father and the Spirit. The above-mentioned types are not mutually exclusive of each other nor are they meant to exclude other approaches to prayer. What is important is that persons of faith incorporate personal prayer into their routine in order to make more their own their religious experience and their mediation of Christ Jesus.

Religious Conversion

This chapter has been studying religious experience as the subject's immediate encounter with the realm of mystery. More precisely, with Lonergan, religious experience as well as interpretation of it may be identified as a mediated immediacy in which an individual experiences data immediately but more and more knows oneself to be in contact with divine mystery.[30] Religious experience, however, does not stand alone. As something which happens to a person apart from willing it to happen, religious experience calls for a response. As it invades consciousness, and draws the person beyond the meanings, truths, and values she currently professes, religious experience leads to the further step of religious conversion. It is in the process of religious conversion that the full meaning of religious experience is attained.

Religious conversion is submission to the cogency of religious experience. The subject of religious experience opts for the transcendent values urged by the experience, the values of faith and hope and love. He or she affirms the religious truth of the realm of mystery. If their mediation of Jesus of Nazareth meshes with their religious experience, individuals opt for the values of Jesus' Gospel and affirm the truth that Jesus is the incarnate presence of the divine mystery. Religious conversion enables persons to whom Jesus is mediated to affirm the veracity of the witnesses to Jesus and the transcendent mediation of Christian liturgy. But now we are moving into the dimension of doctrine, and that is the topic for the next two chapters.

NOTES

1. W. Norris Clarke, S.J., "The Natural Roots of Religious Experience," *Religious Studies* 17 (1981): 511.

2. In his essay, "Is a Natural Theology Still Viable Today?" in *Prospects for Natural Theology*, ed. Eugene Thomas Long (Washington: Catholic University of America Press, 1992), W. Norris Clarke, S.J. points to paths of philosophical religious affirmation toward which wonder can direct scientists (151–82).

3. Blaise Pascal, *Pensées*, trans. and intro. by A. J. Krailsheimer, rev. ed. (New York: Penguin, 1995), 290 (#919): "Take comfort: you would not seek me if you had not found me."

4. Lonergan, *Method in Theology*, 105.

5. Lonergan, *Method in Theology*, 113.

6. Munch writes about "The Scream": "I was walking along the road with two friends—then the sun went down—the sky became suddenly a bloody red. . . . I remained behind, shaking with fear—and experienced the great, endless scream of nature." See Alf Bøe, *Edvard Munch* (New York: Rizzoli, 1989), 20.

7. Lonergan, *Method in Theology*, 111.

8. E. Allison Peers, ed., *The Complete Works of St. John of the Cross* (Westminster, MD: Newman Press, 1964), 141.

9. Marc Sulzman seems to be probing such fear in his novel, *Laying Awake*, about the religious experience of a Discalced Carmelite, Sister John of the Cross (New York: Alfred A. Knopf, 2000).

10. I learned of Ms. Lavate through an article in the *Boston Sunday Globe*, 28 January 1996, "India's Accursed Children," A25 and A27.

11. Paul Ricoeur's work on *The Symbolism of Evil* (Boston: Beacon Press, 1967) makes an important contribution to contemporary reflection on guilt and shame, but his argument is far too complex to be incorporated into this brief section.

12. Elie Wiesel, *Night*, trans. Stella Rodway (New York: Bantam, 1960).

13. More poignantly expressive of a transcendent sorrow throughout the entire composition is Shostakovich's less well-known Piano Trio No. 2 in E minor, Op. 67. Written in 1944, it received its premiere performance later that year in the city of Leningrad, whose citizens were suffering the terrible effects of war.

14. Betty and Charles Gifford, "A Duty of Delight," *Catholic Worker,* May 1996, 8.

15. Lonergan, *Method in Theology*, 268.

16. For a philosophical study of religious experience which also employs the transcendental method of Bernard Lonergan, see Jerome A. Miller, *In the Throe of Wonder: Intimations of the Sacred In a Postmodern World* (Albany: State University of New York Press, 1992). Some philosophers who acknowledge that experience can convey a sense of mystery are not, however, "willing to define the mystery in terms of a transcendent being." Thus, Eugene Thomas Long reports on the philosophy of experience of J. J. C. Smart and Karl Jaspers in "Experience and Natural Theology," in *Prospects for Natural Theology*, 213.

17. Lonergan, *Method in Theology*, 341.

18. Bernard Lonergan discusses religious experience as the authentic starting point both of theology and of philosophy of religion in *Philosophy of God, and Theology*, 203–5.

19. Clarke, "Natural Roots of Religious Experience," 513. Later Clarke writes: "I am proposing that man could not be oriented toward union with God by the innate drive of his spirit unless there were some kind of profound ontological affinity or similitude, imperfect though it may be, between the human spirit and the reality of the divine" (515–16).

20. See Clarke, "Natural Roots of Religious Experience," 515.

21. Lonergan, *Philosophy of God, and Theology*: "A fourth form of the question of God arises when one reflects on religious experience. No doubt, such experience takes many forms. No doubt, it suffers many aberrations. But it keeps recurring. Its many forms can be explained by the many varieties of human culture. Its many aberrations can be accounted for by the precariousness of the human achievement of authenticity. Underneath the many forms and prior to the many aberrations some have found that there exists an unrestricted being in love, a mystery of love and awe, a being grasped by ultimate concern, a happiness that has a determinate content but no intellectually apprehended object. Such people will ask, With whom are we in love?" (207).

22. Rudolf Otto, *The Idea of the Holy: An Inquiry into the Non-Rational Factor in the Idea of the Divine and Its Relation to the Rational*, trans. John W. Harvey (London: Oxford University Press, 1923).

23. See Lonergan, *Method in Theology*, 6–9.

24. Lonergan, *Method in Theology*, on the notion of mediation of meaning, 28, and 177 on the psychological present. See also Frederick E. Crowe, "The Power of the Scriptures: Attempt at Analysis," in *Word and Spirit: Essays in Honor of David*

Michael Stanley, S.J. on his 60th Birthday, ed. Joseph Plevnik, S.J. (Toronto: Regis College Press, 1975).

25. How the Gospel stories should be judged that deal with the appearances of the risen Jesus and with the empty tomb is the subject of the third chapter of James D. G. Dunn, *The Evidence for Jesus* (Philadelphia: Westminster, 1985). Dunn provides a balanced discussion of the debate on the historicity of these accounts.

26. How the reality of Jesus' resurrection itself is to be judged is a distinct, but related question. For a discussion of some of the issues, see Robert W. Jenson, *Systematic Theology*, vol. 1, *The Triune God* (New York: Oxford Univ. Press, 1997), chapter 12.

27. William Johnston's works on prayer study its exercise according to the pattern of Lonergan's operations of consciousness. See *The Mirror Mind: Spirituality and Transformation* (San Francisco: Harper & Row, 1981) and *Being in Love: the Practice of Christian Prayer* (San Francisco: Harper & Row, 1989). Johnston elaborates the types of prayer I describe in the following paragraphs.

28. Thomas Keating is a major contemporary teacher of centering prayer as a way to contemplative prayer in books such as *Open Mind, Open Heart: The Contemplative Dimension of the Gospel* (Rockport, MA: Element, 1993).

29. Thomas Torrance names this type of meditation "indwelling" the Scriptures, particularly the New Testament, in *The Christian Doctrine of God: One Being Three Persons* (Edinburgh: T. & T. Clark, 1996), 37–38.

30. Longergan, *Method in Theology*, 29, 77, and, esp., 112.

4

Faith: Knowledge Born of Love

Charles Hefling chose as his title for a 1984 book on the function of religious belief, *Why Doctrines?*[1] It is an important question. For some, religious doctrine is simply a ploy of religious authorities to exercise control over the lives of the faithful. For some, doctrine, which etymologically means "teaching," is quite acceptable as a guide for the religious thinking and action of the faithful *for the time being*, but it should never be construed as possessing permanent value. Some accept the need to express in concepts and words and propositions what we believe, but, for them, doctrine is abstract, unconnected with religious experience, which is the heart of faith, and, therefore, doctrine is of quite limited value in its actual service of faith.

The three criticisms are peculiarly modern/postmodern. The response offered in this chapter and the next is to connect religious doctrine to religious experience, demonstrating how (1) both are the fruit of the patterned operations of the human quest for meaning, truth, and value, yielding some knowledge of reality; (2) with religious experience serving as a partial touchstone to test the authenticity of religions. Doctrine is integral to religious faith.

RELIGIOUS EXPERIENCE, FAITH, BELIEFS

We can think of religious experience as an inner word of God addressed to a person. It is a word that is quite personal, although it can be shared by many, and it is spoken in love. It is a word that invites and draws the recipient into the realm of mystery.[2] In the case of Christians, religious love is engaged by one's affective encounter with Jesus, whom we can name an outer

word of God in history. Unrestricted love is experienced in one's attraction
to Jesus of Nazareth, as he has been communicated to the recipient in a variety of possible ways. Whether the encounter is sudden or gradual, dramatic
or quiet, is not relevant. Religious faith is a response both to inner and outer
words that call forth faith.

When people let religious experience of this sort guide them, they become
people of faith, growing in their conviction that they know. Know what? Persons may not be able to say. Or, they may say something like: "I know/sense
life's deepest meaning." Perhaps a more explicit response is possible: "I
know the mystery of the universe," "I know the Lord Jesus," "I know God."
This is, as Bernard Lonergan writes, a "knowledge born of religious love."[3]
In the same context, Lonergan recalls Blaise Pascal's famous dictum that the
heart has reasons for its knowledge which the knower does not know
through the act of understanding.[4] It is an affective knowledge, functioning
on the fourth, evaluative, level of human consciousness. Faith, then, is
knowledge that is rooted and grounded in love (Eph 3:14–17). Religious faith
is knowledge of the divine in a loving, interpersonal encounter. Faith includes commitment to the one whom I know in love; no matter that the faith
functions in the midst of a "cloud of unknowing."

Commitment in faith cannot be separate from the work of daily living. If
in my heart of hearts I am in love with divine mystery, I want my commitment to influence my attitudes, thoughts, and actions. For this to take place
consistently, I need to move from fourth-level operations of intentionality to
third-level operations, where reasonableness becomes engaged. More must
be discerned about the one whom I know in loving faith and what the implications of this faith might be for the rest of my living. I am pressed to make
some judgments about what and who divine mystery is, about proper ways
to celebrate this reality in my life and with others of like faith, about appropriate attitudes and behaviors. Thus, faith becomes the hinge between religious experience and religious beliefs.

Religious beliefs are judgments affirming the realities of loving faith. They
are motivated from within persons of religious faith by the intentional character of the instances of religious experience. Belief is self-motivated because it is a free act of and from within the subject; it is relied upon as affir-
mative of reality because of the intentional dynamism of religious
experience. However, beliefs are not solely self-motivated. They also emerge
from the trust of believers in others. These others can share the religious experience of the subject. Or these others can inform religious seekers more
fully about Jesus, the object of their religious attraction. Thus, the writings of
the New Testament assume their importance, among which the Gospel narratives play the particularly important role of telling the story of Jesus.

One might ask: Which comes first? Religious experiences, narratives provided by the New Testament or one's community of faith, or beliefs? Histor-

ically there is a developmental progression from experience to narrative to belief.[5] As for actual persons of faith, however, the three are interchangeable. For many, the narratives have been heard from infancy in the settings of family and local congregation. A corpus of beliefs has been handed on in the setting of catechetical instructions. Religious experiences have been named in passing: trust, sorrow, love; one may have been able to identify one's own feelings as described by the names. Faith gradually has taken shape.

Sooner or later, however, at least with very many living in these times, if faith does not receive assistance from self-understanding, it wanes and possibly withers away. This is the reason for the importance of sorting out the operations of the human subject as they are implemented in religious faith. One needs to recover how and why the grounds of one's religion are to be found in experience, the conviction of religion in faith, the articulation of religious reality in judgments of belief. Without applying intentionality analysis to the religious dimension of human intentionality, many persons of faith cannot go on with the assurance that their faith is intelligent, reasonable, and responsible. Thus, chapters 3 through 8 of this book. The previous chapter examined religious experience. In the present chapter and the next, the operations of evaluation and judgment are studied insofar as they have been implemented historically in the formation of Christian beliefs in the triune God. Current believers must follow along and test for themselves if their beliefs are confirmed.

Belief in God as Triune

How did Christians come to the belief that the one God is at once Father, Son, and Holy Spirit? The question asks how the Christian community arrived at its firmly held judgments about God, by which we can profess that God *is* what we claim God to be.

As we sort out the process, we will not respond successfully to those who are convinced that no claims about reality can be made which are not the result of strict application of the methods of the natural sciences. Nor may we satisfy those people of religious faith who cannot fathom how one can say anything about the divine Other, beyond naming it "mystery." But we may be able to sort out to our own satisfaction why it is reasonable to believe. Further, we can use the analysis to assist us in our discernment of beliefs that are permanently valid and beliefs we maintain currently but which may be confirmed or revised at some future time.

Reasonable beliefs are never a matter of individual conviction alone. This becomes evident when we consider, once more, that beliefs are motivated by trust. We are told about something inaccessible to knowledge generated totally by ourselves. In enormous numbers of instances, belief based on trust is *simply a matter of fact.* I believe the news announcer who communicates the event of a bomb blast in London, although I am sitting at my desk on the other side of the Atlantic Ocean. Why should I doubt the announcer? Announcers get it wrong quite often, but I have learned that straightforward events such as a bomb blast are normally reliably reported, so I trust the report and believe. The way I have learned such reliability, however, is not from checking various instances of news reporting by traveling to a distant location to examine the evidence for myself. Theoretically, it would be possible to investigate the report myself, but practically it is out of the question. I may tune in to reports of the same incident on other TV or radio stations or by reading a newspaper. In this case, my trust is bolstered by the reports of other, possibly rival, news gatherers and reporters. The journalistic community is trustworthy in this sort of event, I believe.

To take another instance, I believe a colleague who calls the office to say that he is ill and won't be reporting for work today. The man could be lying. But I have come to know that this worker is consistently diligent in carrying out his responsibilities, and by working side-by-side with him over the years I have come to regard him as honest. I could do some investigation and verify the facts for myself, but I trust my colleague's statement by telephone and wish him good health. Notice how belief brings together experience (my awareness of myself as trusting) and appropriation of data gathered over time about my coworker (confirmed instances of honesty).

I could find out the truth in the above two instances by conducting a personal investigation. But the world would grind to a halt if everyone investigated personally every possible meaning before making a judgment about its truth. The human world cannot go on without belief in other human beings whom we choose to trust because we judge them to be trustworthy.

Trust in others leads people to believe propositions of religious truth. Proximately, we believe parents, preachers, teachers, church leaders, friends. Several steps removed, we believe biblical authors and the communities that gave rise to the Bible. At the core, we believe Jesus, and we believe Jesus to be revealing the truth about God.

By means of extant scriptures, various religious communities of the first century in the Common Era have handed on narratives about the mission and ministry of Jesus of Nazareth. They have also handed on names expressive of their faith, such as Son of Man, Son of God, Savior, Father, Spirit, Advocate. Confessions of faith are included in Scripture too.[6] Investigations conducted according to modern methods of historiography confirm that the redactors of the New Testament narratives, names, and confessions express the religious convictions not just of individuals, but of communities of faith. People who profess Christian faith trust the individuals and communities that produced the biblical texts. Further, they trust the words and acts of Jesus to be words and acts of God. It is never a matter of proving that God is in Jesus the Christ. It is a matter of concluding that it is reasonable to believe; indeed, for the believer it is more reasonable to believe than not to believe.

From the Gospel narratives we learn that Jesus may well have addressed the God in whom Jews believe, that is, Yahweh, as Father.[7] "I thank you, Father, Lord of heaven and earth" (Mt 11:25). "Father, for you all things are possible" (Mk 14:36). "Father, into your hands I commend my spirit" (Lk 23:46). While Yahweh is understood to be Father to all human beings (Heb 2:11), with Jesus there is a unique relationship, which the Letter to the Hebrews expresses in terms of Psalm 2:7: "You are my Son; today I have begotten you" (Heb 1:5). Paralleling Jesus' invocation of Yahweh as Father, certain passages in the Synoptic Gospels (Mt 11:27/Lk 10:22, Mk 13:32, Mk 12:1–12) indicate the likelihood "that Jesus spoke and thought of himself as 'the Son,' implying a very special relationship to God that is part of his identity and status."[8]

Additionally, according to the Gospels, Jesus claims divine attributes for himself. Raymond Brown writes: "The Gospel traditions agree in depicting him as a man who thinks he can act and speak for God. . . . His implied relationship to God was more than that of an agent; God was acting not only through him but in him."[9] Who can forgive sins, but God alone? Yet, Jesus forgives sins (Mk 2:7f). Who can interpret Torah with definitive authority except God? In the Sermon on the Mount, especially in the Matthean version, Jesus interprets Torah definitively. In John's Gospel, Jesus says directly, "The Father and I are one" (John 10:30), one interpretation of which is identity in some ontological sense.[10]

The New Testament can be interpreted to attest that Jesus also named a third person in conjunction with the Father and himself, namely, the Spirit, who would be the advocate sent from the Father through Jesus after the departure of Jesus (see John 14:16–17, 26; 15:26; 16:7–11,13–14). Beyond Jesus' own naming of the Spirit, New Testament writings are replete with references to the distinctive role of the Spirit in the lives of the faithful (see, e.g., Eph 1:3–14; 2:18; 3:1–6 and 14–19; 4:3–5; 4:30–5:2; 5:18–20).

My point is that Christian belief in the triune God rests upon the judgment that Jesus himself revealed the triune God, and that Jesus is trustworthy. By naming God his Father, by identifying the Spirit as distinct and yet in union with the Father and himself, by claiming divine prerogatives for himself, Jesus communicates that God is triune. These, at least, are the claims being made by many communities whose beliefs are mediated by the New Testament scriptures.

In turn, these beliefs are confessed doxologically. Thus, baptism is conferred "in the name of the Father, and of the Son, and of the Holy Spirit" (Mt 28:19), a confession whose specificity so early in the life of the Christian community continues to puzzle scholars of the New Testament.[11] But perhaps the great commission at the end of Matthew's Gospel is not so strange when it is placed alongside the narrative of the baptism of Jesus himself, with

its triune symbolism: Jesus standing in the water, with the Spirit of God hovering overhead in the form of a dove, while a voice from the heavens proclaims: "This is my Son, the Beloved, with whom I am well pleased" (Mt
3:16–17). Perhaps the faith of the first-century Matthean community was
more explicitly trinitarian than scholars are sometimes inclined to maintain.
To offer an example of doxology in another context, Paul offers a valedic-
tory blessing in one of his letters to Corinthian Christians: "The grace of the
Lord Jesus Christ, the love of God, and the communion of the Holy Spirit be
with all of you" (II Cor 13:13).

The New Testament offers several more texts, as well as themes, which
could be highlighted to indicate the belief, widespread if not universal, in
early Christian communities that Jesus revealed God somehow to be three
and that God is active in human history, sharing the gift of divine life in accord with the threefold divine character.[12]

Why do Christian faithful of later ages find the witness of the biblical authors, and, even more, of the communities they represent, trustworthy when
they claim that Jesus has revealed God to be three? At least for some whose
beliefs are an articulation of the knowledge born of love, the explanation is
that the later recipients of the biblical witness down through the centuries
find that their religious experience resonates with the narratives and doxologies and other trinitarian texts in the New Testament. Even more, when it
comes to belief that Jesus is the divine revelation of God, Christians can go
back to their original attraction to Jesus, before explicit faith in him and
surely before any beliefs about him. Religious experience confirms the reasonableness of Jesus' claims. It leads the Christian faithful to cull the Bible
further, sifting through the other trinitarian texts, for the wherewithal to develop more complete statements about the God whom Jesus reveals.

Standing by themselves, the distant figures of the early Christian communities could hardly create a strong enough presence to mediate belief for
contemporary persons of faith, even if it is Jesus and his revelation that they
mediate. The living community in the present hands on these beliefs in its
liturgies, when word and symbol, brought to life within a community at worship, nourish faith. Prayer is addressed to the Father through the Son in the
Holy Spirit, or to the Father and to the Son and to the Holy Spirit, throughout Christian sacramental liturgy, at least in most Christian churches. The dynamic of the eucharistic prayers is trinitarian. The effects of the sacraments
are proclaimed in trinitarian terms. The creed of the councils of Nicea and
Constantinople, which codified Christian trinitarian faith, marks the end of
the liturgy of the word at Sunday Eucharist in many churches. In summary,
belief in the triune God pervades the church when it gathers for worship. As
early as the third century, the church is described concretely as "a people
brought into unity from the unity of the Father, the Son, and the Holy
Spirit."[13] This trinitarian character of the church community is celebrated

every time there is a gathering of Christians for worship. At times more directly, at times more obliquely, it is communicated to the worshipers.

Conflicts of Interpretation

One could imagine that belief in the triune God might develop on a smooth trajectory from the original witnesses to the early creeds and beyond. But that would be to ignore the actual complications that attend the development of human history, including the history of the doctrine of God. One important reason for the complications that accompany the interpretation of religious meaning is the character of religious beliefs as expressive of truth that transcends the world accessible to the natural, as well as to the human, sciences. Thus, while it plays a role in all of human life, as was noted in the previous section, belief is an equivocal term.

As is noted above, a distinction is necessary between beliefs that are *matters of fact*, which, at least theoretically, human beings could investigate to their satisfaction if they chose to do so and were endowed with requisite resources of various kinds (e.g., intelligence, access to data, specialized education), and beliefs which are beyond our investigation. The latter are instances in which belief is required *in principle*. In such instances the trustworthiness of those who claim to know and hand on the truth proposed for belief grows in importance. Truths of religious faith, which are judgments about reality that absolutely transcends the human mind, belong to the group of beliefs in principle. In fact, they are the chief instance of such beliefs. Let us reflect on the actual functioning and relationship of these two sorts of belief in the daily life of a typical modern person.

While every human being's functioning in the world remains coherent on the basis of a wide-ranging array of beliefs, very many of these beliefs have no proximate relationship to the core meanings of life. To believe that the polar cap is covered with ice has no connection with my choice of a spouse or whether I allow physicians to equip me with life-sustaining machines in the case of dire illness. Simultaneously, it may be quite tragic for the long-term future of the human race if a significant number of earth dwellers dismiss their belief about ice on the polar cap so totally that they fail to take seriously those scientists tracking the melting of the polar ice cap and their related warnings about global warming.

Thus, with regard to the many, many beliefs as *matters of fact* that function to keep our daily living moving along, some are of greater value in the short run, some in the long run, and some will never be of much consequence at all. In the first instance, my belief that my physician knows what she needs to know about medicine is tested when a family member becomes a candidate for artificial life support. In the second instance, belief in those scientists promoting the hypothesis of global warming may have no consequences until some decades after the death of everyone currently inhabiting the earth, although, if true, it should influence some behaviors now. In the third instance, my belief in those scientists who claim to know that the island of Nantucket, off the coast of Massachusetts, is gradually being eroded away, will never matter much to me or to most human beings, except insofar as I may be sympathetic to residents of Nantucket who may one day actually be affected.

One difficulty with religious beliefs is that they can seem to be of little or no significance for daily living. Although they address issues about the very source and final goal of life, one can go about much of life without being concerned about religious beliefs. Or so it can seem until major issues confront individuals or a society. Even then, however, since the beliefs are beliefs *in principle*, they admit no possibility of investigation that might prove them to be true or false. For this reason it happens that some moderns, with their devotion to the methods of natural science, reject any statements based upon religious belief since they cannot be verified empirically, while some postmoderns dismiss the possibility of objective transcendent truth because all truth statements are compromised by bias or, at least, by relativity.

For many, however, it is evident that there are too many vital questions that demand answers and decisions, both individually and socially, for human living to move forward with some meaning without religious faith and beliefs. Technology gives human beings far more effective control over important aspects of human living than was possible just fifty years ago. With the new technological possibilities new questions of value arise. Is it valuable to terminate a pregnancy, or engage in nuclear warfare, or maintain terminally ill persons indefinitely by mechanized interventions? Is it valuable to computerize and mechanize the production of goods or shift the production of goods from high-paying to low-paying countries, so that vast numbers of the higher-wage work force lose their jobs?

Moreover, in a democracy, where individual freedoms are so highly prized, is it possible to achieve enough consensus about truths and values that decisions satisfactory to the majority are possible in these difficult areas and in many others besides, ranging from offshore fishing to divorce and remarriage to international arms trade? It seems that the common good cannot be promoted without invoking beliefs, including perhaps religious beliefs, that are *in principle* beyond experimental investigation in the manner of the natural sciences.

It is my contention that if we accept Bernard Lonergan's advocacy of the position that meaning, truth, and value can be achieved in every area of human life, with no exceptions, then we are off to a good start. On Lonergan's account, meaning, truth, and value can be achieved by employing a generalized empirical method, the method I have described briefly in the second chapter, a method that relies not only on the data of sense but also the data of consciousness to discover reality.[14] Moreover, if generalized empirical method can be employed satisfactorily when the data of consciousness are drawn affectively by an intentional dynamism into the realm of mystery, as I have argued in chapter 3, then religious beliefs not only can, but must, be brought into the discussions of how to go about one's daily living. For those data of consciousness intimate some dimension of reality.

Sooner or later civil discourse will not be able to enclose the question of God within exceptive parentheses. For the questions of meaning, truth, and value regarding the issues of life and death can be finally settled only when the question of God, by which we refer to the ultimate source and goal of meaning, truth, and value, is answered. Sooner or later the question of religious belief must be addressed.

This is all the more reason for Christians who live by religious faith in the modern/postmodern context to sort out how, within our faith tradition, we have come to a belief in God expressed in a doctrine of the Trinity. In our investigation, we find that even the premoderns who developed the doctrine had to deal with conflicts of interpretation on their way to the doctrine, although nearly everyone accepted the value of religious belief. Moreover, the same premodern Christians also needed to relate to their religious experience what they heard proclaimed and read for themselves in the scriptures of the Hebrew and Christian testaments and what they celebrated in their liturgies. They needed to do this for their faith, the knowledge born of love, to make sense to them and ultimately to become articulate.

This, then, is another reason for the conflict of interpretations. The religious experience of persons who were attracted to Jesus in the early centuries was interpreted in some fashion by Jewish faith or faith in one of the mystery religions or one or other Hellenistic philosophy. As they employed the images, symbols, and concepts familiar to them to interpret their new experience of attraction to Jesus and the new images and concepts expressed in the new narrative of the Christian Gospel, it is not surprising that they would experience conflict within their own minds and hearts and also with one another.[15] The most pressing question was also the ultimate question. What kind of person is this Jesus to whom we are so drawn in loving faith? Since most accepted that Jesus was somehow divine, the question was how.

How would the early Christians adjudicate conflicts with the hope not only of achieving personal peace of mind and social peace within the church, and on Constantine's part within the empire, but also the truth about God? We find that these Christians of the first four centuries of the Common Era did three things. First, on the basis of their newfound faith they adopted entirely new beliefs. Second, they appealed to convictions they brought with them from their former religious and philosophical faiths to support their new faith. Third, they could not consistently and did not retain all former beliefs, but only those that they considered to be unassailable; they let their new faith lead them to eliminate some former beliefs.

We are led to ask, however, what guided all the picking and choosing that took place, all the accumulated negotiations that eventuated among Palestinian Jewish Christians and Hellenistic Jewish Christians, and devotees of various mystery religions, and Greek and Roman philosophical types, members of Gnostic sects, and others, all of whom cast their lot with the new faith in Jesus of Nazareth.

On the basis of generalized empirical method, I maintain that two things happened. Basically, what was going forward was a move toward making judgments on the operational level of weighing the evidence. That meant, on the one hand, checking convictions of the new faith and their formulations against both one's own already held convictions and those of one's partners in dialogue who were equally committed to faith in Jesus. On the other hand, what most fundamentally motivated the outcome of weighing the evidence was its compatibility or resonance with the feelings of wonder, awe, longing, trust, joy, fear, sorrow (and other religious experiences), but mostly love. For, swayed by overwhelming love, the faith conviction becomes firm that the ultimate witness, acting through all the other intermediary witnesses, is divine, personal mystery itself.

Factoring religious experience into the development of doctrine was very difficult. First, no explicit advertence to it was evident, since religious experience was not an articulated category. Second, the catalysts of various religious experiences led different people to different dimensions of the one mystery which all were seeking. So some focused on God's creative power, some on the suffering of Jesus, some on God's otherness relative to this world and humanity, and so on.[16] Thus, even after judgments were made at Nicea in 325 C.E., they could not be consolidated until fifty-six years later. Indeed, they needed to be consolidated anew many times over throughout the centuries of Christian faith. They need to be consolidated in our own time, which is the purpose of this part of my investigation.[17]

Dialectical Development

What might strike a contemporary Christian as odd is that some of the key biblical texts at the heart of the controversies about Jesus and his relation to God are not at all the texts contemporary Christians find revelatory of plurality within the one God. A popular text among early Christian theologians is Proverbs 8:22: "The Lord created me at the beginning of his work." Proverbs, of course, is not one of the New Testament writings at all, preceding by some five or six centuries the birth of Jesus. Nevertheless, Christians whose background was Alexandrian Judaism found that verse to be quite congenial to their view of Jesus as Word (logos) of God in creation, as proclaimed in the prologue of John's Gospel. Word and wisdom are similar, and Paul declares Christ to be the wisdom of God in I Corinthians 1:24. The personification of wisdom (*sophia*) and wisdom's role as an instrument of creation seemed to confirm a preexistent life on the part of the Christ.

Other passages of Old Testament wisdom were also employed to demonstrate the role of Christ vis-à-vis God. In the Book of Wisdom, much closer to the time of Jesus but still predating his birth by about one hundred years, we read that *sophia*/wisdom is "a breath of the power of God and a pure emanation of the glory of the Almighty . . . and an image of his goodness" (Wis 7:25–26; see Heb 1:3).[18]

Upon reflection we should not be surprised to discover a use of Old Testament texts, for the Hebrew scriptures were, at first, the only scriptures proclaimed in the early Christian assemblies. The scriptures that we call the New Testament, while they were being written and read already in the first century and collected in the second and third centuries, did not become a fully accepted part of the canon or rule of faith in their present form until the fourth century. Not surprisingly, as the oral traditions faded, the written tradition gained in prominence. If one wanted to refer to a canonical book, Old Testament scriptures were acceptable without question.

New Testament texts, of course, were employed, but they can be as ambiguous as the Old Testament texts just cited. John's prologue declares that the word is God, but when it does so in the opening verse of chapter 1 it omits the definite article used for God in the previous phrase. Thus, the Greek literally says that while the logos is God, it somehow differs from *the* God with whom it coexisted in the beginning. This omission of the article gave pause to some early theologians. Is John indicating that the logos is not God in the same sense or as much as *the* God is God?

Or take John 10:30: "The Father and I are one." That is quite straightforward. Or is it? Does it mean that Jesus and the Father are identical? In every way, or only in some ways? Or does it mean intimately united while still distinct? Or do they have different natures, but prove to be of the same mind about things (moral union)? Add to this John 14:28: "for the Father is greater than I." Or take Mark 13:32: "But about that day or hour no one knows, neither the angels in heaven, nor the Son, but only the Father." Is Jesus God or not? If so, is Jesus God as fully as the Father is God? Shouldn't he, then, know all as God knows all? If not, wherein lies the difference? Various theologians interpreted these texts variously. Communities, too, emphasized Christ's divine-human qualities variously. Little wonder that conflicts of interpretation arose.

Contemporary Christians improve their chances of understanding the development of beliefs in the early church when we recognize that some issues about God which were of pressing concern in the first four centuries are not so pressingly felt in our time. Some early Christians shared with some of their contemporaries great concern about God as creator and about the world as distant from God. They wondered how Christ fit into God's creative activity in the world. Today we are more concerned with God's redemptive activity in Christ, and we are concerned about this in interpersonal terms on the one hand and political terms on the other.

For some, the different concerns of the early Christians and especially the answers to which they led pose a conflict of interpretations on several counts between the Christians of the first four centuries and ourselves. However, while our concerns may be different, and while we may ardently hope to develop theology of God further than it was developed by the end of the fourth century, this is not a reason to ignore or, even less, to reject the development that the dialectical conversation of the first four centuries achieved.

Indeed, we have the benefit of hindsight. We can observe the conversation from afar. We can appreciate more clearly than was possible at the time the reason for different styles of conceptualization and linguistic expression. And we can uncover more fundamental developments taking place perhaps beyond the notice of anyone at the time. So we move on to a brief survey of key moments in the development of belief in the triune God.

DEVELOPMENT OF THE DOCTRINE OF GOD

The history of the theological development regarding the truth about God inherent in religious faith in Jesus achieves a high point in the judgments of the Nicene-Constantinopolitan Creed (or the comparable Apostles' Creed). It is helpful to distinguish three moments: the original experience of the event of Jesus; a period spanning more than three centuries of questions and answers about Jesus and his relationship with God; and the Christian community's discernment of the truth about God and Jesus in the conciliar decrees of the fourth century.

Being Attracted to Jesus, Listening to Him

Here we combine what was said about experience of Jesus in the previous chapter with what was said in the earlier section of this chapter, "Belief in God as Triune." I have contended that, in the final analysis, everyone who comes to genuine faith in Jesus does so because they feel an attraction to his person. This faith begins as one feels oneself being drawn by wonder, awe, longing, love, fear, trust, shame, guilt, sorrow, joy, and perhaps other feelings. In these experiences of oneself, the person sometimes feels drawn into the realm of mystery in which there is no this-worldly object that is or likely can be motivating these feelings. In these cases, feelings possess a religious dimension. Finally, one realizes that it is in the psychological presence of the person of Jesus that one's feelings of mystery are more or less intensely awakened. At this point one cannot say how or why, but one is attracted beyond normal human attraction to the wandering preacher of Galilee. This is the case no matter how one became acquainted with Jesus, whether having met him in person in first-century Capernaum, or having heard about him from an excited friend in a later century, or having sensed his presence at a eucharistic liturgy, or having been introduced to him in a private reading of a New Testament passage. This is the meaning of specifically Christian religious experience.

For many who have met him through the centuries, attraction to Jesus has included falling in love with him in that all-embracing way characteristic of falling in love with mystery, the mystery which has been named God. Thus, when we read the texts of those who wrote up the convictions of early Christian communities, and we discover them telling the story of Jesus' relationship with God, we pay attention. In our love of Jesus, we affirm with these authors what Jesus tells of God and of his relationship with God. God is the Father of Jesus in a unique way. Yet somehow God is our Father, too. Jesus and the Father are one, and yet the Father is greater than Jesus. No one can come to God the Father except through Jesus; Jesus reveals the Father to anyone who cares to take notice.

Furthermore, with the Father and Jesus there lives or dwells a Spirit. This Spirit is depicted in a distinct symbol, that of a dove, at the baptism of Jesus. Perhaps the placement of the hovering Spirit of God at his baptism might not mean a distinct individual in God if there were no other references. But in John's Gospel, Jesus multiply speaks of the Spirit who will be sent from the Father or from the Father and himself. Is this Spirit the spirit of Jesus or of the Father in the sense of their indistinct spirit? Or is it a distinct spirit? Pauline writings make frequent reference to the Spirit as well, but it is a more complicated task to sort out when Paul might mean the spirit that is the personal power of the risen Jesus and when he might mean a distinct spirit.

Sorting Out the Options

The particular nature of the indwelling divine Spirit was not much discussed during the period up to the year 325. Jesus was the obviously historical figure who could readily be recognized to be attracting adherents. The role of Jesus in the divine realm had to be articulated if his followers were to continue to relate to him honestly and maintain coherent beliefs about God. After Jesus' place relative to God was sorted out, then the question of the Spirit could be taken up in earnest, as it was in the decades following the formulation of the Nicene Creed.

Moreover, until the role of Jesus is sorted out, there can be no specifically Christian judgments about God at all. At the same time, early Christians brought with them to their interpersonal encounter with Jesus beliefs about God that had been confirmed in their prior religious experience. These beliefs were variously cast depending upon their backgrounds. As the conversation with Christians of other backgrounds took shape within the several geographical centers of Christian faith, positions formed, accumulated, clashed, added new elements, subtracted previous elements, reformed. There is development in the sense of moving from one position to another, but the stages cannot be distinguished until after the development reaches its term.

Studies of this interesting and important period of Christian history abound. Thus, it is not necessary to go into detail here. Instead, the purposes of the present chapter are served by highlighting the contribution to the conversation of three prominent theologians who wrote before the end of the second century: Justin Martyr, Athenagoras, and Irenaeus. Then, the next chapter will begin by attending to two third-century theologians, Tertullian and Origen, and, finally, from the beginning of the fourth century, the famous Arius, who became the proximate catalyst of the Nicene Creed. In these six we can observe the progress of the development. To remain true to our purposes, two aspects of the theological reflection of each of these thinkers will be highlighted: (1) what they brought to the discussion from their previously formed constellation of judgments; and (2) how their commitment to Jesus interpreted in their reading of the witnesses to Christian faith led them to make new judgments articulated in concepts that, for them, were relatively satisfactory.

It is not difficult to flag where clashes might erupt. If the previously formed constellations of convictions of one thinker differ from those of another, and both remain firmly held, disagreement is sure to characterize the distinct authors. On another front, interpretations of the witnesses of faith, whether those of the written scriptures or those within the thinker's contemporaneous living community, may vary from individual to individual. In a third area, less easy to flag, feelings of wonder and awe may predominate in one thinker's religious experience, while feelings of trusting and restful contemplation predominate in another's, while the fear of yielding to unrestricted love may motivate the reflection of a third thinker. Although it is not easy even for the subject of feelings to distinguish and name them, let alone the observer who simply has access to a thinker's writings, still all can acknowledge that feelings influence thinking, and it may be possible to identify feelings of our chosen thinkers to some extent and thus appreciate more adequately the positions taken. We begin the review with Justin.

1. Justin, surnamed Martyr because he died for the faith in the reign of Marcus Aurelius, wrote in the middle years of the second century. Originally from Nablus in Palestine, he eventually settled in Rome. Justin was a philosopher who, by his own declaration, longed to know God. In our language of religious experience, he was drawn by wonder and longing into the realm of mystery. This was the motivation of his intellectual quest. Justin tried to learn from several philosophical schools of his day, settling finally on the "philos-

ophy" of Christianity. Justin closes his *Dialogue with Trypho* with the judgment: "Jesus is the Christ of God."

Justin reports that he was disillusioned in his quest for God until he met an elderly man who promised that in the Old Testament prophets and especially in Jesus he would find the enlightenment he was seeking. With that promise Justin's heart was set on fire. Justin's religious experience was resonating as he encountered Jesus the Christ.[19]

Justin's study of Plato had convinced him about God's transcendence of the created world and about God's Word/Logos, which mediates between the transcendent God and the created world. How is the Word able to function in this way? Here Justin brings with him a conviction he appropriated from Stoic philosophy. The Word is the word of the mind of God. It resides first in the mind of God and then, when spoken, it creates the world.[20]

His philosophical convictions, then, led Justin to recognize the oneness of the Word with the Mind in which it dwells both before and after being spoken, and at the same time to take the Word to be distinct. When, in turn, after his conversation with the man who introduced him to Jesus, Justin read the Old Testament from within his loving faith in Jesus (both because the old man had told him he would find enlightenment in the "prophets and in Christ" and because the Old Testament books were the only God-given scriptures accepted in the Christian community at the time), he had no trouble interpreting the two uses of the divine name, "Lord," in Genesis 19:24 to refer to the Father (the Lord of heaven) and Jesus (the Lord who executes God's judgment upon Sodom and Gomorrah).[21] Both are Lord, but they are distinct from one another. As the word is distinct within the mind in which it resides, so the Logos who is God's agent in the world is distinct from God who acts upon the world.

Besides confirmation of convictions he brought with him from his Greek philosophical background, Justin found something remarkably new in Christ. Not only was God's instrumental agent active as the preexistent Logos, it also became incarnate, became human, suffered and died in this flesh, and in the same flesh ascended into heaven. Justin goes on about the life of Jesus in the flesh at great length in his *Dialogue with Trypho*. He does so to highlight God's redemption of humanity from its sinfulness by means of the incarnate activity of the preexistent Word. For God to become human would be scandalous both for the Jews (Trypho is an Ephesian Jew) and for the Greek philosophers for whom the physical is the dimension of reality farthest removed from God. But once Justin was committed to Jesus in loving faith, some of his philosophical convictions were abandoned.

2. Arriving on the scene just a little later than Justin, Athenagoras is much less famous. Still, his *Plea for Christians* is a valuable expression of the developing Christian doctrine of God. Probably written in 177 C.E., the *Plea* is addressed to two Roman emperors, Marcus Aurelius and his son, Commodus.

Like Justin, Athenagoras seems to be well-versed in both Stoic and Middle Platonist philosophy, or perhaps in Stoic philosophy as filtered through Middle Platonist philosophy.

Just what religious experience drew Athenagoras to his strong commitment to Christian faith cannot be ascertained, but it would not surprise a reader of the *Plea* if Athenagoras had discovered that Christian doctrine provided the best answer to the wonder he experienced as he asked some of the central philosophical questions of his day. This is implied by one of Athenagoras's commentators, Leslie W. Barnard, when he makes a general statement: "The immediate concern of the second century Apologists was to present Christianity as the crowning perfection of the highest ideals of the Graeco-Roman world by a skilful adaptation to contemporary philosophical trends."[22]

One reason that Christians were so despised by the cultured elites of the Roman Empire was a conviction they shared with the Jews, namely, their strict monotheism. Athenagoras takes great care to claim that God is at once utterly transcendent Creator and yet a provident Father of all creatures. And he calls upon Plato, Aristotle, and the Stoics to support his claim.[23] He summarizes his position on the oneness of God by naming several transcendent divine qualities:

> We have brought before you a God who is uncreated, eternal, invisible, impassible, incomprehensible, and infinite, who can be apprehended by mind and reason alone, who is encompassed by light, beauty, spirit, and indescribable power, and who created, adorned, and now rules the universe through the Word that issues from him. I have given sufficient evidence that we are not atheists on the basis of arguments presenting this God.[24]

Furthermore, Athenagoras finds Christian trinitarian doctrine of God to be well suited to his defense of his faith, for in that way he can both claim strict monotheism and yet concede plurality in God. One Athenagoras translator, William R. Schoedel, puts it this way: "Athenagoras concentrates on an aspect of trinitarian thought which prepares the ground for a theology capable of uniting the biblical emphasis on God as Creator, the Greek fascination with a world interpenetrated by Logos, and a doctrine of prophetic authority rooted in the activity of the Spirit who touches the deepest recesses of the human intellect."[25]

So, Athenagoras insists: "Who then would not be amazed if he heard of men called atheists who bring forward God the Father, God the Son, and the Holy Spirit and who proclaim both their power in their unity and their diversity in rank."[26]

This brilliant effort to profess monotheism while yet commending his fellow Christians to the emperor for their appreciation of plurality in God motivated Athenagoras to continue to express unity in diversity and diversity in unity in God. He writes: "We are attended only by the knowledge of him who is truly God and of the Word that issues from him—a knowledge as to what is the unity of the Son with the Father, what is the communion of the Father with the Son, what is the Spirit, what is the unity of these powers—the Spirit, the Son, and the Father—and their diversity when thus united."[27] Later in the treatise he will repeat his point: "We say that there is God and the Son, his Word, and the Holy Spirit, united in power yet distinguished in rank as the Father, the Son, and the Spirit, since the Son is mind, reason [word], and wisdom of the Father and the Spirit an effluence like light from fire."[28]

In short, Justin, Athenagoras, and other apologists find that their philosophical convictions and their Christian convictions happily coincide in important areas. Their purpose is to defend the rule of Christian faith, not to make Christianity into another version of Greek philosophy. To quote Barnard again: "The Apologists did not scruple to use technical philosophic terms which were the current stock-in-trade of educated pagans. It is however an error to believe that in doing this they so hellenized Christianity as to dilute its central doctrines. They were first and foremost Churchmen and their object was to christianize Hellenism, not to hellenize Christianity."[29]

3. Irenaeus is similar to Justin and Athenagoras in his defense of the faith against threats. He differs from the first two of our thinkers in that those against whom he defends the faith themselves claim to be the faithful interpreters of the Christian Gospel. Irenaeus also differs in that his theology is not articulated in philosophical terms for the most part. It is a straightforward exposition of the faith, a commentary on what he is sure is the traditional statement of Christian belief.

A native of Smyrna in Asia Minor, Irenaeus made his way to Gaul, along with many other Asian Christians. In Gaul, Irenaeus became the leader (bishop/presbyter) of the church in Lyons, where he wrote in defense of the Christian faith against those *within the church* who, he was convinced, were promoting a false interpretation of Christian faith. Before his death in the last years of the second century, Irenaeus had written memorable summaries of what, he insisted, was the authentic Christian tradition, the order of faith handed on by the apostles through the succession of bishop-teachers of the church.[30]

We can ask what inspired Irenaeus to be so passionate in his defense of the faith. We might even say that he was consumed by his project when we realize that, originally, he had intended to write two books in opposition to what he deemed to be the false teachings in vogue in his day. But eventually *The Detection and Overthrow of Knowledge Falsely So-Called* (the actual title of what is commonly known as *Against Heresies*) expanded from two volumes to five.[31] Perhaps Irenaeus's passion for the faithfully handed-on tradition comes from his upbringing in Smyrna, a church addressed by John the Seer in the Book of Revelation (2:8–11). The Seer was inspired to encourage the church at Smyrna to be steadfast and faithful to Jesus who is first and last, who was dead and has risen.[32] This they were to do even in the face of persecution. Maybe this was the form that Irenaeus's religious experience took.

Whatever the motive of his preoccupation with the authentic Christian tradition, Irenaeus proclaims it in an early style of creed, recognizable by Christians of every later era. On several occasions throughout his interpretation of the faith in *Against Heresies*, Irenaeus repeats the basic structure of the faith, namely, belief in God, Father, Son, and Holy Spirit.[33] However, because of its clarity, I include here a statement of the order of faith from a later and shorter work of Irenaeus, *The Demonstration of the Apostolic Preaching*.[34] It is an appropriate way to conclude this chapter.

> And this is the order of our faith, the foundation of [the] edifice and the support of [our] conduct: God, the Father, uncreated, uncontainable, invisible, one God, the Creator of all: this is the first article (*kephalaion*) of our faith. And the second article: the Word of God, the Son of God, Christ Jesus our Lord, who was revealed by the prophets according to the character of their prophecy and according to the nature of the economies of the Father, by whom all things were made, and who, in the last times, to recapitulate all things, became a man amongst men, visible and palpable, in order to abolish death, to demonstrate life, and to effect communion between God and man. And the third article: the Holy Spirit, through whom the prophets prophesied and the patriarchs learnt the things of God and the righteous were led in the path of righteousness, and who, in the last times, was poured out in a new fashion upon the human race renewing man, throughout the world, to God.
>
> For this reason the baptism of our regeneration (*palingenesia*) takes place through these articles, granting us regeneration into God the Father through His Son by the Holy Spirit: for those who bear the Spirit of God are led to the Word, that is to the Son, while the Son presents [them] to the Father, and the Father furnishes (*peripoieo*) incorruptibility.

NOTES

1. Charles Hefling Jr., *Why Doctrines?* (Cambridge, MA: Cowley, 1984).
2. See Lonergan, *Method in Theology*, 112–13.
3. Lonergan, *Method in Theology*, 115.
4. Blaise Pascal, *Pensées,* trans. Krailsheimer, 127 (#423).
5. My statement here is comparable to David Tracy's suggestion that within the New Testament itself there is a development of styles expressive of faith in the event of Jesus the Christ, beginning with proclamation and moving on to narrative, then symbol, and finally more elaborate thought. See *The Analogical Imagination: Christian Theology and the Culture of Pluralism* (New York: Crossroad, 1981), 268f.
6. Anthony Kelly discusses in detail different New Testament expressions of faith in and about Jesus and his revelation of God in *The Trinity of Love*, ch. 2.
7. Raymond Brown, writing from a "moderate conservative" point of view, puts the thesis this way in *An Introduction to New Testament Christology* (New York:

Paulist, 1994): "If Jesus presented himself as the first of many to stand in a new and special relationship to God as Father, that priority implies that his sonship was in some way superior to the sonship of all who would follow him" (87).

8. Brown, *Introduction to New Testament Christology*, 89. In a summary section a few pages later, Brown makes the strong suggestion that Jesus had "an emphatic filial relationship to God as the Son" (102). Craig A. Evans offers another approach to "son" language, this time in the title son of man. See "Jesus' Self-Designation 'The Son of Man' and the Recognition of His Divinity," in *The Trinity: An Interdisciplinary Symposium on the Trinity*, ed. Stephen T. Davis, Daniel Kendall, S.J., and Gerald O'Collins, S.J. (Oxford: Oxford University Press, 1999).

9. Brown, *Introduction to New Testament Christology*, 101.

10. All New Testament texts on God originate as functions of God's saving activity on behalf of humanity. That is the chief concern of New Testament texts. There is no interest in talk of God for its own sake. In the case of John's Gospel, see David Stanley, "The Purpose of the Fourth Evangelist and the 'Trinification' of the Christian," in *Trinification of the World: A Festschrift in Honour of Frederick E. Crowe in Celebration of His 60th Birthday,* ed. Thomas A. Dunne and Jean-Marc Laporte (Toronto: Regis College Press, 1978).

11. See Nils Alstrup Dahl, "Trinitarian Baptismal Creeds and New Testament Theology," in *Jesus the Christ: The Historical Origins of Christological Doctrine*, ed. Donald H. Juel (Minneapolis: Fortress, 1991).

12. Some contemporary texts that develop this statement are Peter Toon, *Our Triune God: A Biblical Portrayal of the Trinity* (Wheaton, IL: Victor, 1996); Boris Bobrinskoy, *The Mystery of the Trinity: Trinitarian Experience and Vision in the Biblical and Patristic Period* (Crestwood, NY: St. Vladimir Seminary Press, 1999); Thomas F. Torrance, *The Christian Doctrine of God: One Being, Three Persons*, chs. 2 and 3 (Edinburgh: T. & T. Clark, 1996).

13. Cyprian, bishop of Carthage, *On the Lord's Prayer*, 23. This phrase is quoted in article 4 of the Second Vatican Council's Dogmatic Constitution on the Church (*Lumen gentium*).

14. On Lonergan's meaning of the phrase, "generalized empirical method," see *Insight: A Study of Human Understanding*, 268–69.

15. David Tracy notes that the New Testament itself provides a background for later conflicts of interpretation by its wide array of expressions of the Christ-event. See *The Analogical Imagination*, 250.

16. Robert Sokolowski claims that the key to the Christian doctrine of God is the distinction made by Christians between God as creator and the created world. See *The God of Faith and Reason: Foundations of Christian Theology* (Notre Dame: University of Notre Dame Press, 1982). Jaroslav Pelikan concurs that the faith confessed at Nicea is premised on the Creator God who saves humankind from its sinfulness. Thus, Nicea's is at once a "cosmological confession and a soteriological confession." See *The Emergence of the Catholic Tradition (100–600)*, vol. 1 of *The Christian Tradition: A History of the Development of Doctrine* (Chicago: University of Chicago Press, 1971), 203.

17. A complementary effort to revisit and consolidate Nicene Trinitarian belief is offered in Christopher R. Seitz, ed., *Nicene Christianity: The Future for a New Ecumenism* (Grand Rapids, MI: Brazos, 2001).

18. For further discussion of Old Testament texts such as these see Robert M. Grant, *The Early Christian Doctrine of God*, (Charlottesville: University Press of Virginia, 1966), 37–53. William J. Hill claims that Alexandria is the provenance even of John's use of Word/Logos in the Prologue of his Gospel, and that Logos is thus already related to Wisdom in the Gospel. See *The Three-Personed God: The Trinity as Mystery of Salvation* (Washington: Catholic University of America, 1982), 11.

19. Justin Martyr, *Dialogue with Trypho*, 8, in Thomas B. Falls, trans., in *Writings of Justin Martyr*, vol. 5 of *The Fathers of the Church* (New York: Christian Heritage, 1948), 160.

20. Martyr, *Dialogue with Trypho*, 61, in which Justin quotes Proverbs 8 at length. For complementary reflection on Justin Martyr and other thinkers highlighted in this text, see Hill, *The Three-Personed God*, 30f. See also J. N. D. Kelly, *Early Christian Doctrines* (NY: Harper & Row, 1958), 95–101.

21. For a report on the use of this Old Testament passage by other thinkers as well as Justin, see Pelikan, *The Emergence of the Catholic Tradition (100–600)*, 181.

22. Leslie W. Barnard, *Athenagoras: A Study in Second Century Christian Apologetic* (Paris: Beauchesne, 1972), 11.

23. In the *Plea* 6:2, Athenagoras writes: "Plato says: 'It is a hard task to find the Maker and Father of this universe, and having found him it is impossible to declare him to all.' Here he understands the uncreated and eternal God to be one." In 6:3, he writes: "Aristotle and his school bring before us one God whom they liken to a composite living being and say that he consists of soul and body." And in 6:4: "The Stoics, although they multiply names for the divine being by means of titles corresponding to the permutations of matter through which they say the Spirit of God moves, in reality think of God as one." These quotations are from *Athenagoras, Legatio and De Resurrectione*, ed. and trans. by William R. Schoedel (Oxford: Clarendon, 1972), 13 and 15.

24. *Plea*, 10:1, in *Athenagoras, Legatio and De Resurrectione*, 21.

25. William R. Schoedel, introduction to *Athenagoras, Legatio and De Resurrectione*, xviii.

26. *Plea*, 10:5, in *Athenagoras, Legatio and De Resurrectione*, 23.

27. *Plea*, 12:3, in *Athenagoras, Legatio and De Resurrectione*, 27.

28. *Plea*, 24:2, in *Athenagoras, Legatio and De Resurrectione*, 59.

29. Barnard, *Athenagoras: A Study*, 11.

30. See Irenaeus's famous statement on apostolic succession in *Against Heresies*, Bk IV, 3. The complete text of *Against Heresies* in English is included in vol. 1 of *The Ante-Nicene Fathers*, ed. Alexander Roberts and James Donaldson (Grand Rapids, MI: Eerdmans, 1985; originally published 1885).

31. Dennis Minns, O.P., *Irenaeus* (Washington, DC: Georgetown Univ. Press, 1994), 6–7.

32. Cf. Jean Colson, *Saint Irénée: Aux origins du christianisme en Gaule* (Paris: Éditions Ouvrierès, 1993), 8–9.

33. See *Against Heresies*, Bk I, 10, 1; Bk IV, 33, 7 & 33, 15; Bk V, 18, 1 & 20, 1.

34. St. Irenaeus of Lyons, *On the Apostolic Preaching*, trans. and intro. by John Behr (Crestwood, NY: St. Vladimir Seminary Press, 1997), nn. 6 and 7 (43–44). Just how Irenaeus understood the relation of the three in God to the oneness of God, a central question in the early church, is a further question. On this matter, see Dennis Minns, *Iraneus* ch. 4.

5

The Achievement of a Creed

As the second century waned and the third followed, Christianity became more firmly established. The number of Christians increased. Questions about Christian faith in God were less about defending the new faith against nonbelievers and more about Christians clarifying their faith in God for themselves. How could a human being truly save someone from sin? How could the one God truly live at once in the one whom Jesus called Father, and in Jesus himself, and in the Spirit? How could baptism into the one God, and yet into the Father, the Son, and the Holy Spirit, make sense? Christians became fully engaged in discussion and debate among themselves on how to interpret faith in the one God, the identity of the preincarnate Word, the meaning of the incarnation of the Word. Of course, as previously with the apologists of the second century, it was not simply a matter of interpreting biblical faith, but a matter as well of relating biblical faith to current philosophies, especially in the Hellenistic context within which most Christians lived.

THIRD-CENTURY DEVELOPMENTS

It would be difficult to overestimate the influence of three thinkers to whom we now direct our attention. Tertullian and Origen wrote at the beginning of the third century, and Arius preached and argued at the beginning of the fourth century. Tertullian and Origen made great strides in moving from trinitarian awareness toward precise trinitarian belief, although each one's thought needed further refinements. Arius, on the other hand, forced the definition of Nicea because he insisted upon his own interpretation of trinitarian awareness over what was determined to be the communal consciousness of the wider church. What follows is one view of how the dialectic unfolded.

1. Tertullian, a lawyer, arrived on the scene of trinitarian theology at the beginning of the third century in a North African capital of Christian faith, Carthage. Tertullian seems to have been attracted to faith in Jesus by the heroism of Christian martyrs, for he writes that "everyone in the face of such prodigious endurance feels himself, as it were, struck by some doubt, and ardently desires to find out what there is at the bottom of this matter; from the moment that he discovers the truth he forthwith embraces it himself."[1]

Sometime around 213 C.E. Tertullian wrote a treatise against the theories of a certain Praxeas. Interestingly, at the time of writing, which was late in his career, Tertullian had taken up with a sect that was not in favor in mainstream circles. He had become a follower of Montanus, a Christian who perceived himself to be a prophet specially designated by the Holy Spirit. Perhaps Tertullian became so concerned about trinitarian theology because of the prominence in Montanism of faith in the Holy Spirit. If this is true, it is of great importance since, as has been noted, most pre-Nicene Christian thinkers were so preoccupied with the relationship of the Word to the Father, either in its earthly existence or in its pre-earthly existence, that they paid little attention to the Spirit.

There is no question about the deeply affective quality of Tertullian's faith. So devoted is he to Jesus that repeatedly and sternly he calls his fellow Christians to fidelity in various areas. Indeed, it was Tertullian's dismay with the laxity which he perceived on the part of many Christians that led him to affiliate with the stricter Montanists.[2] Johannes Quasten claims that Tertullian had a "fanatical passion for truth."[3]

Zealous in his defense of the three-in-one God, Tertullian's efforts in this regard have won him an important place in the development of the doctrine of the Trinity. In fact, Tertullian is credited with coining the time-honored term *Trinity*. The catalyst for Tertullian's reflections was the fuzziness of some Christians regarding whether the second and third manifestations of God acknowledged by Christians, and named the Son/Word and the Spirit, were really a distinct second and third, or whether they were simply different appearances of the one God at the various times in which God chose to reveal the divine reality in history. Thus, it was a popular concept that God appeared as Father at one moment, as Son at another, and as Spirit at a third, but that there were not three really distinct in God; this interpretation is named modalism.

Tertullian knew where his faith and the faith of the church (both that of the Montanists and that of the wider church) had to come down: on three really distinct ones in the one God. But he also appreciated that there were two problems: how to express this conviction of faith in a clearly stated belief, and, because of this need, how to find a suitable terminology. Tertullian's treatise against Praxeas represents his effort to address the issue on both fronts.[4]

Although he disparaged the so-called wisdom of philosophy in comparison with the true wisdom of the Gospel, Tertullian's thought is much influenced by the Stoic philosophy with which he was familiar. As Justin did before him, Tertullian finds the Stoic view of the two words of the mind a helpful way to conceive the two modes of the existence of the Word of God before the incarnation. First, the Word exists within the divine mind as the Word of the Father. In this sense, the (inner) word is reason. Then, at the time of creation, the divine Word is spoken. In this sense, the (spoken) word is discourse.[5] Finally (here Tertullian moves beyond Stoicism), at the time of the redemption, the Word becomes flesh.

What Tertullian brings to the discussion is the way in which the Son and the Spirit could be distinct from the Father and yet be fully God as the Father is God. His solution is to understand the Father as a symbol of what is both first in God and the source of the other two. The Father is the monarch, from whom the Son and the Spirit come forth and with whom they share divinity. Does this mean that the Father is superior to the Son? Not at all, in Tertullian's view. And he explains it by making a comparison between the divine Son and an earthly king's son. When the king chooses not to be present to a group in person, but wants to be fully present to them nevertheless, he sends his son as regent. In the king's son, the group knows that the king is as good as present; the son possesses all the power of the father and all the other kingly qualities of his father, although the Father remains the monarch and the Son remains the regent.[6]

Lawyer that he is, Tertullian finds that the legal term *person*, with its emphasis upon a responsible individual, is especially appropriate to distinguish the three in God. To express what the three share, the chosen term is *substance*, meaning that which upholds the three persons in common. Thus, three persons, one substance, making up the divine Trinity. Tertullian also expresses individuality in God by speaking of each of the three as *alius*, a term of masculine gender to name one thing, and *aliud*, the same term but in the neuter gender, also expressing one thing. The former, for Tertullian, is used to express the three distinct ones in God, and the latter to express the one thing which the three share. Substance, person, Trinity—these terms, clarified by Tertullian's and later precisions, became the stock-in-trade for trinitarian theology in the Latin world.

Bernard Lonergan notes that there is a significant dialectical tension present within Tertullian's valuable contributions. Lonergan names it "naive realism."[7] By this he means that Tertullian's view of substance, also taken over from Stoic philosophy, effectively cancels God's transcendence. Tertullian assumes that every substance is somehow corporeal, bodily. The body of God may be quite rarefied so that one can't see it or hear it or touch it. But it is no less a body for all that.[8] Thus, Tertullian espouses the naive realism of those, who live in every age, who assume that if you can't somehow relate to a reality as a body, there is, in fact, no reality to which to relate. Tertullian's failure to grasp spirituality renders crass his conception of the monarchical image of Father and Son. Tertullian's "materialism" calls out for correction.

2. Tertullian's correction comes not long after in the early third century. Origen, hailing from another seaport of North Africa, Alexandria, taught there in the Christian catechetical school. Origen's reputation is that of a thoroughly devoted follower of Jesus, and why should he not be so regarded, for he not only witnessed his own father's martyrdom when Origen was an impressionable seventeen, but he also accompanied some of his students when they were led off to be martyred.[9] Finally, he was himself tortured mercilessly.

Philosophically, Origen was a Platonist through and through. There would be no chance that he would conceive God as in any way corporeal. God is totally spiritual. Each of the three in God is totally spiritual. The Son and the Spirit proceed from the Father in a totally spiritual manner, not unlike the way that the mind, which is spiritual, generates thoughts, which participate in the mind's spiritual nature.[10]

Because of his appreciation of the meaning of spirituality, Origen is also remarkably lucid in his understanding of unity and distinction among the three in God. He names the quality common to the three "goodness," by which a transcendent goodness is surely meant. Origen is prescient about distinction: the Son is born and the Spirit proceeds.[11]

Unfortunately, while Origen's Platonist philosophy helped him provide a corrective to any material conception of God, the same philosophy led him to interpret important biblical passages in such a way that the Son, while divine, is conceived to be so in a participatory and diminished way. The same is even more true of the Spirit. For Origen, the Word and the Spirit proceed from the Father as emanations of God, with the Father retaining a higher level of divinity. When Origen read the first verses of John's Gospel, he took the word God with the definite article to refer to the Father as more fully divine, while the Son, to whom reference is made without the definite article, is divine, but less so. When Origen read John 14:28: "the Father is greater than I," he applied it not just to the relation of the human Christ to God the Father, but to the relationship of the eternal Word to the Father as well, in the sense of subordination. And if the Word was a diminished participation of the divine reality, the Spirit was an even more diminished participation.[12]

Origen's conception of the participatory divinity of the Son and the Spirit also has implications regarding God's transcendence. Perhaps only the Father is transcendently free. Moreover, transcendence for Origen includes the utter distance of the Father from humanity; God the Father cannot come close to humanity. The Son and the Spirit may thus be regarded as bridges to the physical order of reality. This may go some way to explain Origen's view of the Son and Spirit as on a lower plane than the Father.

3. Early in the fourth century, another Alexandrian, a presbyter named Arius, finds his name at the head of a group who push to its logical conclusion the subordinationist sense of the Son as divine in a diminished way.[13] The Son must in some sense be a creature of God, not the transcendent creator along with God. Arius's formula, expressed in a letter to his bishop, Alexander, denies what Origen claimed.[14] Origen had claimed that the Son is eternal as the Father is eternal: There is no time when he was not. Arius claims that, since the Son is subordinate to the Father, he must somehow be creature. Therefore, there was a time when the Son was not, although it is not time like the temporality of physical creation, but a sort of transcendent time.

History has not communicated any sense that Arius was lacking in devotion to Jesus, the incarnate Word. His difficulty was not different from that of Origen. His presuppositions about the utter transcendence of God made it impossible for him to conceive God's creative, instrumental Logos as sharing the same transcendent nature as God. Even in the face of the opposition of church leaders, Arius stood his ground. Moreover, there were many likeminded Christians whose influence endured for several centuries.

THE COUNCIL OF NICEA AND ITS AFTERMATH: MORE SORTING OUT OF OPTIONS

Arius alerts us to a recurrent problem in the church. How are disputes to be adjudicated? Maintaining fidelity to God's self-revelation is the issue. But the content of divine self-revelation is not so easily determined, and less easily expressed in human terms, which, in any case, fall short. Images and symbols that resonate with shared religious experience and, in this way, mediate revelation can lend themselves to incompatible interpretations, even among people who share faith. The response in the case of the dispute with Arius was for a synod to be called, in this case by the Emperor Constantine. Perhaps three hundred bishops gathered at the emperor's summer villa in Nicea. Their conclusion was that the faith inherited from the apostolic age, the faith which earlier generations had attempted to interpret, required the affirmation that the preexistent Son is as much divine as the Father, although the two remain distinct. There has been no time when the Son was not.

The difficulty that the bishops encountered at Nicea was partially a matter of faith and partially a matter of finding the right words to express the faith. The party which insisted that the Son is divine as much as the Father won the day. But even those bishops had trouble articulating their conviction. Finding suitable words to express divine mystery is never accomplished in a completely satisfactory way.

In addition, the passions of the bishops and theologians for one or another position, along with the political considerations of Constantine and the ambitions of various bishops, all played their role in the adjudication of the dispute. No doubt the fathers of the council devoted themselves to prayerful discernment and sought to be faithful to the Gospel. But the transcendent dimension is not readily apparent in the great imbroglio.[15] Here the long-term reception of the council's creed is evidence that the doctrine is faithful to the teaching of the Holy Spirit.

The word upon which the bishops finally settled was not an unproblematic choice. *Homoousios*, of the same being or substance, had to be taken in just the way the bishops meant it, namely, the Son is fully God just as the Father is God, but it took further time even for the bishops to figure out what they meant. A creedal statement was adopted at Nicea that became the touchstone of authentic Christian faith. The moment of judgment had arrived. Religious experience and the tradition confirmed one another in the words of the Nicene Creed, with the phrase "one in being" (*homoousios*) rendering a coherent meaning to the other affirmations about the unity and identity of Christ with God. It was a matter of working out in explicit knowledge what was implicitly known all along and gradually became more explicit.[16]

After the Council of Nicea proposed its creed in 325 c.e., Athanasius, also of Alexandria, emerged as the figure who championed that interpretation of *homoousios* which allowed no subordination of the Son. At the expense of his personal comfort, Athanasius painstakingly promoted this doctrine, demonstrating how the biblical texts support it.[17] Thus, John 10:30 teaches the equality of Father and Son to which *homoousios* refers. On the other hand, John 14:28, with its statement about the Son's subordination to the Father, refers to the Father as source of the Son.[18] Throughout his defense of Nicea Athanasius's guiding concern is the conviction that humanity can only be saved if the one true God really becomes human. A lesser God will not do. To be savior, Jesus must be divine, fully divine.

Athanasius also invites greater attention to the Holy Spirit. The creed of Nicea mentioned the Holy Spirit as a kind of afterthought: "And [we believe] in the Holy Sprit." Nothing further than this is affirmed. Athanasius highlights that the Spirit, too, is *homoousios* with the Father and the Son. How else is it possible to make a trinitarian invocation of God as Christians have been doing from the beginning? Athanasius explains that "there is a sequence in revelation whereby the Father is perfectly and totally imaged in the Son and the Son in the Spirit" and "there is a sequence of sanctification which is from the Father through the Son in the Spirit."[19]

As the century progressed, Athanasius was joined in the defense and development of Nicea by three theologians of Cappadocia in Asia Minor: Basil, metropolitan bishop of Caesarea; his younger brother, Gregory of Nyssa; and a close friend of Basil, Gregory Nazianzen. The three provided important further clarifications of the Christian doctrine of God. As is frequently the case with thinkers struggling with the mystery of God revealed in Jesus, the Cappadocians are not entirely consistent in their use of images, concepts, and language. They fail to sort out the theology of the triune God to the complete satisfaction probably of anyone. Still, they make important contributions that move the development along. It is worth adding that they do so by taking over and expanding upon the best of Origen's theology.

All three theologians strongly argue the transcendence of God. For example, in his treatise on the Holy Spirit, Basil writes that "[f]orm, shape, and bodily position cannot be invented for God; these factors are alien to the absolute, the infinite, the incorporeal."[20] Gregory Nazianzen writes about "the incomprehensibility of deity to the human mind and its totally unimaginable grandeur."[21] Despite the divine transcendence, the Cappadocians affirm that it is possible to come to some true statements not merely on how God works in our historical world, but also on the very nature of the divinity in itself. In this the Cappadocians are agreed upon something of profound importance for all the later life of the church: While human beings, no matter how learned or faithful, will never grasp the full meaning of what it is for God to be a communion of three persons, nevertheless our faith leads us to profess that they are three in themselves as the one God and that certain distinctions are important for us to maintain about the triunity of God if we are to be faithful to the mystery Jesus reveals to us.

Whereas Nicea affirms that the Son shares divinity equally with the Father, and Athanasius reasons that the Spirit in whom we profess our faith must equally be *homoousios* with the Father and the Son, it is the Cappadocians who turn to the reason for distinction among the three in God. The Latins, by way of Tertullian, had already come up with a term somewhat suitable to name each of the three in God: *person*. The Greeks had come up only with a more superficial word, *prosopon* (which, while it can be loosely translated into the word *person*, actually is more properly a mask, as an actor in a Greek play wears a mask to portray a person). Greek-speaking Christians also used the word *hypostasis* to refer to the distinct three in God, but that word could just as easily be equated with the Latin word *substantia* (substance, referring to what there is one of in God), so it could not be used without carefully clarifying its use. These inadequate words perhaps forced those who spoke Greek to work out more adequately the meaning of distinction in the Trinity.

Unanimously, the three Cappadocians posit distinction in God in the relationships which obtain within God. Thus, there is communion in nature but distinction by reason of *hypostasis*, the word chosen originally by Origen to render the threefold individuality within the one God. Gregory Nazianzen writes that while there is "numerical distinction" in God, there is "no division in the being."[22] "*Father* designates neither the substance nor the activity, but the relationship, the manner of being, which holds good between the Father and the Son."[23] To this day, the church retains, as the most satisfactory expression thus far devised, that distinction in God is by reason of relationship.

Clarifying the manner of distinction in God enabled fuller reflection upon the Holy Spirit's activity within the divine being. Basil devoted an entire treatise to the Holy Spirit. Before embarking upon his specific theology of the Holy Spirit, Basil engages a few important preliminary questions. He notes that in praise and public worship Christians use various prepositions to refer to the relationships of the three in God to each other. Thus, in liturgy the doxology might be offered "to God the Father with the Son and with the Holy Spirit" (to indicate difference two distinct words for "with" are employed in Greek) or "to God the Father through the Son in the Holy Spirit."[24] Basil's community used both doxologies, much to the chagrin of some other bishops. Basil claims that the first formula is more suitable when praising God as God is in the divine self, while the second formula more appropriately celebrates God in the divine action on behalf of humanity. Both doxologies are in praise of three equal, yet distinct, divine persons (*hypostases*).

Basil is also concerned that when we understand the Father to be the source of the Son and the Spirit we do not mistakenly think of before and after, or of superior and inferior. We must simply understand distinction in terms of relationship. This is evident when, for example, we take note of God's action in the world: "The Originator of all things is One: He creates through the Son and perfects through the Spirit."[25]

When Basil takes up the Holy Spirit specifically, he is concerned that his readers appreciate that the Holy Spirit is really God in a distinct individuality. The Spirit is not simply a manifestation of God in the world for the sake of humanity. "But the Spirit is organically united with God, not because of the needs of each moment, but through communion in the divine nature."[26]

The Cappadocians find that the names Father and Son lend themselves to the word *generation* to specify the relationship that obtains between them. When it comes to the Spirit, they do not have such an easy time of it. Ultimately, the word employed is *procession*, the word used in John's Gospel to name the way in which the Spirit, who is to be sent into the world by the glorified Son, comes forth from the Father (Jn 15:26).

Obviously, the language of the New Testament is the most readily available to employ when the desire is to describe the relationships among the three in God, and it enjoys a certain normativity. For more precise language to articulate the relationships as they obtain within God, the Cappadocians employ more abstract, but no less existential, terminology. One of the more successful attempts, in my view, is that of Gregory of Nyssa. In his short treatise addressed to Ablabius, Gregory writes that he is disinclined to conceive what the three in God share as their "nature."[27] Rather, noting that we come to know God from the activity of the divine creative and redemptive economy, we better conceive God to be "activity." The divine activity is expressed in each instance according to the particularity of each of the divine persons. Thus, Nyssa writes that "every activity which pervades from God to creation and is named according to our manifold designs starts off from the Father, proceeds through the Son, and is completed by the Holy Spirit."[28]

The Council of Constantinople (381 c.e.)

The Cappadocians made a tremendous contribution to the linguistic expression of beliefs which are relatively adequate to express for Christians our loving faith in Jesus and the living God whom Jesus reveals. The contributions of Athanasius and the Cappadocians helped to form the additions to the Nicene Creed that are affirmed in 381 at the Council of Constantinople. The creed's most significant addition is an elaboration of the terse line on belief in the Holy Spirit that appears in the Nicene Creed. The Spirit is professed to proceed from the Father and to be equally worthy of adoration along with the Father and the Son. In the Creed of Constantinople, the belief of Christians in God as triune achieves a unifying resolution of the various and diverse expressions of the New Testament and of the theological development of the three centuries subsequent to the apostolic age.

ON TO THE PRESENT

What influence should the hard-won belief expressed at Nicea and Constantinople exert in the present upon faith and beliefs in the God of Jesus Christ? After all, most contemporary Christians do not give a thought to whether the Son and the Spirit are "one in being" with the Father, nor do they worry about just how each of the three divine persons is distinct from and relates to the others. So much is this the case that it has led Walter Kasper to warn: "The vital historical faith of scripture and tradition threatened to rigidify into abstract formulas which are materially correct but which, isolated from the history of salvation, become unintelligible and functionless for an existential faith."[29]

Still, the history of salvation is of a piece. And while the formulation of beliefs, and the concepts and words in which they are cast, is conditioned to some degree by the culture in which the beliefs took shape, their truth has a staying power from one culture to the next, at least insofar as beliefs state propositions about God that are supported in religious experience as it resonates with the developing witness to Christ Jesus. Let us examine this claim in three steps by acknowledging the achievements of the past, welcoming new questions as they arise, and recontextualizing past achievements.

Acknowledge Past Achievements

Why would we want to be sure to retain past formulations of belief? The answer was given in the preceding paragraph: because they represent genuine achievements of the truth. If truth has been achieved, it is not wise to let go of it, since it puts us in touch with reality, with the way things are.

Why would people even think of rejecting or ignoring past formulations of belief? One reason would be that further investigation has shown that the belief did not express a truth after all, but merely a supposed truth. In this case, the belief of a former age needs to be rejected. It does not put us in touch with reality. It is invalid. Another reason would be that noted by Kasper: Although expressing truth, the belief formulated in the past has no bearing upon existential concerns of the present. In this case, the belief is irrelevant in contemporary culture. It can be ignored, although not consistently rejected.

If we accept that the patterned operations of consciousness have the possibility of arriving at the truth when affective experience not only urges the operation of reason to state the truth, "I love you," but also to state who "you" is, and if we accept that religious experience urges the truth, "I am in love with mystery," indeed, "I am in love with mystery in Jesus," then it makes sense to strive to state, to the extent that we are able, who mystery and who Jesus are. This is not to deny that mystery remains always elusive of our best attempts to state its truth. It is not to deny that Jesus remains elusive of our best attempts to state his truth. Nevertheless, as Jesus and the witnesses to him resonate with the religious experience of women and men of many times and places, gradually something can be said truthfully. The beliefs about God's oneness in being and triune distinction by means of relation are among the first Christian truths requiring more precision than is attained in images and symbols. This sort of formulation makes explicit the truth(s) implicit in image and symbol, but only insofar as the doctrinal formula and the image and the symbol resonate with religious experience.

If the doctrinal statements of the Nicene and Constantinopolitan creeds are valid, they say something true about God. Christians of later generations would be foolish to abandon any statement of truth about God, especially when we realize that it is highly unlikely to be proved untrue at a later time, although one cannot be absolutely certain about this but only relatively certain, since only God is absolute. But the truths formulated in the beliefs of the two great fourth-century councils come as close as we Christians are likely to get to irreformable doctrine.

Even if we retain these beliefs, might we put them off to the side, ignoring them while we attend to questions about God that strike people in our culture as more relevant? This does not seem to be any wiser than abandoning past achievements of true statements about God. First, what could be irrelevant about God at any stage of human affairs? It is one thing if we haven't yet discovered something of the truth of God. In this area, of course, there is infinitely more that we do not know than that we know. So, in fact, we have learned to articulate very little about God. But we ought to hold on for dear life to the little we know and value its contribution to our love of God, to our pilgrim journey of faith, and to the pressing questions of our day.

People of Christian faith who lived during the first four centuries of the proclamation of the Gospel gradually won the ability to make a few clear statements about who God is in Godself. These statements say something about what it means that both unity and plurality coexist in the transcendent God. They explain that the activity of God on behalf of humanity, which is described in the witness of the Hebrew and Christian testaments, implies a few truths about God's very nature. They demonstrate that people of faith need not feel separated from God either in love or in knowledge, but rather that by knowledge as well as by love human beings are welcomed to be intimate with God. These are truths that are, or can and should be, relevant in every human culture.

Let New Questions Arise

Development takes place as an actual unfolding of what has been potential. Questions provoke development. Questions are the eros of the mind reaching out to meaning that is as yet not grasped.[30] Just as new questions continue to arise about every other reality, even more may new questions be expected to arise regarding divine mystery. It is part of the gift of being human to search, trusting that the unfolding meaning of mystery will enrich humanity.

So the twentieth century has seen myriad new questions about God arise. Advocates of process philosophy and theology have asked whether God changes along with the rest of the being(s) of the world. Doesn't a changing God, affected by the human world, better satisfy biblical teachings on God as compassionate and merciful than the doctrine of the transcendent God?[31] Carl Jung and his followers ask whether God should be affirmed to be dichotomous with evil; is not evil necessary for human growth and therefore somehow so intimately related to goodness that good and evil are contrary, but not contradictory?[32] Others wonder whether God might not be relativized by the relativity of human thinking. Some, like Raimon Panikkar with regard to Hinduism and William Johnston with regard to Buddhism, ask whether the triune God affirmed in Christianity might not be comparable to conceptions of mystery in

those Eastern religions.[33] Catherine Mowry LaCugna wonders how much harm
has been done because the theological tradition's concern with the immanent
life of God has led to a sad neglect of God's revelation of the divine activity
within human history.[34] Sallie McFague and Elizabeth Johnson ask about affirmations of God that are not limited by gender specificity, or that include transcending qualities of both genders.[35] Liberation theologians have attempted to
find suitable language to affirm God in God's care for the poor, the oppressed,
and the marginalized of the world.[36] There are and will be many other questions about God, for questions dynamically move human subjects toward all
that can be known and all that can be understood.[37]

From the perspective of professing faith in the triune God, two responses
are appropriate to all the possible questions. First, let every question be pursued as long as it is profitable for insight or judgment. Second, let the
achievements of the past, that is to say, relatively adequate beliefs already attained, be taken into consideration as the new questions are pursued. Let the
achievements of truth and understanding of those who have gone before us
inform our quest.

It seems to be at least unfortunate, at worst disastrous, to dismiss those who
have gone before us and their tested achievements because we consider our
questions superior to theirs. Does not such an attitude set us up as those who
"really" know? Is this a variation of gnosticism? Instead, is it not better to do
as Lonergan has counseled: grasp the operations of consciousness in the patterns by which human beings come to understand and to know, and test
whether they have been adequately implemented in any instance of pur-
ported understanding and knowledge? Thus, one acknowledges that others
have come to know truths of importance before ourselves, and we want to
learn from them, even as new questions are posed and investigated.

Recontextualize Beliefs

The trinitarian doctrine of the first Nicene and first Constantinopolitan
councils was worked out in the context of Greek and Roman antiquity. A
philosophical mentality prevailed in the culture, even among people who
weren't educated to be philosophers.[38] The mentality keenly sought to know
the innermost being of things. Members of the church who lived in this context wanted to know the inner essence of God. They needed to know it if
they were to affirm what needed to be affirmed about Jesus of Nazareth
whom they knew by faith to be human and whom they knew by faith to be
their Savior. They were attracted to Jesus because their religious experience
resonated with his communication of the divine mystery. They became increasingly sure that he is divine even as he is human. Moreover, he revealed
that he had a quite unique relationship with God whom he called Father, and
with God whom he named Holy Spirit. In their love become faith, people

needed to know, in order to live their faith consistently in their culture, what to believe about these various convictions.

Christians of later times and places, including ourselves, need to know no less than the early Christians, even if our questions may not be formulated in just the same way as those Christians of the first centuries or may not be directed toward quite the same answers.

At the same time, as the beliefs formulated in the first centuries have been received into later contexts, their reception may have overemphasized or underemphasized or mistaken dimensions of the truths affirmed in the first councils. These receptions need to be investigated to determine whether the danger noted by Walter Kasper at the beginning of this section might be at work, namely, an abstraction of the beliefs from the historical action of God in Christ. In such instances we seek corrections to recover and redirect the meaning, in accord with religious experience resonating with the biblical witness and the ongoing interpretations judged to be faithful to them.

So, for example, when divine transcendence seems to mean that the triune God is so far removed from the human world that God does not relate to the whole, as has happened in some cultural contexts, then either the meaning of transcendence or of love or of both need to be more accurately understood in order to retrieve what is obviously the strongly emphasized truth of religious experience and biblical witness that God both loves the human world and transcends it.[39] Or if, in particular cultural contexts, it is forgotten that the triune God is beyond gender, despite the masculine, symbolic language often used of the first two among the three in God, then correctives are in order.[40]

Besides corrections, the already articulated beliefs about the inner nature of God are often enriched for Christian believers by relating them to concerns and discoveries at various historical moments. In this way, for example, the doctrine of the church taught in the documents of the Second Vatican Council is grounded in a skeletal way in the doctrine of the Trinity, thus presenting an invitation to reflect upon the interrelationship of both doctrines for the enrichment of each.[41] The same may be said of efforts to reflect upon the church's missions of evangelization and of social justice as grounded in the missions of the triune God.[42]

More often what is needed are not new beliefs about God, but rather more penetrating and more wide-reaching appreciation of beliefs already affirmed. To this question of understanding what we affirm in trinitarian belief we turn in the three next chapters.

NOTES

1. Quoted in Johannes Quasten, *Patrology*, vol. 2, *The Ante-Nicene Literature after Irenaeus* (Westminster, MD: Newman Press, 1953), 247.

2. The title of Cahal B. Daly's book on Tertullian is itself illustrative of Tertullian's character, *Tertullian the Puritan and His Influence* (Dublin: Four Courts, 1993).

3. Quasten, *Patrology*, 2:247.

4. Ernest Evans, intro., trans., and commentary, *Tertullian's Treatise against Praxeas*, including the Latin text (London: SPCK, 1948).

5. Tertullian, *Against Praxeas*, in Evans, 5 (134–36).

6. Tertullian, *Against Praxeas*, in Evans, 3 (132–33).

7. Bernard Lonergan, *The Way to Nicea: The Dialectical Development of Trinitarian Theology*, trans. Conn O'Donovan (Philadelphia: Westminster, 1976), 43–48.

8. Tertullian, *Against Praxeas*, in Evans, 7 (138).

9. Thus, Henri Crouzel, *Origen*, trans. A. S. Worrall (San Francisco: Harper & Row, 1989), 6.

10. The chief source of Origen's systematic reflection on the triune God is his text, *On First Principles*. Here I refer the reader to the translation by G. W. Butterworth, *Origen: On First Principles* (Gloucester, MA: Peter Smith, 1973). The entire first chapter of *On First Principles* deals with the issue of the spiritual nature of God.

11. Charles Kannengiesser, "Divine Trinity and the Structure of the Peri Archon," in *Origen of Alexandria: His World and His Legacy*, ed. Charles Kannengiesser and William L. Petersen (Notre Dame: University of Notre Dame Press, 1988), 243.

12. Crouzel, *Origen*, 56f. Origen was hardly alone in his subordinationist interpretation of John 14:28. Tertullian interpreted the text similarly. See the *Treatise against Praxeas* in Evans, 9 (140). But having clarified divine spirituality, Origen's subordinationism is more problematic than Tertullian's. At the same time, Origen's reflection on John 1:1 demonstrates how subtle his thought is on the Father as "the" one God because he is ungenerated, and on the Word as God (without the definite article) because he is the word/image of the Father. See *Origène, Commentaire Sur Saint Jean I* (Paris: Cerf, 1966), 12–33 (214–29). It is not a surprise that both Arius and the Cappadocians found much to ponder in Origen.

13. R. P. C. Hanson provides an exhaustive study of the efforts to work through the implications of Arius's teaching in the fourth century in *The Search for the Christian Doctrine of God: The Arian Controversy 318–381* (Edinburgh: T. & T. Clark, 1988). Curiously, Hanson rejects Lonergan's characterization of trinitarian doctrinal development as dialectical, 873.

14. Arius's letter to Alexander of Alexandria can be found in William G. Rusch, trans. and ed., *Sources of Early Christian Thought, The Trinitarian Controversy* (Philadelphia: Fortress, 1980), 31–32.

15. Richard L. Rubinstein tells the story of the Arian controversy and the attendant development of doctrine in an engaging way in *When Jesus Became God: The Struggle to Define Christianity during the Last Days of Rome* (San Diego: Harcourt, 1999).

16. Charles Hefling writes in *Why Doctrines?*: "Because the specifically Christian message takes the form of a narrative, the meaning is felt before it is figured out. Its meaning is not primarily informative, but affective, not a generalization about human life, but the drama of one particular life" (69).

17. That Athanasius was deeply committed to faith in Christ Jesus does not gainsay that he was perhaps also quite a difficult fellow. See Hanson, *Search for the Christian Doctrine of God*, ch. 9.

18. Manlio Simonetti chronicles the use of this controversial New Testament text in "Giovanni 14:28 Nella Controversia Ariana," in *Kyriakon: Festschrift Johannes Quasten*, ed. Patrick Granfield and Josef A. Jungmann, vol. 1 (Münster: Aschendorff, 1970), 151–61. For reference to Athanasius's use of the text, see 158. Gregory Nazianzen agrees with Athanasius, but also interprets the text to claim the Father to be greater by reason of divinity to the Son in his humanity. See Oration 30.7 in Frederick W. Norris, ed. and commentary, *Faith Gives Fullness to Reasoning: The Five Theological Orations of Gregory of Nazianzen*, trans. of Orations by Lionel Wickham and Frederick Williams (Leiden: Brill, 1991), 266–67.

19. George Dion Dragas, "St. Athanasius on the Holy Spirit and the Trinity," in *Theological Dialogue between Orthodox and Reformed Churches*, vol. 2, ed. Thomas F. Torrance (Edinburgh: Scottish Academic Press, 1993), 46.

20. Basil of Caesarea, *On the Holy Spirit*, trans. David Anderson (Crestwood, NY: St. Vladimir's Seminary, 1980), 15 (31).

21. Gregory of Nazianzen, Oration 28:11, in Norris, *Faith Gives Fullness to Reasoning*, 228.

22. Gregory of Nazianzen, Oration 29:2 in Norris, 245–46.

23. Gregory of Nazianzen, Oration 29:16, in Norris, 255.

24. Basil, *On the Holy Spirit*, 3 (17).

25. Basil, *On the Holy Spirit*, 38 (62).

26. Basil, *On the Holy Spirit*, 30 (52).

27. Gregory of Nyssa, "Concerning We Should Not Think of Saying That There Are Not Three Gods to Ablabius," in Rusch, *The Trinitarian Controversy*, 149–61, at 153–54.

28. Gregory of Nyssa, "Concerning We Should Not Think," in Rusch, *The Trinitarian Controversy*, 155. For a clear, brief summary of the Cappadocians' trinitarian theology, see Anthony Meredith, *The Cappadocians* (Crestwood, NY: St. Vladimir's Seminary Press, 1995), 102–10.

29. Kasper, *The God of Jesus Christ*, 260.

30. The phrase, "eros of the mind," is Bernard Lonergan's. It expresses the desire to know. See *Insight: A Study of Human Understanding*, 97 et passim.

31. For examples, see Joseph Bracken, *The Triune Symbol: Persons, Process and Community* (Lanham, MD: University Press of America, 1985), and Santiago Sia, *God in Process Thought* (Dordrecht: Martinus Nijhoff Pub., 1985), which examines the thought of Charles Hartshorne.

32. See John P. Dourley, "The Religious Implications of Jung's Psychology," *Journal of Analytical Psychology* 40 (1995): 177–203; and Robert M. Doran, S.J., "Psyche, Evil, and Grace," *Communio* 6 (1979): 193–211.

33. R. Panikkar, *The Trinity and the Religious Experience of Man: Icon-Person-Mystery* (London: Darton, Longman & Todd, 1973); William Johnston, *The Inner Eye of Love: Mysticism and Religion* (San Francisco: Harper & Row, 1978), 57–60, and *The Mirror Mind: Spirituality and Transformation* (San Francisco: Harper & Row, 1981), 26–48. See also Roger Corless and Paul F. Knitter, eds., *Buddhist Emptiness and Christian Trinity: Essays and Explorations* (New York: Paulist, 1990).

34. Catherine Mowry LaCugna, *God For Us: The Trinity and Christian Life* (San Francisco: Harper & Row, 1991).

35. Sallie McFague, *Models of God: Theology for an Ecological, Nuclear Age* (Philadelphia: Fortress, 1987); Elizabeth A. Johnson, *She Who Is: The Mystery of God in Feminist Theological Discourse* (New York: Crossroad, 1992).

36. Leonardo Boff, *Trinity and Society*, trans. Paul Burns (Maryknoll, NY: Orbis, 1988). More recently, Boff has written a popularization of his theology in *Holy Trinity, Perfect Community* (Maryknoll, NY: Orbis, 2000). See also, Matthew L. Lamb, *Solidarity with Victims: Toward a Theology of Social Transformation* (New York: Crossroad, 1982).

37. On the central importance of questions, Bernard Lonergan writes: "Negatively, then, the unrestricted desire excludes the unintelligent and uncritical rejection of any question, and positively the unrestricted desire demands the intelligent and critical handling of every question" (*Insight: A Study of Human Understanding*, 661).

38. In *Method in Theology* Lonergan names this a postsystematic context within which to interpret Christian faith (304, 312, 314).

39. Robert Grant, in *The Early Christian Doctrine of God*, claims that "[f]ew early theologians really took love seriously, as far as we can tell from their writings" (64). Acknowledgment of this claim should not lead one to leap to the doctrine of a changing God, as some theologians suggest, for that may entail inaccurate interpretations of both love and transcendence.

40. I write "forgotten" because the sense of divine transcendence among early Christian theologians led them to be quite specific about affirming that God is beyond gender. See Grant, *Early Christian Doctrine of God*, 17; and Gregory Nazianzen, Oration 31:7, in Norris, *Faith Gives Fullness to Reasoning*, 282.

41. See Peter Drilling, "The Genesis of the Trinitarian Ecclesiology of Vatican II," *Science et Esprit* 45 (1993): 61–78.

42. See Second Vatican Council, Decree on the Church's Missionary Activity (*Ad gentes*), articles 2–4, and Pastoral Constitution on the Church in the Modern Word (*Gaudium et spes*), 24.

6

Understanding the Triune God: God in Godself

Implementing the method of theology elaborated by Bernard Lonergan, we progress from religious experience (chapter 3) through religious affirmation (chapters 4 and 5) to religious understanding (chapters 6, 7, and 8). Beliefs about God that are motivated by the religious experience of encounter with the risen Jesus in the community of the church lead some believers to ask an apparently simple question: Can we achieve some understanding of the God in whom we believe?

One way to approach the question for understanding is to try to understand how God acts in human history. What has God done or is God doing for humankind, for me? Almost every person of committed faith asks this question in various ways throughout a lifetime. Another way to ask the question is to wonder about the how of God in Godself. How is the triune God the triune God? This is a more speculative inquiry. And, indeed, can we think and say anything reliable about God apart from religious faith which believes in divine revelation?

In either type of question, if the search intends a comprehensive, satisfactory understanding, the answer is *no*, we cannot understand the God in whom we believe. It is not possible for finite minds to comprehend an infinite reality. But if we take understanding to be finite glimpses into what God means, and, indeed, glimpses that are useful for relating to God and working out how to live in this world according to the meaning, truth, and value that is God, then the answer is *yes*, some understanding is possible and fruitful.

Any understanding of the infinite triune God is sure to be analogical. It will take notice of some similarity between the infinite reality, God, and finite realities that are accessible to the human mind without religious faith and, perhaps, that are accessible with great exactitude. But even as the human search discovers similarity, it also realizes that there must be difference, in fact, an infinitely vast difference, between those realities that the mind can know and the reality of the infinite God whom the mind can only approach. It is the similarity-in-difference that makes such understanding analogical.[1]

The present chapter reflects upon the affirmations of the Nicene-Constantinopolitan Creed. It is a more speculative search for some understanding of the God of Jesus Christ. It first asks about four terms that are embedded in the Christian tradition to express God's unity and trinity: *homoousios*, procession, distinction by relation, and person. That brief investigation will yield an understanding of how these terms are used. But then a further understanding is sought. What is the dynamic of divine trinity within divine unity? Two fruitful analogies are highlighted: the time-honored, although not universally appreciated, psychological analogy, and a more recent biblical analogy of the divine self-emptying. I suggest that the two analogies complement one another.

The next chapter seeks to understand the implications for the human social order of the Christian doctrine of God as triune. The entire Judeo-Christian tradition is firm in its belief that humans are created in the image and likeness of God. That being so, the Christian conviction of God as a communion of divine persons must offer directions for the order of human society. Toward an understanding of the order of human society from the perspective of faith in God, the issue of gender in God and of God indwelling the world are addressed briefly. Then the reflection moves on to some consideration of the influence of trinitarian faith on church and society.

A third chapter pursues two complementary philosophical approaches to understanding who God is and how God acts in the world. The three chapters together are not by any means exhaustive of ways to pursue some understanding of God—in fact we could add chapter 9 on interreligious dialogue to these reflections on understanding God—but they indicate how rich and varied such pursuits can be.

THE TRIUNE GOD: SOME IMPORTANT TERMS

God is not a collective noun like family or community. Nor is God a union that can be likened to the union of marriage. For in the collective instances the one family or community is constituted by individuals separated from one another by their discrete organic and spiritual identities. The same is true in a marital union. In God, however, the three persons are distinct while yet being but one actuality.

The last two chapters include consideration of how these terms to express this doctrine of God emerged in connection with the debates surrounding the first councils of Nicea and Constantinople. Now their meaning is summarized in order to be clear what we believe to be one and three in God. This is important if we are to appreciate the theological analogies that follow.

Homoousios

Later Christians need not adhere to the word employed by the Council of Nicea. In fact, Christians who profess the Nicene-Constantinopolitan Creed around the world today do not utter *homoousios*, unless they are Greek-speaking Christians. The rest of us use a translation. Translating words often entails translating not just foreign languages but foreign concepts into concepts more congenial to people living at another time and place. Thus, for a time, English-speaking Christians professed that the Son is "consubstantial" with the Father; currently, many profess that the Son is "one in Being" with the Father.

Whatever words are used, and whichever concepts are employed as satisfactory within a culture, the point of the affirmation is that the three persons in God are equally divine. None is superior and none is inferior. Each is totally God and all are totally God. It is not a matter of the sum being greater than the parts. A further dimension of the divine *homoousios* is that the three are totally present in each. Where the Son is, there are the Father and the Spirit, and so on with all three persons.

Procession

Again, the word *procession* is not itself so important. If a more adequate word can be found, so much the better. The point is what is important. In the one God the persons proceed in an ordering progression. Thus, in the one God there is an order by which the Father is the principle of the Son. In some sense the Son originates in the Father. The word *generation* has been used to designate the specific procession of the Son from the Father, the origin of the reality of the Son in the Father, because the word relates well to Jesus' invocation of Yahweh as Father and because the New Testament names Jesus God's Son in various ways. There is a procession of the Son from the Father. Specifically, the Father is said to generate the Son. Of course, it is not a matter of physical, but of spiritual generation, which is to say that there is no sense of a process of becoming in God, no before and after.

Moreover, there is also a procession of the Spirit. As well as the Son, the Spirit originates from the Father but not in a sense similar to generation, rather in a sense proper to the Spirit. No one has come up with a satisfactorily specific term to designate the Spirit's procession from the Father through the Son. So the redundant term *spiration* is often used. In the Creed of Constantinople, the biblical word in John 15:26 designating the historical mission of the Spirit is also used of the eternal act by which the Spirit originates in the

Father, namely, *proceed* ("who proceeds from"). In the development, *procession* became the term to designate both the Son's and the Spirit's origin in the Father.[2]

What must be kept in mind is that the Father is the one in whom the Son and the Spirit originate, but this does not make the Father superior, for the truth of *homoousios* remains. Nor does it give the Father priority over the other two, certainly not temporal priority, since time does not pertain to God's actuality, nor any priority in being, because in God there is no greater or less, nor any sense that the Son and the Spirit participate in the being which the Father shares with them. As *homoousios* declares, each of the three is fully divine.

Distinction by Relation

What makes the three in God distinct each from the other has nothing therefore to do with the divinity they all possess equally. By their divinity the three are one in the strict sense. What makes them distinct are the relationships grounded in the processions. As the Council of Florence put it in 1442, in God everything is one except where there is the opposition of relation.[3] The Son is Son in relation to the Father, and the Father is Father in relation to the Son. The Father relates to the Spirit as the Spirit's spirator, and so does the Son, but each distinctly according to the difference of personality. As the tradition has often expressed it, the Spirit proceeds from the Father but through the Son.

The differentiation of the three in God on the basis of the relations resulting from the processions renders the three to be distinct from each other. Thus, the Father is not the Son, the Son is not the Spirit, and the Spirit is not the Father. Each exists distinctly and yet together they are the one divine being. God is a total noun and does not signify a universal in which individuals somehow participate without themselves being the universal; each of the distinct three in God is God in the sense of the one and only. The most successful term coined thus far to express the personal three-in-one may be communion.

Person

The English word *person* derives from the Latin word *persona*, which, as already noted, Tertullian employed to name the three in God. The word functioned in the Roman context, but surely with Greek influence too, since the Latin word *persona* is comparable to the Greek word *prosopon*, meaning "mask" or "face." Person refers to a "someone."

We need to be more careful. The one God is personal, and within the one God there are three persons who are distinct from one another by their relations to one another.

First, the affirmation that God is personal is centrally important to Christian faith, as it is to Jewish and Muslim faith. God is someone, not something. Of course, God is personal beyond all the limitations of human personality. For while it is part of the richness of human persons that we are historical beings, with choices to make throughout our lives in the process of becoming ourselves, nevertheless, the potential of any individual human person is such that no one ever becomes all that he or she can be, but rather becomes a limited person in a particular time and place. The understanding and knowledge and loving and interpersonal relations of each human being are limited by the historicity that attends being human. God, however, knows, understands, loves, and relates personally without restriction.

To say that God is personal needs a further development within Christian faith (which it does not within Jewish and Muslim faith). Within the one personal God there are three persons. The one personal God exists in a person who is conscious, intelligent, and loving in relationship to a second person who proceeds from the first person as a full expression of the first person, except that this person proceeds from the first in a manner that can analogously be described as generation. A third conscious, intelligent, and loving person also exists as the one God, but in a relationship of proceeding from the first person by way of the second.

Is there anything in human experience that can make these four terms of *homoousios*, procession, distinction by relation, and person more intelligible and then be applied to God to offer a glimpse of God? I suggest that what has come to be called the psychological analogy provides a good deal of understanding, offering the best comprehensive analogy in the strict sense.

GOD IS TRIUNELY PERSONAL: THE PSYCHOLOGICAL ANALOGY

From early on in Christian history, preachers and theologians who professed firmly their belief in the triune God have sought metaphors and analogies serviceable for some understanding of their belief. Is there a reality accessible to human understanding that is distinctly one and yet includes within itself three somehow genuinely distinct identities which are, nevertheless, the one reality? Perhaps every Christian has heard of the image of the clover, with its one stem and three leaves, or of the geometric figure of the single triangle composed of three sides. In the early third century, Tertullian of Carthage proposed that believers could understand something of how God could be a Trinity by noticing how the same sun is active in the celestial body, which, in turn, is the source of the ray, which in turn warms things, or how the same water runs from its source in the spring to the river and the rivulets (or canals), or how from the one root a shrub proceeds which in turn bears fruit.[4]

More significantly, the naming of a distinct Word within the one God at the beginning of the prologue of John's Gospel has intrigued Christian thinkers from the start. It has made great sense that there should be a second in God, the divine Word that can be understood by analogy with the human word. I have already cited Justin Martyr, Athenagoras, and Tertullian in this regard. But here I turn to Augustine first, then to Thomas Aquinas, and, finally, to Bernard Lonergan.

Augustine

The most famous early Western theologian, Augustine of Hippo, reflects that if any somewhat satisfactory analogy of the divine Trinity is available it is most likely to be found in that creature made in God's image and likeness, the human being.[5] To this end, Augustine invites his readers to distinguish the spiritual center of human being. In this way we come to the possibility of a proper analogy, for the human spirit actually participates in the divine spirit, even to the point of communion with God.[6]

In book 15 of his great work, *On the Trinity*, Augustine alerts the reader to a trinity in God: divine wisdom and its knowledge of itself and its love of itself. He goes on to say: "We found a similar trinity in man, namely the mind, and the knowledge it knows itself with, and the love it loves itself with."[7] More specifically, Augustine takes the first activity of mind to be the mind's presence to itself, for which he uses the word *memory*. Today we might speak of this activity as self-awareness.[8] Thus, there are self-awareness, self-knowledge, and self-love.

In his trinity of mind, Augustine claims to have found the analogy that is most serviceable. For the mind is of the same spiritual character as God. Admittedly, the human mind is conditioned by its ties to the corporal, material dimension of human being, but it is not totally contained within the corporeal. Moreover, the human mind or spirit is one; it is the spirit of the individual person. Finally, while the three activities are of the one mind in its self-consciousness, they remain three distinct activities.

Augustine goes on to claim that the analogy of human spirit is closest to God when human spirit in its three dimensions is directed to God.[9]

Aquinas

Thomas Aquinas is another major proponent of the psychological analogy to understand threefoldness concomitant with unity in God. Reflecting upon Augustine, Aquinas also searches for a relatively adequate analogy of the divine trinity in the world accessible to the human mind. For Aquinas, too, rational psychology provides the analogy.[10]

In my opinion, Aquinas makes two significant advances upon Augustine. Both are due to his keener analysis of human rational psychology. First, he clarifies how the spiritual activity of consciousness is activity within and of the one consciousness. Second, he specifies how the word and love proceed within consciousness. This last advance has especially important implications for understanding the procession of the Holy Spirit.

Aquinas gets hold of the unifying element when he examines the meaning of procession. When there is a spatial movement of one thing from another or a temporal movement of one action from another, then the effect is different from the cause. Thus, the physical generation of children from parents is not serviceable, strictly speaking, as an analogy for procession in God; physical generation relates to discrete physical entities that generate other discrete physical entities in a process of becoming. But as we move into the realm of spirit, then procession of one activity from another is actually an identity of that which proceeds with that from which it proceeds. Two quotations of Aquinas make the point. The first indicates how procession takes place in the spiritual activity of understanding. "In the act by which someone understands, something proceeds from that act of knowing, and it is the concept of the thing understood. . . . This is said to be the word of the heart."[11]

The second quotation emphasizes that procession, when it is spiritual, is an act of identification. "It is evident that the more something is understood, the more intimately identified is its intellectual concept with the one who understands; for by its act of understanding the intellect becomes one with that which it has understood."[12]

How does Aquinas conceive the processions of knowing and of love? The first quotation above describes how human rational consciousness, after questioning what something means or is, understands. Understanding can be of objects other than the subject seeking understanding, or it can be of the one who understands; it can be self-understanding. When a subject understands, it expresses this understanding in concepts and confirms it in judgment, in short, in a mental word, what Aquinas names the word of the heart.[13] It remains within the person; it is a spiritual word. The person may also find a way to express the truth at which it has arrived in a gesture or a spoken or a written word, thus formulating an external word, but originally there is an interior word. This procession of the inner word from the act of understanding is, for Aquinas, an analogy for the procession of the Word from the Father.

A second spiritual procession takes place within the rational subject. Aquinas speaks of it as the operation of the will in which love proceeds, so that "what is loved is in the one who loves."[14] Once rational consciousness arrives at love, it has completed a sequence: from understanding to truth to love. Thus, Aquinas clarifies that the intellectual subject acts both through the intellect in expressing understanding and truth, and through the will which loves. Since it is a process of act from act in both instances, and since the act of love follows from the act of knowing, a certain orderly dynamism can be discerned in the processions of word and of love.

So now we have Aquinas's version of the analogy working in this way: As the rational consciousness of the human person becomes active in self-understanding, a further act of self-understanding may follow and a joyful approval of the reality of the self that is healthy self-love.[15] This provides a way to understand the divine Trinity as perfect spirit that is at once infinitely intelligent and infinitely loving. The Father is infinite intelligence who speaks an infinite Word of self-affirmation within the divine consciousness and then in and through that Word joyfully loves the divine being in an act of self-love that is the Holy Spirit.

Lonergan

Bernard Lonergan is a third theologian whose theology of the Trinity includes the psychological analogy. Lonergan, a student of both Augustine and Aquinas, has benefited from their conceptions of the analogy and offered his own developments to advance the analogy and make it more cogent for contemporary use. Lonergan begins, as had Augustine in the fifth century, with the statement of I John 4:8 and 16 that "God is love."[16] By starting with love rather than understanding, Lonergan attributes to the personal God something of primary significance to human persons, namely, loving relationality. Religiously speaking, too, love is primary: The enduring ground of a living relationship with God is the experience of falling and being in love in an unrestricted way. The human subject is caught up in a love far greater than the human being and its world. This love is recognized to be God. Thus, love becomes a way into some understanding of God as one and as triune.

It was toward the end of his scholarly life that Lonergan developed the affective analogy; earlier he had followed Aquinas more closely with the intellectual analogy.[17] While both approaches are enlightening, the former is more attuned to the foundations of interpersonal communion. Thus, the subject is a lover who is in love (the Father), acknowledges this to be self-love (the Son), and thus loves the reality of the self (the Holy Spirit).[18] Human subjects are in love; they express their love interiorly and exteriorly in the affirmation, "I love you"; they go on to show in a variety of ways that their affirmation of love is sincere. The three acts are of the same human subject; they are one with the subject. Among the loves of the subject is self-love.

While it is the one God affirming and loving Godself in the divine self-consciousness, nevertheless there are three distinct personal acts: a first, the lover in love; a second, the lover's word of love; a third, love proceeding from the lover through, or mediated by, the word. The analogy of love highlights the dynamically interpersonal character of God. It is also precisely at this point that we find the mystery of it all. As Lonergan wrote, it is three conscious subjects of one divine consciousness.[19] There is nothing identical to it in the created order, nor can human reason comprehend the divine Trinity, but by studying the three distinct acts of human self-love believers can gain some foothold onto understanding how the one God is three.

From time to time theologians criticize the psychological analogy as being too abstract, too unrelated to the warp and woof of human living, or not connected sufficiently with divine action in the world.[20] That is undoubtedly true insofar as few human subjects take the time and put in the necessary effort to sort out their own operations of knowledge and of love. Yet, the philosophers of human subjectivity, such as Immanuel Kant, have had an enormous effect upon the modern and postmodern cultural milieu, despite massive lack of knowledge of their thinking. How can it seem of little or no value to analyze human intentionality and then relate that analysis to some understanding of the God in whom we believe? In fact, the analogy connects quite successfully. What some discover after putting in the effort to understand the psychological analogy is that a peculiar rest in the wondrous reality of God is produced. The understanding and subsequent rest have no further goal than to marvel and rejoice in the mystery of divine transcendence revealed in the Three-in-One, although there are further practical implications to be exploited in due time. Indeed, as would be hoped, the analogy can keep further, more practical, reflections faithful to orthodox belief in the triune God. In any case, for the time being, to rest in God brings calm to our restless hearts, as Augustine so astutely observes at the beginning of his *Confessions.*

GOD IS TRIUNELY PERSONAL: THE ANALOGY OF THE CROSS

Employing an apparently more dramatic and existential but no less intellectually demanding imagery, Hans Urs von Balthasar developed a strict analogy of faith to gain some understanding of the trinitarian dynamic of God. By a "strict" analogy I mean that von Balthasar moves from one mystery of faith in the order of human history, namely, the ignominious death of Jesus on the cross, to another mystery, namely, the total self-emptying of the Father in the generation of the divine Word. As with Augustine's and Lonergan's rendition of the psychological analogy, "God is love" is the guiding concept. Everything in God is love, both immanently and economically.

Von Balthasar begins with imagery drawn from the theatre, which he finds helpful to express the relationship between the triune God and the world, both the world of creation and the world of redemption. He calls it all a theo-drama, beginning with the processions and relations and persons that constitute the immanent Trinity and continuing with creation and the divine missions on be-half of human salvation and sanctification.[21] However, the drama becomes known to human beings in the economy of redemption. The economic Trinity reveals the immanent Trinity.

The elements of the theo-drama are author, actor, and director. "Naturally, God the Father is and remains the Author from whom everything comes and who accepts responsibility for it all; he is prior to the play and above it, but the very fact that he has written it means that he is most deeply and irre-versibly involved in it. Yet it is not he who acts in the play but the actor, who gives the Author's word a real presence in the form of action."[22]

Primarily, of course, the Actor is the eternal Word who, in human history, becomes incarnate in Jesus of Nazareth. But other human beings are "fellow actors of the primal Person (the Son of God)."[23] The Holy Spirit is the Direc-tor of the drama. The Holy Spirit is the "indispensable Person who brings the Author's text into the actuality of the performance. . . . The Spirit is indis-pensable since he is Holy: the Father entrusts his play to him to be translated into real life."[24] Both Jesus and the members of the church who are united to his person submit themselves to the direction of the Holy Spirit.

This image of the triune God as Author, Actor, and Director functions as the guiding image in the background of the entire drama of salvation history. In the foreground of von Balthasar's trinitarian theology a highly biblical im-age functions. The traditional doctrine of the divine missions of the Son be-ing sent by the Father to redeem humanity, and of the Spirit being sent from the Father to animate and guide the Son, and through the Son to make the divine action effective in humanity, is applied to the drama of the cross. Here von Balthasar reflects upon the artistic rendition of the Trinity popular in Eu-ropean Catholic sensibility from the medieval through the Renaissance and post-Tridentine periods: As Jesus hangs upon the cross, the Father, regularly pictured as an elderly, white-bearded man, holds the arms of the cross in his own outstretched arms, while the Holy Spirit hovers above the scene in the form of a dove.[25]

First, God so loved the world that he gave his only Son in a self-emptying act of love (John 3:16). Then, the utter self-emptying of Jesus in love in his excruciating death upon the cross is followed by the even more exhaustive emptying of Jesus' total alienation from his beloved Father in the descent into hell.[26] Only after Jesus has been abandoned by his Father so devastat-ingly in death by crucifixion and in the wretched separation of hell is he re-stored to the bosom of the Father in glory through the resurrection. Through-out the action of the cross (which includes the descent into hell and the resurrection), the Holy Spirit empties itself in the self-gift by which it directs all the events of Jesus' entire human life. Then, as Jesus returns to glory as the risen Lord, the Holy Spirit continues its self-emptying self-gift by direct-ing the application of the divine salvific activity to the rest of humanity. All

God's action on behalf of creation, and most of all God's action to save humanity and bring human beings to a share in the divine communion, are acts common to all three persons of the Trinity, but each person acts in its distinctive way. This is preeminently evident in the event of the cross.

In the self-emptying event of the cross, von Balthasar finds a marvelous analogy of faith. From the mystery of the economic Trinity acting in Jesus' death, descent, and resurrection, the person of faith can catch a glimpse of the dynamics of the inner divine life. "[W]e must see the doctrine of the Trinity as the ever-present, inner presupposition of the doctrine of the Cross."[27] Von Balthasar's theology of the inner trinitarian dynamic shows how this is so. The first self-emptying in God, the first *kenosis*, is that of the Author of everything, the Father. The Father empties himself totally by generating the Son. Then, "[a]lmost automatically this first kenosis expands to a kenosis involving the whole Trinity."[28] Thus, the Son/Word eternally empties himself in his total expression of all that the Father is; the second person is the Word speaking everything the Father is. Finally, the Spirit pours itself out as the total manifestation of the love of the Father and the Son. "This primal kenosis makes possible all other kenotic movements of God into the world; they are simply its consequences."[29] At this point the psychological analogy and the analogy of the cross can be related to one another as complementary. Although, as I note above, the psychological analogy has been found wanting by some prominent twentieth-century theologians, I remain convinced of its usefulness. For, as developed by Bernard Lonergan, it elegantly demonstrates how three distinct acts of conscious love can, and do, in the human person, implement one loving self-consciousness. All the more so in the three loving persons of the one divine consciousness. Complementarily, von Balthasar clarifies how the one God, in fact, expresses self-emptying love, according to the witness of the New Testament, in the action of the three distinct persons of God on behalf of sinful humanity. In turn, von Balthasar demonstrates how the economic love of the Trinity can shed light on the dynamic self-emptying love of the persons of the Trinity in their immanent life. It is not a matter of either the psychological analogy or the analogy of the cross; it is a matter of both.

NOTES

1. This brief statement leaves many questions about how any understanding of God, analogical or otherwise, is possible. For a detailed exposition of analogical understanding of God, see W. Norris Clarke, S.J., "Analogy and the Meaningfulness of Language about God," in the author's anthology, *Explorations in Metaphysics: Being, God, Person* (Notre Dame: University of Notre Dame Press, 1994), ch. 7.

2. For a careful statement of the nuances of the terms "procession" and "generation" and why there has been acrimonious debate at times between the Roman and

Orthodox Churches on the procession of the Holy Spirit, see the statement of the Pontifical Council for Promoting Christian Unity, "The Greek and Latin Traditions Regarding the Procession of the Holy Spirit," *L'Osservatore Romano* (English language weekly edition), 20 September 1995, 3 and 6.

3. Council of Florence, Bull of Union with the Copts, in Norman Tanner, S.J., ed., *Decrees of the Ecumenical Councils*, vol. 1, *Nicaea I to Lateran V* (Washington, DC: Georgetown Univ. Press, 1990), 570–71.

4. Tertullian, *Against Praxeas*, chapter 8.

5. Saint Augustine, *The Trinity*, intro., trans., and notes, Edmund Hill, O.P., Vol. 5 of *The Works of St. Augustine* (Brooklyn: New City Press, 1990), Book IX, throughout.

6. Augustine, *The Trinity*, Book XII, 12.

7. Augustine, *The Trinity*, Book XV, 10.

8. Augustine defines his meaning of "memory" in Book X of the *Confessions*. See Peter Brown, *Religion and Society in the Age of St. Augustine* (New York: Harper & Row, 1972), 28–29.

9. Augustine, *The Trinity*, Book XIV, 15.

10. The analogy is extensively developed in the *Summa contra gentiles*, Book IV, chs. 11 and 24, and more summarily in the *Summa theologiae*, as indicated below.

11. Thomas Aquinas, *Summa theologiae*, I, q. 27, a. 1, reply.

12. Thomas Aquinas, *Summa theologiae*, I, q. 27, a. 1, response to 2nd objection.

13. Most helpful for understanding Aquinas's inner word is Bernard Lonergan, *Verbum: Word and Idea in Aquinas*.

14. Thomas Aquinas, *Summa theologiae*, I, q. 27, a. 3, reply.

15. Here, I accept Frederick E. Crowe's interpretation of the first meaning of love in Aquinas, and of its application to God. See "Complacency and Concern in the Thought of St. Thomas," *Theological Studies* 20 (1959): 1–39, 198–230, 343–95; esp. 221–24: "God, however, loves Himself and delights in Himself" (221). This study has been reprinted in Frederick E. Crowe, *Three Thomist Studies*, Supplementary issue of *Lonergan Workshop*, vol. 16 (2000): 73–203.

16. It is noteworthy that Augustine also conceived one version of the psychological analogy within the framework of divine love, thus thinking of the Trinity as lover, what is loved, and love (*The Trinity*, Book VIII, 14). It should be added, however, that neither Lonergan nor Aquinas would conceive the second person in the Trinity as "what is loved" (*quod amatum*). Rather, the second person is the word of understanding through which the first person acknowledges the divine self to be the beloved.

17. I do not mean to diminish the cogency of the intellectual analogy. In a 1963 article, "Consciousness and the Trinity," Longergan articulated the analogy thus: "There is only one act, but there is a distinction because the three persons have the same consciousness differently: the Father is God in a manner analogous to the grasp of sufficient evidence that necessitates one to judge; the Son is God in the same consciousness but now a consciousness analogous to that of the dependence of the judgment on the grasp of sufficient evidence; the Holy Spirit is the same consciousness in a third manner, namely, as the dependence of the act of love on the grasp of sufficient evidence and the rational affirmation." See *Philosophical and Theological Papers 1958–1964*, vol. 6 of *Collected Works of Bernard Lonergan*, ed. Robert C. Cro-

ken, Frederick E. Crowe, and Robert M. Doran (Toronto: University of Toronto Press, 1988), 135.

18. Bernard Lonergan, "Christology Today: Methodological Reflections," in *A Third Collection*, 93–94.

19. Lonergan, "Consciousness and the Trinity," 132.

20. Anne Hunt notes this criticism in her chapter (6) on the psychological analogy in *What Are They Saying about the Trinity?*, but she goes on to review Tony Kelly's and Bernard Lonergan's efforts at retrieval (New York: Paulist, 1998). See also Karl Rahner's comments on "The Problem with a 'Psychological Theory of the Trinity,'" in his *Foundations of Christian Faith: An Introduction to the Idea of Christianity* (New York: Crossroad, 1978), 135.

21. See his presentation of the immanent trinitarian self-emptying in Hans Urs von Balthasar, *Theo-Drama: Theological Dramatic Theory*, vol. 4, *The Action*, trans. Graham Harrison (San Francisco: Ignatius Press, 1994; original German 1980), 323–24.

22. Hans Urs von Balthasar, *Theo-Drama: Theological Dramatic Theory*, vol. 3, *The Dramatis Personae: The Person in Christ*, trans. Graham Harrison (San Francisco: Ignatius Press, 1992; original German 1978), 532.

23. von Balthasar, *Theo-Drama*, 3: 533.

24. von Balthasar, *Theo-Drama*, 3: 533–34.

25. This depiction expresses the "throne of grace" of Hebrews 4:16. See Gerald O'Collins, S.J., on the throne of grace theme in *The Tripersonal God: Understanding and Interpreting the Trinity* (New York: Paulist, 1999), 50–51, 197, 200. For a study of Masaccio's early-Renaissance fresco of the "Trinity" in relation to the text of the Letter to the Hebrews, see Rona Goffen, "Masaccio's Trinity and the Letter to the Hebrews," in *Masaccio's Trinity*, ed. Rona Goffen (Cambridge: Cambridge University Press, 1998). Albrecht Dürer's woodcut of the Trinity and his painting of the same, dated 1511, even features God the Father wearing a tiara. El Greco followed by putting his own characteristic stamp on the throne of grace in his painting of the Trinity, dated 1577–78.

26. See I Peter 3:19.

27. von Balthasar, *Theo-Drama*, 4: 319, 331–38, 361–67.

28. von Balthasar, *Theo-Drama*, 4: 331.

29. von Balthasar, *Theo-Drama*, 4: 331.

7

Understanding the Triune God:
In the Image of the Divine Trinity

The first account of creation in the Book of Genesis exalts God's human creation. "Then God said, 'Let us make humankind in our image, according to our likeness.'"[1] Since God is a triune God whose reality is to be in communion, then, the human vocation—in the image and likeness of God—is communitarian, as the Second Vatican Council's Pastoral Constitution on the Church in the Modern World puts it.[2]

GOD BEYOND GENDER

Throughout this text, when speaking of the persons of God, I have been generally using the traditional language of Father and Son to name the first two persons in God. It is language rooted in the New Testament. It is more than probable that Jesus thought of and addressed Yahweh as Father. Likewise, Jesus commended to his followers that they address Yahweh by the same name. The early community of his disciples thought of Jesus as God's Son and eventually identified him as such quite distinctly. When, eventually, theologians got around to conceiving the procession of the second from the first person of the Trinity, the word at hand was *generation* (cf. Ps 2:7).

On the face of it, this language identifies God as male, at least with reference to two of the three persons in God. That identification has not been without its influence in the church community and in Christian civilization generally. Today, particularly, gender issues are alive, and virtually every thinking Christian recognizes that God-language and gender matter a great deal for the understanding of communion in church and society.

For this reason alone, it is valuable to recall that theologians from very early on in the tradition make it a point to state that God is spirit, while gender is a matter, first of all, of biology.[3] Gregory Nazianzen, the great Cappadocian theologian, for example, states emphatically in one of his theological orations that God is without gender.[4] Augustine simply assumes that his readers appreciate that God is beyond gender.[5] Anselm of Canterbury (d. 1109) was so unconcerned about gender specificity that he even images Jesus as a mother.[6] Aquinas takes pains to demonstrate that while the procession of the Son from the Father can be called generation, it has nothing to do with material generation; it is the sameness of nature of the one proceeding from its source that specifies generation, not bodily likeness.[7] Today, we would point out that not only can there be no actual generation of son from father when one is dealing with the realm of spirit, except metaphorically speaking, but that, furthermore, human generation requires the active participation of two parents, so the father-son relationship does not provide a particularly useful analogy for the first procession in God unless a variety of mental adjustments are made.

The psychological analogy comes to the rescue, assisting us to employ biblical terms that nicely avoid naming God according to the masculine, father-son relationship. The first person in God is the one who is in love, God as loving. The second person is the affirmation or word of love, "I love you." The third person is the love of the one acknowledged to be infinitely loved. The language, while gender-free, is quintessentially personal, indeed, interpersonal.

At the same time, the New Testament is replete with references to the Father and the Son. So are the prayers of the liturgies. So is the catechetical and theological tradition. It hardly seems necessary to seek to abandon the language entirely. The wiser strategy, it seems to me, is to discern carefully when a language change is appropriate and when the traditional language is best left in place. For example, when making the sign of the cross at the beginning of the liturgy and at the final blessing, the traditional language ought to be retained. Similarly, new Christians are baptized in the name of the Father and of the Son and of the Holy Spirit. The eucharistic prayer is addressed to the first person of the Trinity as Father or sometimes as Lord. On the other hand, in public but spontaneous prayer, the prayer might be directed to God who is both Mother and Father. And Jesus might be invoked as Word and Wisdom, or even referred to as a mother, in the sense that Anselm so referred to Jesus. In any case, it is important to communicate that Christians understand God to be eminently personal but beyond gender.[8] Homilies and catechetical classes offer such opportunities of communication, as do theology classes on the Christian doctrine of God.

A TRINITARIAN SPIRITUALITY

The love of God overflows in creative activity to bring the world into being and in the regenerative activity of healing human sinfulness and drawing human beings into interpersonal communion with the divine Three. Communion with God can be, and often is, conceived generally. But it is more faithful to Christian reality to conceive of communion as specifically interpersonal, relating to each of the divine persons within the one communion. Thus, we conceive of God's action on behalf of the world and its human inhabitants as proceeding from the Father. This divine activity takes place in history, most notably in the visible entrance of the Word into human history as a human being, and in the invisible entrance of proceeding Love into human history by acting upon the interiority of human subjects, and through them affecting societies and nature.[9] This loving activity of God creates a capacity in human subjects to enter into an interpersonal exchange of truth and love with the divine Three.

When we think of God's life in itself, we usually think first of the Father and then of the Son and then of the Holy Spirit. But when people respond to the divine initiative in human history, we think of the movement of love starting with the Holy Spirit, who in turn leads us to love the Lord Jesus and listen to him and follow him. In turn, the ministry and dying and rising of the Lord Jesus introduce us to God the Lover, thereby leading us into the very core of the divine mystery. In and through the Love of God and the Word of God's love we enter into communion with the divine Lover.

Divine Absence

Frederick E. Crowe employs the psychological analogy to highlight further dimensions of God's own life and of human response to God. Crowe's work indicates how a trinitarian spirituality can be formed that specifically employs the dimensions of human psychology.[10] The Word of love is the ultimate ground of all meaning, even the most limited human meaning, and the Spirit is at the heart of all genuine love. Moreover, at the beginning and goal of communion with God, there is the experience of transcendent mystery. It is the experience of being drawn into love in an unrestricted way and the experience of resting in that love. The divine person most associated with this experience is the divine Lover, or, in traditional terms, the Father.

However, as I have discussed in the chapter on experience of the transcendent, experience of divine mystery is not confined explicitly to love. There is also awe and wonder, longing, trust and joy, sorrow, fear, guilt and shame. Crowe suggests another experience, closely associated with the person of the divine Lover: absence. While divine Word and Spirit have entered on mission into human history, the Lover is not conceived as having done the same. Crowe invites us to recognize this as the experience of the divine absence. "There is an experience of the dark night of the senses and of the human spirit; it is the absence, the lack, the need, the hunger, the emptiness, the longing, the abandonment, experienced in our human condition as long as we are separated from the presence of the Father in our world. . . . [This is] the absence of God our eschatological hope."[11]

People of faith may be inclined to wonder why God does not intervene more forcefully and evidently to make things better in the human world, whether the concern is peace among warring nations or the health of a loved one or oneself. Experiencing God as absence is an authentic indicator that God's wisdom is beyond human calculation (see Isa 55:8–9).

Divine Kenosis and Human

In another dimension, there is the decision to let go of our self-centeredness and to become ourselves generous in love in the direction of the divine mystery to whom we hope to be faithful at all costs. Here we touch upon the resonance in human life of the analogy of the cross that was discussed in the previous chapter. In the teaching of St. Paul, this is the activity of the Holy Spirit moving us toward the divine mystery. It is the Holy Spirit, divine Love, poured out in our hearts enabling us with Jesus to call God, Abba (Rom 5:5; 8:15). It is the divine Love groaning with unutterable longings within our spirits and within all creation as the whole world longs to be set free (Rom 8:19–27). In the same act, divine Love touches our spirits so that they are enabled to become generous in love of our fellow human beings of every race and language and way of life,[12] for it makes no sense to love the God who creates every human person out of love if we do not also love all those whom God loves.[13]

In his own human living, Jesus is the witness of this kenotic spirituality. Jesus came to be the servant of all to the point of giving his life as a ransom for many (Mark 10:45). Jesus' human witness was in the image and likeness of the eternal divine relations of self-giving that constitute the persons of God.

In imitation of Jesus, each human being individually and human beings socially become most authentically themselves when they pour out themselves in love for the others. Implementing the psychological analogy of the Trinity on the human level, such self-giving leads to the formation of many human communities in pursuit of meaning, truth, and value. Just as the Father speaks the truth of love that is the Son, and then through that truth loves the divine being, so humans on their own level collaborate for the true and the good in human affairs, leaving behind their selfish interests.

The analogy of the cross adds to this dynamic the image of all the disciples of Jesus being enabled by the divine Trinity to embrace their own crosses to the point of giving their lives.

The Role of the Word

It is Jesus as the intelligible Word of God who leads humans to the awareness of the trinitarian dynamic of their lives. The New Testament has Jesus introducing his followers to Yahweh as Father. He invites them to pray to Yahweh as Father. Moreover, the Synoptic Gospels, particularly Luke, reveal that Jesus was inspired and guided throughout his life by a holy Spirit. In turn, the Pauline and Johannine Jesus introduces his followers to the Holy Spirit and his role in the postresurrection order of things. Moreover, by the way he lives and by what he says, the Jesus of the New Testament reveals that he himself shares in divinity, as has been noted above in chapter 4. In sum, Jesus reveals to his followers a triune God of love.

Jesus functions economically as the Word that renders God's activity intelligible.[14] Just as the role of the "word" in human psychology is to express understanding and truth, first interiorly to the intelligent and reasoning subject and then by that person's language and gestures to the people with whom the person communicates, so, by analogy, linguistic expression is also the particular function of the Word of understanding and of knowledge within God and in the divine self-communication to humanity. Jesus is the Word of understanding and truth, both in his eternal generation and in human history.

Since God indwells the world as a trinity of persons, and most especially the interiority of human beings, people of trinitarian faith are blessed with opportunities to relate their personal experiences, understandings, judgments, and decisions to the divine Three. These opportunities can be exploited most explicitly when we stop to think about the specifics of the interpersonal relationships with God that are entailed in the life of grace. We can come, confident and unafraid, to God as to a loving parent. We interface with God as a revered, boundlessly admired older sibling. We can relish God as Spirit touching us in our depths with an overwhelming love.

Trinitarian Structure of the Eucharistic Prayers

Explicitly trinitarian prayer is especially rich. The church's liturgy offers just such trinitarian prayer in the celebration of the sacraments, especially the eucharistic prayers of the Mass. Each eucharistic prayer is addressed to the Father; commemorates the Lord Jesus in his life, death, and resurrection; and expresses its prayer confidently in the Holy Spirit, whose power is invoked to transform both the elements of bread and wine and to transform the diverse human participants into one body and spirit in Christ.[15]

The eucharistic prayer is the prayer of the entire Body of Christ. Christ Jesus, the head of the body, is the leader of the prayer. It is he who addresses the prayer to his Father (the entire prayer is named the *anaphora*, the offering up). As mediator of the covenant between God and the people saved by the Lord's dying and rising, the risen Lord Jesus is high priest of this perfect prayer to the Father. Jesus brings his whole body with him in his prayer.

The ordained priest stands at the altar and says the words of the prayer in the person of Christ the head (*in persona Christi capitis*) and in the person of the members of the body (*in persona ecclesiae*). The priest's role is not unimportant, but it is "insignificant" because he is to lose himself (another form of *kenosis*) in Christ, the actual leader of the prayer. The congregation, in turn, is to ignore the priest and see the actual leader who is leading them in prayer, Christ Jesus.[16]

On two occasions during the eucharistic prayer, the Father is asked to send the Holy Spirit (*epiclesis*). Before the words of the institution of the Eucharist, the Father is asked to send the Spirit upon the bread and wine so that they may truly become the Body and Blood of Christ. Then, when the death and resurrection of the Lord are remembered, they become effective for this congregation here and now. After the prayer of remembrance (the *anamnesis*), the Father is asked again to send the powerful Spirit, this time to change the congregation into the body of Christ for the transformation of the world of daily living.

In its entirety, the eucharistic prayer is an act of praise, adoration, and thanksgiving to the Father, through the Son and in the power of the Holy Spirit. It is a foretaste of the eternal praise of God in the realm of glory. This is expressed in the final words of the eucharistic prayer, the doxology.

Flowing from the trinitarian structure of the eucharistic prayer, personal prayer can become more trinitarian as the pray-er focuses on the distinct divine persons not as disparate but as trinitarian community. Such prayer is a multifaceted interplay of feelings of participation in the triune, divine communion. Gradually and subtly, it can lead to a trinitarian lifestyle, something discussed in the next section.

SOCIAL IMPLICATIONS OF TRINITARIAN FAITH

Instinctively, human beings seem to have a longing for peaceful and harmonious unity in diversity. No doubt, this instinct is a communication of the distinct divine Three who are the one God in their very act of creating human beings in the divine image and likeness. Despite the instinct, at every turn human beings find that their diversity is divisive, often leading to outrageous fractures within human society. Christians believe that this sorry state is attributable to human rejection of divine grace. Happily, God is at work recreating humanity to live up to its inherent meaning as the image and likeness of God. Still, the celebration of unity in diversity remains more a goal to be hoped for than a reality dynamically in place. The present section draws on the virtue of hope to sketch a trinitarian-based view of the church as communion, all human society as communitarian, and socially responsive and responsible ethics as instances of friendship.

The Church as Communion

Christian thinking about the meaning of church has come a long way in the course of the last one hundred years. In the wake of the Protestant Reformation, several church orders emerged in Christian denominations, from episcopal to presbyterian to congregational, with variations of each structure. In Catholicism, characterized by an episcopal church order, a theory of the church as the perfect society took hold from the seventeenth century until the mid-twentieth. The Catholic church was thought to contain within itself all that was necessary for people to participate in the saving work of Christ: right teaching, right worship, right authority. From this quite juridical view, a more expansive theory developed, which was endorsed by Pope Pius XII in his 1943 encyclical, *On the Mystical Body (Mystici Corporis)*. On this view, whose core is proposed by St. Paul in his letters, notably I Corinthians 12, as well as Ephesians and Colossians, the church is the extension of Christ Jesus in subsequent centuries and in millions of people. The church is the Body of Christ, with Christ himself as the head of the body. The risen Jesus is in glory, but he remains present in the world through the mediation of those incorporated into his life, death, and resurrection by their baptism. The bishops, and to a lesser extent ordained presbyters and deacons, represent the head-functions of Christ; the other baptized faithful represent the other parts of the body.

The Second Vatican Council did not reject the view of the church as the mystical body of Christ, nor the notion that the church is a society which includes all the means necessary for salvation, but it placed those approaches to ecclesiology within one that is trinitarian.[17] The somewhat exclusively hierarchical perspective fostered by the image of the mystical body, at least as currently favored in the middle of the twentieth century, was tempered by a more universally participatory view. The chosen image of the Second Vatican Council to express the more trinitarian view is People of God. A description of the people of the covenant (Ex 19:6) transformed for application to the assembly of baptized faithful (I Pet 2:5–9), this image has the advantage of first stressing the participation of all the faithful as a single people in the gifts of God's covenant. The diversity of leadership and other roles accruing to individuals are secondary.[18]

Taking a cue from the Council's adoption of the image of People of God, together with its many explicit references to the church as the work of the divine Trinity and as formed in the image of the same Trinity, it has become increasingly common to think of the church as a communion analogous to the divine trinitarian communion.[19] As there is no superior or inferior among the persons of God but all are equally divine, so in the church, no matter what a person's function, all are equally recipients of the divine favor of forgiveness and friendship and all are equally invited to share the full life of heaven. The diversity of services on behalf of the mission of the church does not render some members of the church more important, while others are less significant. Instead, all work in fidelity to the one Lord Jesus by the power of the one Holy Spirit to serve the glory of the one God of love (cf. I Cor 12:4).[20]

Of greatest importance in the view of church as trinitarian communion is precisely the aspect of communion. Each member of the church is called to see herself or himself as a follower of Jesus precisely in generous self-giving. Service in the spirit and name of Jesus is the heart of discipleship. Every member of the church is empowered to feel so intimately one with all the other members that the greatest joy is to give, and equally it is a joy to receive the ministrations of others, according to the needs of each. Such giving and receiving is inspired by the life of interpersonal communion with the divine Three that all the baptized are empowered to share.

When approached from this perspective the diversity of roles does not dissipate. Authoritative leadership, of the ordained and of the baptized, is still necessary. Some individuals undertake new initiatives, while others guide their progress; some individuals introduce new ideas and theories; some individuals emerge from the body of the faithful to issue the timely challenge or encouragement or consolation. Each of these ministries can be recognized as leadership. But in none of these instances does leadership need to imply a diminishment of those church members who exercise ministries other than leadership. All the ministries are mutually beneficial. The key is service within communion. Ambition, self-aggrandizement, envy, and jealousy are antitrinitarian.

Society as Communitarian

Christians who think through the implications of their belief that God is a communion of Three who are distinct from each other within the one divinity cannot fail to envision not only the church but broader society as well as somehow analogously communitarian. We rarely think in this communitarian way. More commonly the image of God within human beings has been recognized in the intelligence, love, and freedom of individuals. Nor need we deny this more individualized understanding of the human person as image of God. But to be consistent in their faith, Christians will broaden their view to include human social relationships.[21]

Implementing the trinitarian view politically is not easy, even if we assume agreement on the desirability of a communitarian society. The contemporary church understands itself to be a communion, but political society has no such view of its social bonds. Currently, democracy is widely the political structure of choice. The major value of democracy, however, at least in its current post-Enlightenment variety, puts most stress on individual rights, primarily equality and liberty. Important advances in political democracies have seen increased sensitivity to civil rights of citizens, including minorities, and some concern to offer all citizens a share in the material standards that some individuals have attained. One disadvantage of such focus upon the individual is that the rights of all have to be continually defended against the encroachments of individuals, which encroachments are often motivated by greed or desire for power. Another disadvantage of a too-enthusiastic individualism is that it becomes difficult to determine what the common good is or whether discernment and pursuit of a common good is even a worthwhile venture.[22]

Citizens whose basic attitudes are formed by faith in God as triune and an ecclesial polity of communion will not be comfortable with political democracies that exaggerate individual rights while downplaying a search for shared human truths and values. But, undoubtedly, genuine trinitarians would be no less at home with authoritarian forms of government that diminish the equal worth of every citizen or anarchists who reject any sort of social order and authority. The resolution of the tension is not to search for a style of civic government adequate for every time and place, but to search for ways to incorporate within the style of government at hand the truths and values of human society as trinitarian, translating the theological meaning into civic meaning.

Implicit in the above paragraphs is the notion of society as nation. But there are other social realities that would benefit from reflection upon human society formed in the image of the trinitarian God. Marriage and family is one. Economic groups, such as corporations, firms, factories, and farms are others. Educational institutions qualify, as do recreational clubs, and even such loose societies as neighborhoods. Moving from intermediate to overarching society there is the so-called international community. Technological developments of communication make it unavoidable that nations be interdependent and therefore cooperate among themselves, not just in groupings according to interests conceived narrowly, but as a global society. How to work out that interdependence to the mutual long-term benefit of all is an invitation for at least some of the influential participants to reflect on society as communitarian in the image of God.

Friendship as a Model for Socially Responsible Ethics

Recognizing that increasingly the human inhabitants of the planet live in societies dominated by free-market capitalism, one could easily question how realistic for society the communitarian view can be. The question is cogent in civic, and even ecclesial, situations in which the rights of individuals have been the main focus increasingly since the late eighteenth century. Despite the odds, the guiding symbol thus must be the creation, restoration, and enhancement of the image of God in humanity.

In the thirteenth century, when a communal vision of humanity was more prevalent, Thomas Aquinas conceived of the divine-human relationship established by the twofold divine mission of Word and Spirit as analogous to human friendship.[23] Human beings are not only called by their creation, but they are enabled, in the world redeemed by Christ Jesus, to enter into friendship with the divine Three. Only God could create this possibility; in fact, God does create this possibility. In freedom, human persons may choose to accept or to reject the divine offer in their actual living.

In the contemporary context, Bernard Lonergan has revived the sense of salvation and sanctification as the establishment of new interpersonal relationships of friendship between the triune God and humanity.[24] It is the establishment of a shared life among God and humanity based upon friendship. For Lonergan, the precise mission of the Word is to make us friends of God. This is the purpose of Jesus' reconciling activity (Jn 15:5f; Eph 1:14). Concomitantly, the mission of the Holy Spirit is to initiate interiorly those intimate relations by which we belong totally to our beloved, the triune God (I Cor 6:19).[25] The gift of God to humanity is to invite and empower human subjects to rejoice in communion with God. Celebrating the marvel of it all, Lonergan was wont to say that we live in a friendly universe.

In his recent book, L. Gregory Jones takes to the next stage the meaning of the divine-human friendship, together with its consequence that we live in a friendly universe. He concludes that the theological context of human living leads to a moral imperative by which human persons are called to treat as friends all the other human persons with whom they share the friendly universe. "The task and goal of Christian life is to grow in friendship with God so that people are increasingly able to see every other human being as loved uniquely by God. The goal of the Christian is to be able to see each and every stranger as a friend in God, and as a friend of God."[26]

From this perspective of human life being gathered up into the life of the divine Trinity and patterned after it, human society is to be formed and moral judgments are to be made on the basis of inspiration by the Spirit who lovingly leads believers to follow Jesus, who, in turn, teaches, both by his words and by his living, how the kingdom of God can be enacted in human history.

In societies marked by free-market capitalism and globalization of trade, with their tendencies to stress the rights of individuals, the model of society as friendship invites the members to understand that discernment of the rights of individuals and respect for them are not for the sake of isolating people from one another, but for the sake of appreciating that all members of society are solidary with one another because each is equally valuable as created by God and redeemed in Christ Jesus and in the Holy Spirit, and because all are together innately called to form both broader as well as more particular communities of friendship in the divine image. From this perspective racial, ethnic, gender, economic, and whatever other falsely based belittlements of the world's citizens are simply immoral. That is the negative side. On the positive side moral life formed along the lines of extending the divine-human friendship into social life is welcoming, inclusive, and characterized by solidarity.

There is no single way to express moral relationships in society as analogous to the divine-human friendship. Since human persons and the societies they form are historical, they undergo continual change. Jones views this changing character of human life as the precise juncture at which "the Spirit is at work in the Christian community's puzzlement over its own as well as its individual members' existence and character."[27] For Christian members of society, the Spirit assists in the interpretation of the recorded message and ministry of Jesus. This is part of the meaning of the mediation of the risen Jesus in the tradition. Respect for their non-Christian friends leads Christians to carry on conversation with their fellow citizens for the sake of forming the family or neighborhood or economy or nation or the international community. Without attempting to impose the Christian belief-system, but rather with generous attitudes of self-forgetfulness and appreciation of the beauty and worth of every other individual, Christians seek to be friends with all society's members.[28]

Society and its members are never untainted by evil, including egregious evil. Christians will respond in the Spirit of Jesus, not seeking an eye for an eye, but with an even greater love. Although in the past Christians have all-too-frequently fallen far short of the attitude of Jesus, we always hope to do better.

Calling to mind once again the absence of the Father, that is, that historical societies still await eschatological union, there is no room for euphoria. If the moral life of societies and individuals is most healthy when inspired by the paradigmatic divine communion, nevertheless no group of human beings can expect to achieve perfect society within the limitations of history. Since, however, the future is God's future, hope for the future rests upon a sure foundation.

NOTES

1. Genesis 1:26. Cf. Psalm 8.

2. Second Vatican Council, Pastoral Constitution on the Church in the Modern World (*Gaudium et spes*), 24.

3. See John 4:24: "God is spirit. . . ."

4. Gregory of Nazianzen, Oration 31.7, in Norris, *Faith Gives Fullness to Reasoning* (282): "Do you take it . . . that our God is a male, because of the masculine nouns

'God' and 'Father'? Is the Godhead a female, because in Greek the word is feminine? Is the word 'Spirit' neuter, because the Spirit is sterile? If you want to take the joke further you could say. . . ."

5. St. Augustine, *The Trinity*, Book XII, 12: "After all, the authority of the apostle as well as plain reason assures us that man was not made to the image of God as regards the shape of his body, but as regards his rational mind. It is an idle and base kind of thinking which supposes that God is confined within the limits of a body with features and limbs" (translation of Edmund Hill, O.P., 328–29).

6. "An Thou, Jesus, dear Lord, art Thou not a mother too? . . . Indeed Thou art, and the mother of all mothers, who didst taste death in Thy longing to bring forth children unto life." Quoted in M. J. Charlesworth's introduction to *St. Anselm's Proslogion* (Notre Dame: University of Notre Dame Press, 1979), 16.

7. Thomas Aquinas, *Summa theologiae*, I, q. 27, a. 1, Reply & a. 2, Reply.

8. Happily, the *Catechism of the Catholic Church* (Vatican City: Libreria Editrice Vaticana, 1994) stresses the point: "We ought therefore to recall that God transcends the human distinction between the sexes. He is neither man nor woman; he is God." (n. 239, also n. 370). It would help, however, if the Catechism itself, in its English-language edition, employed gender-inclusive language.

9. From the Christian perspective, God was acting in the world through the Word bestowing meaning and in the proceeding love of the Spirit from the beginning of creation and throughout the years even before the incarnation of the divine Word.

10. Frederick E. Crowe, S.J., "Rethinking God-With-Us: Categories from Lonergan," *Science et Esprit* 41 (1989): 167–88, and "Rethinking the Trinity: Taking Seriously the 'Homoousios'," *Science et Esprit* 47 (1995): 13–31.

11. Crowe, "Rethinking God-With-Us," 176; see also 174 and 182.

12. Cf. the Second Eucharistic Prayer of Reconciliation in the liturgy of the Roman Rite.

13. Cf. Romans 13:8–10 and I John 4:8–16, although there is no direct reference to the Spirit here.

14. Karl Barth conceives of the Trinity as Revelation. God is "Revealer, Revelation, and Revealedness. These are the equivalents for the New Testament symbols: Father, Son, and Spirit. God is the agent, the content, and the state of revelation." See William J. Hill, *The Three-Personed God: The Trinity as a Mystery of Salvation*, 116.

15. For an exposition of the trinitarian dynamic of the church's eucharistic prayers, see Edward J. Kilmartin, S.J., "The Catholic Tradition of Eucharistic Theology: Towards the Third Millenium," *Theological Studies* 55 (1994): esp. 449–55.

16. In this understanding of the priest's role of acting in *persona Christi* in the celebration of the Eucharist, I agree with Dennis Michael Ferrara's analysis of Thomas Aquinas's "ministerial-apophatic" meaning. See "Representation or Self-Effacement? The Axiom In Persona Christi in St. Thomas and the Magisterium," *Theological Studies* 55 (1994): 195–224, esp. 204–6. Ferrara takes up the issue again in "In Persona Christi: Towards a Second Naïveté," *Theological Studies* 57 (1996): 65–88, where Ferrara summarizes: "To fulfill this office [to preside in persona Christi at Eucharist], the priest must be transparent of Christ, his individual person disappearing as it were behind the Word of God so that he may present this word rather than anything of his own to the Church and the world" (88).

17. On the church as the Mystical Body of Christ, see the Dogmatic Constitution on the Church, 7. On the church as the visible society that includes all the elements needed for salvation, see Dogmatic Constitution on the Church, 8 and 14.

18. For a discussion of the juxtaposition of these different perspectives in Vatican II's Dogmatic Constitution on the Church, see chapter 1 of Susan K. Wood, *Sacramental Orders* (Collegeville, MN: Liturgical Press, 2000). See also, Peter Drilling, "Common and Ministerial Priesthood: Lumen gentium, Article Ten," *Irish Theological Quarterly* 53 (1987): 81–99; "The Priest, Prophet and King Trilogy: Elements of Its Meaning in Lumen gentium and for Today," *Église et Théologie* 19 (1988): 179–206, and the already cited article, "The Genesis of the Trinitarian Ecclesiology of Vatican II."

19. Church as communion is a theme of "The Final Report" of the 1985 Extraordinary Synod of Bishops, convoked to mark the twentieth anniversary of the close of the Second Vatican Council. See *Origins* 15 (19 December 1985).

20. Two ecumenical statements on the church as communion are noteworthy. In 1990, the Anglican–Roman Catholic International Commission published an agreed statement entitled "Church as Communion" in Jeffrey Gros, FSC, Harding Meyer, and William G. Rusch, eds., *Growth in Agreement II* (Grand Rapids, MI: Eerdmans, 2000), 328–43. In 2004, the U.S. Lutheran–Roman Catholic Dialogue published a joint statement entitled "The Church as Koinonia of Salvation: Its Structures and Its Ministries," available at USCCB.org/seia/koinonia.htm.

21. See the Second Vatican Council's Pastoral Constitution on the Church in the Modern World, 24. For a philosophically oriented expression of this, see W. Norris Clarke, S.J., *Person and Being*, The Aquinas Lecture, 1993 (Milwaukee, WI: Marquette University Press, 1993), 50, 68, 77, and esp. 88–89.

22. The philosopher Charles Taylor has written cogently on the strengths and weaknesses of contemporary attention to the individual, which he names the "modern rights culture." See *Sources of the Self: The Making of Modern Identity* (Cambridge, MA: Harvard University Press, 1989) and Taylor's Marianist Award Lecture in *A Catholic Modernity?*, ed. James L. Heft, S.M. (New York: Oxford, 1999). See also the quotation of Vaclav Havel in chapter 1 of the present work.

23. See L. Gregory Jones, *Transformed Judgment: Toward a Trinitarian Account of the Moral Life* (Notre Dame: University of Notre Dame Press, 1990), 100–8.

24. Bernard Lonergan, *De Deo Trino*, vol. 2 (Rome: Pontifical Gregorian University Press, 1964), 247.

25. Lonergan, *De Deo Trino*, 2:241.

26. Jones, *Transformed Judgment*, 107. Charles Taylor also calls for an ethics of friendship, likewise on the basis of the creation of human beings in the image and likeness of the triune God, in his essay in *A Catholic Modernity?* He writes: "Our being in the image of God is also our standing among others in the stream of love, which is that facet of God's life we try to grasp, very inadequately, in speaking of the Trinity" (35).

27. Jones, *Transformed Judgment*, 127.

28. Another model that is congenial to that of friendship is proposed by Michael Downey in his book, *Altogether Gift: A Trinitarian Spirituality* (Maryknoll, NY: Orbis, 2000), 137: "The fullness of human life and destiny lies in self-giving as a response to the gift of Love which is the self-gift of the Father, through the Son, in the Spirit. Through the gift which has been first given, we participate in the mission of Word and Spirit, cultivating, nurturing, and sustaining a world transformed in and by Love."

8

Understanding the Triune God: The Way of Philosophy

Theological attempts to understand something of the God of Christian revelation reflect specifically and explicitly on what is accepted as divine revelation formulated in the Christian scriptures, celebrated in Christian liturgy, developed in Christian creeds, and practiced in Christian living. Generally, philosophical attempts to understand something of God reflect on the world in which human beings live without explicit reference to divine revelation.[1]

Is a philosophical approach to understanding God meaningful? Since the human mind must start with what is immediate to it in the data of the five senses or in the data of human consciousness, it might seem that God is not available to human reasoning because God, who transcends this world, is not directly available in the data of sense or of consciousness—except by the direct intervention of divine revelation. Bernard Lonergan counters this line of thought by pointing to the "thrust by which the human spirit moves towards self-transcendence."[2] Lonergan describes a threefold thrust of the human spirit toward self-transcendence: intellectual, moral, and religious.[3] By way of each of the three trajectories the human spirit is not satisfied until it somehow attains God. Specifically, the intellectual thrust especially can yield a natural knowledge of God, which "means that God lies within the horizon of man's knowing and doing, that religion represents a fundamental dimension in human living."[4]

Another question asks whether natural or philosophical knowledge of God, while conducted without explicit reference to revealed religion, is pursuable separate from the religious dimension of the human spirit, if we recognize that the religious dimension refers to the gift of God's grace by which "the love of God is poured forth in our hearts by the Holy Spirit that is given to us (Rom. 5:5)."[5] Lonergan would respond that normally, in fact normatively, philosophy of God is pursued within the ambiance of the gift of God's grace.[6] Of course, theological reflection upon God takes place within the same context. Theologians pick up on the data of the human thrust toward self-transcendence by reflecting upon the data of divine revelation, and in the case of the present work, revelation in and through Jesus the Christ (see chapters 3 and 4). Philosophers pick up on the data of the same thrust by probing the world in which we live and the persons we are who live in it. Both approaches are the work of thinkers convinced of the transcendent dimension of reality. In the previous two chapters, speculative and practical instances of the theological approach were employed. In the present chapter the effort to understand can be characterized as philosophical.[7]

Two philosophical approaches to God are pursued here: one the way of human self-transcendence and one the way of the sufficient reason for the universe in which we live. As developed in the present chapter, both approaches are inspired by the theology of Thomas Aquinas. Two contemporary thinkers who are especially adept at clarifying the approaches are Bernard Lonergan and W. Norris Clarke.

THE WAY OF HUMAN SELF-TRANSCENDENCE

The activities of human consciousness are ecstatic. They lead persons beyond themselves into the wider world. It is through the operations of consciousness that we relate to the things and persons around us. The operations of consciousness may even lead a person to God.[8] At this point we examine how the operations of consciousness find a horizon wherein they open themselves onto the divine mystery. Recall, again, St. Augustine's famous line at the beginning of the *Confessions*: "Our hearts are restless until they rest in you."

Meaning[9]

Human beings delight in asking questions. Sometimes the questions ask "how" and "why." These questions head toward meaning or intelligibility. How are things the way they are? Why are things the way they are?

As human beings of every walk of life and every corner of the globe and every period of time keep asking about the meaning of this particular thing and that particular set of events, some of them inevitably ask whether there is a meaning to it all. Does the universe inhabited by human beings, and every other possible universe, possess some grand intelligibility? Is my pursuit of understanding isolated, unrelated to the pursuit of understanding of others? Is my understanding some lesser participation in an understanding of all that is there to be understood?

If you and I and every other human being understand something of the world in which we live, must there not be an intelligence that understands it all? For if there were not, then what could relate my understanding to yours in a meaningful way? Perhaps my understanding of the meaning of things would make sense to me, and yours to you, but there would be no connection of one to the other. Indeed, this is the position of postmodern relativism, namely, that there is no universal meaning. But if this is the case, how do human beings communicate?

The position taken here is that if there were no universal meaning, no absolute intelligibility, there would be no partial meaning either, no contingent intelligibility. For what would render that intelligibility genuinely intelligible? And since meaning and intelligibility are discerned by minds, the universal meaning and absolute intelligibility must be the product of a mind that not only understands by "an unrestricted act of understanding," but that is the creative source of a meaningful world.[10] Clarke writes that all beings are intelligible "because they have been thought-created by an Infinite Mind."[11] Likewise, intelligent beings are intelligent for the same reason.

Truth

Questions asking "how" and "why" must be followed up by questions asking whether the answers anyone gives really achieve meaning and intelligibility accurately. After all, human beings are prone to make mistakes, and from their mistaken understandings they are prone to make a mess of things. For this reason it is not enough to answer questions for understanding, no matter how thoroughly. The further questions for reflection are necessary, asking about the truth of the matter at hand. Until the question for truth is answered, knowledge is not attained.

Often enough the ideas generated about how the universe works and about its source are mistaken. Natural scientists develop elaborate theories about what is entailed in the construction of spaceships that function effectively and safely while on their missions. But the theories might be mistaken, with dire consequences. Political scientists may be accurate in their studies of the meaning of a democratic style of government and of an autocratic style. But we would want to test their theories and not simply take them at their word. And so on with every idea. As Lonergan teaches, cognitive self-transcendence requires the implementation of acts of reflection as well as acts of understanding.[12] Meanings need to be verified.

How then is it determined that a theory is accurate, is true? Scientists involved in designing and redesigning space shuttles test their theories to ascertain whether the conditions are actually fulfilled that need to be fulfilled for their theory to be accurate. When something goes wrong, they work further to correct their mistaken conclusions. Scholars studying the meaning of democracies and autocracies, often with the prodding of those proposing contrasting theories, strive to devise ways to demonstrate the accuracy of their theories. Otherwise, their theories may be dismissed by reasonable reviewers. But once an idea or an elaboration of ideas into theories has been verified, then a judgment about the truth of a theory can be made and it moves from being just an idea or a theory to becoming a true grasp of reality. Space shuttles can be constructed so that they shuttle safely between planet Earth and a destination in outer space. Members of a society can come to know what they are getting themselves into if they choose a democratic form of government or if they find themselves under an autocratic government.

Inevitably, some persons reflecting on the need for truth if our world is to function beyond half-baked ideas and fantasies are going to ask about God. For if human beings go to a lot of trouble and expense to be propelled into space to find out and affirm the full reality of our universe, don't we want to know if there is some reality underlying this and all possible universes, and what that reality is? Likewise, if human beings want to know the relative merits of political democracy and autocracy, don't we want to know the final truth of human society, if there is one? Such a truth, such a reality will transcend our minds' grasp because it won't be true in the limited sense of realities whose conditions happen to be fulfilled, like space shuttles and political orders. But does a world full of realities that are true in a limited way make sense if there is not a reality that is absolutely true, the ground of all limited truths? Indeed, limited truths of all sorts make no sense without an overarching, transcendent truth that is the ultimate condition of all more limited truths. Such is God, who is an unlimited act of judgment, knowing all that is true because God is the Truth, creator of all that is.

Value

Beyond cognitive self-transcendence there is moral self-transcendence.[13] To understand meaning and to know truth is one thing. To choose and to do the good that is truly affirmed is a further step along the path of human self-transcendence. Decision to act is at issue here. But on what are decisions based? Is it worthwhile to take the risks entailed in space exploration? Unless people are rash and willing to treat human lives casually, their decision will at least partially relate the good that is likely to be achieved by space exploration and the risks of the same. Their decision will be determined on the basis of verified theories of what went wrong on those ships that exploded, how successfully the flaws can be corrected, and, in uncertain conditions, how much risk is worthwhile. Or, again, is it more worthwhile to establish a political democracy or an autocracy? The determination of worth will rely on the verified meaning of each type of government. The question will be answered whether one type of government is more worthwhile than another, what human values each promotes and what values are short-changed or ignored. But the decision to establish one type or the other is a further step beyond verification.

That further step is a matter of deciding which course of action is good or better. It is a matter of values. Values are limited. Depending on how one values space exploration, it may be more or less worthwhile to put the lives of astronauts at risk, or to spend large sums of money collected from taxpayers, or to probe the universe when the outcome of the probe remains unforeseen. But how much risk to take, how much funding to provide, which elusive goals to pursue—these are questions of value. When it comes to a type of government for a society, both democracy and autocracy are limited in their value. Both can be useful and both can be harmful to the common good. For example, does a group value personal liberties more or an orderly, predictable way of life? A choice must be made for the relative value of the one over the relative value of the other.

Are all values relative only to you and me, here and now? Are there values that transcend what might be comfortable or convenient for you and me, here and now? What about truth, justice, compassion, mercy, forgiveness, generosity, love? These are values that are highly desirable for human beings to embrace whether or not it is comfortable or convenient. But then there must be a higher good, a common good. Whence does that common good derive? It seems that there must be an Ultimate Good from whom all contingent values derive. Otherwise, what would give them their transcendent worth relative to other values? It must be the Ultimate Transcendent Good that is the norm because it is the creator of goodness in all its forms.

Choices, then, are orderly according to a scale of values. Lonergan offers one way to understand the order of values.[14] First, there are vital values; these have to do with health, and so involve eating properly, resting and exercising adequately, medicating in cases of illness, and the like. Then there are social values, which deal with the relations among people. These would include the more weighty relations such as those of spouses, parents, and children, as well as important but less significant values such as behaving politely in a restaurant or on public transport. Social values are most often directed by cultural values of custom (family, ethnic, religious, national, etc.), law, education, art, civil government, and the like. Then there are personal values by which the human dignity of each individual person is affirmed and respected. Finally, there are religious or transcendent values determined by the Ultimate Good. Apart from their relationship to the Ultimate Good, all other values are underestimated or exaggerated.

God as Pure Act

From the affirmations that God is an act of unlimited understanding and knowing and an act of unlimited good will and love, several further important

qualities of God follow. To start with, we do not say that God possesses understanding and knowing, or that God wills or loves now more and now less.
God *is* understanding and knowing; God *is* love. For these reasons, God is
called by Thomas Aquinas Pure Act.[15] This significant way of expressing the
Being of God emphasizes that the reality that is God is not static but dynamic.

Since God is Pure Act and there is no process of becoming in God (what
would it be for one who is without limit?), God is simple—not made up of
parts; eternal—beyond time and presiding over it; unchanging—there being
no act for God yet to attain; and necessary—the one being whose existence
is not expendable: if God were not, nothing else could be; since God is,
other things can be, but need not be. In addition, as the one who is infinite
understanding and knowing, God knows all that there is to know (past, present, and future, to use paltry human terms of temporality), which is to say
that God is omniscient. As the infinite intelligence and the infinite subject
choosing good, God chooses without limit what is intelligent and reasonable
and responsible and loving. Such is God's provident omnipotence, endow-
ing whatever God does with meaning, truth, and value.[16]

A Personal God

Implied in all that is said above is the reality of God as personal. Intelligent and loving beings are personal subjects. The affirmation of God as
personal is centrally important to Christian faith, as it is to Jewish and Muslim faith. God is someone, not a something. Of course, as Pure Act, God is
personal beyond all the limitations of human personality.[17] For while it is
part of the richness of being human that we are historical beings, with
choices to make throughout our lives in the process of becoming ourselves, nevertheless the potential of any individual human person is such
that no one ever becomes all that he or she can be, but rather becomes a
limited person in a particular historical time and place. The understanding
and knowledge and loving and interpersonal relationships of each human
being are limited by the historicity that attends being human, at least in this
earthly life.[18] God, however, knows and loves and relates personally without restriction.

Moreover, although God is personal, gender does not pertain to God. This
truth is ascertainable both on theological (see the previous chapter) and
philosophical grounds. God who is Pure Personal Act, simple and infinite, is
clearly not physical in any way, since that would limit the divine being. God
has no biological or sensitive characteristics, although the Bible often images
God materially and physically (think of the burning bush of Ex. 3:2 or the
"sound of sheer silence" of I Kgs 19:12) and anthropomorphically in order to
assist believers to relate to God. And since the Bible was written in patriar-
chal cultures, the anthropomorphic imagery is more often masculine (king,

warrior, father, shepherd). But, in fact, God is spirit, and thus neither male nor female.

All the qualities that can be attributed to God by human understanding express divine transcendence. Because the base from which they refer to God is limited human personality, the divine attributes indicate much more what God is not than what God is, that is, they indicate how infinitely far beyond human personality divine personality reaches. All the limitations of such expressions of the divine attributes do not make them incorrect. They indicate something of the intelligibility of God. They offer a glimpse that enables believers to relate to God with an intelligent and reasonable faith. Such glimpses can enhance a believer's love of God. But we do ourselves no service if we forget that our understanding is but a glimpse.

At the same time, once it is posited that God is creator of every finite universe of being, all the qualities attributable to God imply divine immanence as well as divine transcendence. By means of infinite intelligence, truth, and love, God creates and oversees the activity and order of finite beings. Thus, God relates personally to the universe of finite beings, and interpersonally with finite personal beings. However, apart from direct divine intervention in revelation, human beings cannot proceed very far along the way of interpersonal relationship with God.

THE SUFFICIENT REASON FOR THE
UNIVERSE IN WHICH WE LIVE

W. Norris Clarke begins a chapter entitled *The Final Unification of All Being* with the question: "What does the world of my experience demand as its adequate sufficient reason, to render it adequately intelligible?"[19] In this approach to God, the starting point is not the activities of human consciousness, but the many realities that are part of the world in which we live. However, as it turns out, the way of sufficient reason is not so different from the way of human self-transcendence.

In everyday life we approach the many realities at hand in terms of living our lives from day to day and year to year. We must relate to the world pragmatically. How useful are the things and people around us for getting by? We need food and clothes and shelter; we need to earn a living; we need a social life; we need leisure and relaxation. But if I relate to the people and things in my world only instrumentally, from the perspective of their usefulness to me according to what I feel is most useful, then I cheapen my value as a person and the value of the other persons with whom I associate and even the things in my world. I cannot live just pragmatically; I must live ethically, too, with regard for the others with whom and with which I share the world. What are the meaning, truth, and value of these others that I need to take into account? Where do these meanings, truths, and values come from? To be true to the universe, questions of deeper and even ultimate meaning must be pursued.

The pragmatic is one perspective. There are other perspectives. For example, scientists have their own distinctive perspective on the world. They want to know how things work. Within their various disciplines scientists apply their sophisticated strategies to "take apart" the things of the world, including much of what composes human beings, in order to put them back together in different arrangements to produce an increasingly technologically advanced world. Contemporary science and technology keep generating dazzling new wonders. But does the world's meaning extend no further than the latest scientific discoveries and the latest technological innovations? How are the discoveries and innovations to be evaluated?

Besides the pragmatic and the scientific, some people find themselves drawn in yet another direction of questioning. They ask why the many and varied beings of the world exist at all, and why they relate the way they do, and whether there is any order among all the beings of the world or whether they have just emerged haphazardly. They also wonder if the many beings that emerge for a time and then disappear have any further meaning and destiny. These are all metaphysical concerns of a cosmological sort, distinguishing them from metaphysical questions of a psychological sort. In the end, however, even the cosmological questions resolve into psychological questions because they are questions about meaning, truth, and value.

God as Efficient Cause

Every being to which humans have access through sense experience requires other prior existent beings for its origin and it requires various other beings for it to continue in existence. Nothing just emerges from nothing, and nothing can continue in existence without the support of other beings. This principle refers to beings that are limited in space and time. The principle also applies to beings with a spiritual dimension—notably human beings—which are limited in the power of their conscious operations.

There is a major exception to this principle. If every limited being we know is conditioned by requiring a cause other than itself, and if these causes are themselves limited beings, it makes sense that there be a transcendent cause that is unlimited and that empowers all the limited causes.[20] Such is the being that simply exists—again we are at Pure Act. Not only is this being infinite in its existence; it is the only adequate source of all beings that are limited. It is the creator. It is the personal creator. It could not act as an impersonal force, since it must include in a perfect way the constitutive qualities of all the beings of which it is the creator, and among these beings are intelligent and rational human beings, with the freedom to make choices of many sorts. The personal creator chooses not only to create, but also which of the possible universes to actualize. Lonergan puts it this way: the universe of beings that is proportionate to human cognition is the product "of an unconditioned intelligent and rational consciousness that freely grounds the universe in much the same fashion as the conditioned intelligent and rational consciousness of man grounds freely his own actions and products."[21]

God as Final Cause

Every being acts to accomplish something. The more limited the being, the more limited its action to accomplish something. The maple seed has the potential within it to become a maple tree. Assuming that a series of conditions is met, it will grow into a maple tree. Some conditions are that the seed be healthy, that there be soil in which to take root, that the climate be beneficial. Even with all the proper conditions the maple seed can only become a maple tree. On the other hand, the potential of human beings to act is much more open-ended. Just relative to the maple, the arborist might plant a single maple seed or a tract of them, prune a tree to enhance its growth, gather maple sap in the spring, or cut down a tree. Human potential is dazzlingly varied. But human potential, various as it happens to be, is actualized for the sake of accomplishing particular goals.

Is the direction of each finite being without relation to the directions of other finite beings? No, limited beings accomplish their ends only in interaction with other limited beings. The maple seed can only achieve its potential in cooperation with many other limited beings such as soil, moisture, and sun. In addition, human intervention may be conducive to the maple's growth or terminate it. All limited beings require other beings in order to be able to actuate their potential. They are also susceptible to the action of beings that limit their potential. However, since all these beings are limited/finite, one is led to ask whether the many finalities of the vast array of realities in the world are simply random in their relations to one another or even if they are at cross purposes. Neither of these seems to be a reasonable conclusion to draw, at least not as a final answer. Intermediately, however, it seems that there are random events, as well as events at cross purposes with one another. But as an order emerges of greater and lesser realities, and of a range of dependencies, the world can be recognized to be less random and less in conflict.

A more sufficient reason for the multiple purposes of the world's multiple beings is an unlimited/infinite, intelligent, reasonable, and loving being orchestrating the whole, and particularly making sure that no positive thrust of any finite being is wasted. It makes sense that the universe in its entirety be purposeful. This requires a personal overseer, a guide and director, who is the source of order in the universe, drawing forth the universe to realize its potential. And since this being is the intelligent source of all being, it must be the ultimate end as well. But what could that finality be? God is already perfect. How could the created universe enhance the perfect God? For Clarke "the only adequate meaningfulness of the universe is as a gift of its Creator to rational creatures, who are endowed with intelligence to understand consciously the gift and free will to accept it with appreciation and grateful love in return."[22]

Evolution and God

The theory of evolution can seem to challenge the position of God as the ultimate source of all being. An evolutionary view of the universe seems to rely so much on the role of chance. Another challenge to the position that God is sufficient cause is the view that there is sufficient reason for the universe in the minute particles of matter that exist at the start of the evolutionary process. This supposedly sufficient reason is expressed well by John Haught: "Evolutionary materialism locates the source and substance of life's diversity in the purely physical determinism that, allegedly, has led, step by fateful step, out of the dead causal past to the present state of living nature in all its profusion of complexity."[23] Thus, everything was present from the beginning. There is nothing genuinely new under the sun.

On the other hand, evolution is witness to the emergence of ever more complex realities, so much so that earlier stages of development can be called primitive while later stages can be called advanced. Perhaps this elaborate process of development is even greater witness to God's creative power than a more condensed creation would be. Clarke suggests a view other than evolutionary materialism:

> God is constantly working creatively with the ongoing unfolding of the world's own built-in active potentiality, stepping up his creative collaboration at certain key thresholds to inject new information-sets—not necessarily new physical energy—into the process to enable new qualitatively higher ontological centers with new properties to appear on the scene.[24]

Thus, God collaborates creatively in the process of development from the physical to the chemical to the biological to the sensitive, and, finally, infuses the human soul. And there might well be more yet to come, since God can be understood as the Absolute Future, still very much directing the universe, actualizing the world's potential in marvelous ways yet to unfold. Thus, John Haught asserts that "[e]volution happens, ultimately, because of the 'coming of God' toward *the entire universe* from out of an always elusive future."[25]

One way to understand how God could be the creator of all things even as things emerge gradually through the interaction of many causes is by relating primary and secondary causality. God the Creator is the primary cause by which any existing reality comes to be, remains in existence, interacts with others, and reaches its potential. What God wills comes to be as an intelligible being, a being that is true and valuable. But the omnipotent God freely chooses that all contingent beings exercise their own limited causality, mutually influencing one another. All beings exercise a causality appropriate to them, which is a secondary causality. God wills that all these secondary causes effect the ends proper to their natures. If the evolution of the actual universe is, in fact, pertinent to the activities of the vast number of limited beings in the world, that simply indicates a need for the divine creator and provident and loving overseer. The primary cause delights in letting the secondary causes exercise their causality and ultimately, in accord with the finality of creative truth and love, in such a way that no contingent being is wasted.[26]

A challenge has been leveled against the Thomistic view of causality. Joseph Bracken (among others) adopts a Whiteheadian approach to questions of God and the world. Bracken contends that

> [w]ithin the Whiteheadian scheme . . . the primary causality is exercised by the creature, the actual occasion in process of concrescence, not by God as supplying diverse initial aims to enable the creature to make its decision. Contrary to the Thomistic scheme, therefore, in the Whiteheadian scheme divine causality is instrumental to the exercise of primary causality by the finite actual occasion in its self-constituting decision. Moreover, God cannot know the decision of the creature until the creature actually makes the decision.[27]

I contend, however, that positing God the Creator as primary cause need not imply that the freedom of secondary causes is truncated. On the contrary, God who creates all finite beings freely is to be understood to endow them with the freedom proper to their degree of being. Divine providence can mean precisely that: providently allowing all secondary causes their proper, if limited, freedom to act, while nevertheless providing an overarching goal in which infinite (i.e., divine) wisdom and goodness will finally prevail.

God and Human Freedom

If we understand God to allow secondary causes their full, proper freedom, what does this mean for human beings? God lets human beings choose for themselves in matters of both greater and lesser import. Even when human beings choose what they should not choose or fail to choose what they should, thus refusing the path of moral self-transcendence, God allows them this freedom. It belongs to the way that God has created human beings. Of course, with human beings the stakes are higher precisely because human beings are created to be responsible, because of the thrust toward moral self-transcendence. Still, somehow, in ways too mysterious for the human mind to fathom, God will finally bring good even out of seriously flawed human choices.[28]

What is affirmed here is both God's utterly reliable, because infinite, wisdom and love and the appreciation that God's creative power is constructing a future in which the universe will be transformed. Human beings especially, whose being includes a spiritual dimension, may be counted on to achieve their potential beyond what is possible within the limitations of space and time. The details, however, remain hidden in the mystery of God.

In sum, it is reasonable to recognize that God is at the beginning of the process of the developing universe of contingent beings as absolute creator of all of them, that God sustains all things in being as provident overseer of their existence and development, and that God is the final cause drawing all beings individually and corporately into their future fulfillment.

A METAPHYSICS INSPIRED BY THE TRINITY

Having criticized negatively Bracken's rejection of the classical notion of primary and secondary causality, I nevertheless laud his construction of "a metaphysics based on the principle of universal subjectivity,"[29] or, in a happier phrase (in my view), a "social ontology."[30] Bracken intends this metaphysics to be related explicitly to the Christian doctrine of the divine Trinity. Early in his study, *The One in the Many*, Bracken lays out the basic scheme of a social ontology: "Just as the divine persons of the Christian Trinity are one God in virtue of their dynamic interrelation, so all created entities have their identity not in terms of their individual being but rather in terms of their participation in various social groupings or functioning systems of which they are members."[31] Later, Bracken proposes what might be the inner divine logic of the social ontology: "[I]f the divine persons constitute a community of life and love even apart from creation, then their decision to create can be said to be motivated by love, namely, an unselfish desire to share the riches of their communitarian life with creatures, above all, their rational creatures."[32]

While there are a number of specific points at which the positions presented in this chapter and points of Joseph Bracken's intersubjective metaphysics/social ontology disagree, the general outline of this trinitarian metaphysics is intriguing and invites further conversation. Because his references to the triune God derive from revelation as received by Christians, his metaphysical outline could also be included among the analogies reported in chapter 6 of the present work.

NOTES

1. There are philosophical reflections on God that explicitly draw upon doctrines accepted as revealed, including the Christian doctrine of the Trinity, as in Joseph

Bracken, *The One in the Many: A Contemporary Reconstruction of the God-World Relationship* (Grand Rapids, MI: William B. Eerdmans, 2001).

2. Bernard J. F. Lonergan, S.J., "Natural Knowledge of God," in *A Second Collection*, ed. William F. J. Ryan, S.J., and Bernard J. Tyrrell, S.J. (Philadelphia: Westminster Press, 1974), 131. The essay was originally a 1968 lecture to the Catholic Theological Society of America.

3. Lonergan, "Natural Knowledge of God," 128.

4. Lonergan, "Natural Knowledge of God," 130. This hearkens back to Gregory of Nyssa's preference for naming activity as what there is one of in God, rather than nature. Thus, God's oneness is understood in more dynamic terms. One must be careful, of course, not to view the two understandings, of nature and of activity, too dialectically. See above, chapter 5.

5. Lonergan, "Natural Knowledge of God," 129.

6. Lonergan, "Natural Knowledge of God," 133. This idea is also developed in Bernard J. F. Lonergan, S.J., *Philosophy of God, and Theology* in *Philosophical and Theological Papers: 1965–1980.*

7. See *Philosophy of God, and Theology*, 203–5, and, in particular: "Here our basic argument will be that the question of God arises on a series of successive levels, that it may begin as a purely metaphysical question but it becomes a moral and eventually a religious question, and that to deal with all of these levels requires putting an end to the isolation of philosophy of God" (205).

8. W. Norris Clarke, S.J., names this "the inner path, exploring the depths of our own inner conscious life to find God as the Ultimate Goal of one's inner drive toward the fullness of Truth and Goodness (Love)," in *The One and the Many: A Contemporary Thomistic Metaphysics* (Notre Dame: University of Notre Dame Press, 2001), 215.

9. In the sections on meaning, truth, and value, I am returning to the normative patterns of the operations of consciousness discussed above in chapter 2. I am reflecting with Bernard Lonergan in *Philosophy of God, and Theology*, 205–8, and in *Method in Theology*, 101–3.

10. Lonergan, *Insight: A Study of Human Understanding*, 681.

11. Clarke, *The One and the Many*, 296.

12. Lonergan, *Method in Theology*, 104.

13. Lonergan, *Method in Theology*, 104.

14. Lonergan, *Method in Theology*, 31–32.

15. In his *Summa theologiae* I, q. 25, a. 1, reply, Aquinas reasons that God is the utterly perfect being, "pure act, simply and universally perfect; nor in God is there any imperfection." Later, in ST I, q. 87, a.1, reply, Aquinas writes: "The essence of God, therefore, which is pure and perfect act, is simply and perfectly intelligible in itself. Thus, of his very essence God understands not only the divine self, but all things."

16. For Alfred North Whitehead, the founder of process philosophy, God is not the ultimate. Creativity is the ultimate. See *Process and Reality: An Essay in Cosmology* (New York: Free Press, 1978; corrected version of the 1929 edition). In one of several similar statements, Whitehead remarks: "And it is also to be noted that every actual entity, including God, is a creature transcended by the creativity which it qualifies" (88). God is in process of becoming as much as every other creature. God's distinction is that God is the "aboriginal instance of this creativity" (225), and, in this sense, God has some direction of all subsequent beings. Whitehead's student, Charles

Hartshorne, acknowledged a divine ultimacy that enables God to be worshipped, namely, the unsurpassability of God. Unsurpassability names God as perfect, beyond every non-divine reality, while yet recognizing that God changes in interaction with the other realities of the world. Santiago Sia, a Hartshorne commentator, puts it this way: "While there can be no change whatsoever in God's exalted status, there can be change in God himself. He can surpass himself although not in the sense that he can be more divine but in the sense that he can be affected by what others do," in Santiago Sia, *God in Process Thought: A Study in Charles Hartshorne's Concept of God* (Dordrecht: Martinus Nijhoff Publishers, 1985), 37. Thus, God "can grow in perfection, he has potential states. (This is in direct contrast to the philosophical doctrine that God is 'pure act')," 38.

17. For a complementary way of expressing this point, see John Polkinghorne, "Physics and Metaphysics in a Trinitarian Perspective," *Theology and Science* 1 (April 2003): 46: "While finite human language is always being stretched beyond its limits when we try to speak of the infinite reality of God, it will be stretched in the most satisfactory direction when it is used in a personal mode."

18. I prescind here from questions of the suprahistorical qualities of human beings endowed by grace and glory, since these are issues related to specific divine revelation.

19. Chapter 14 of Clarke, *The One and the Many*, 212.

20. Cf. Clarke, *The One and the Many*, 217.

21. Lonergan, *Insight*, 680.

22. Clarke, *The One and the Many*, 309.

23. John F. Haught, *God after Darwin: A Theology of Evolution* (Boulder, CO: Westview Press, 2000), 86.

24. Clarke, *The One and the Many*, 256.

25. Haught, *God after Darwin*, 99. Haught's conception of the divine creative action within an evolving universe is much like Hans Urs von Balthasar's theology of trinitarian kenosis, as discussed above in chapter 6. Haught writes: "Similarly, as I have proposed all along with other Christian and Jewish theologians, it is the 'self-withdrawal' of any forceful divine presence, and the paradoxical hiddenness of God's power in a self-effacing persuasive love, that allows creation to come about and to unfold freely and indeterminately in evolution. It is in God's self-emptying humility that the fullest effectiveness resides" (97).

26. Cf. Thomas Aquinas, ST, I, q. 19, a 8, reply. John Polkinghorne is similar to Aquinas and W. Norris Clarke with his suggestion of a way to understand God's causal action. God's is one, certainly the chief one, among "several kinds of causalities." God's causality is spiritual and provides the primary input of information. See *Belief in God in an Age of Science* (New Haven: Yale University Press, 1998), 58ff.

27. Bracken, *The One in the Many*, 23.

28. I do not here enter into a reflection on the fate of human beings who are seriously and persistently irresponsible. That is beyond the realm of philosophical theology. But see chapter 10 for remarks on a Christian theology of sin and redemption.

29. Bracken, *The One in the Many*, 105.

30. Bracken, *The One in the Many*, 2 et passim.

31. Bracken, *The One in the Many*, 4.

32. Bracken, *The One in the Many*, 200.

9

Interreligious Dialogue on the Divine

At this point a turn is made from reflection on Christian faith standing by itself to dialogue among several religious faiths, each of which claims millions of adherents. Taking into account the specific different genius of each religion, and especially their doctrines of God, how are the several religions to relate to each other? Historically, the religions have related in various ways: with friendly or begrudging tolerance, with ignorance, or with open hostility. The concern of this chapter is dialogical or conversational. That is to say, I want to state the Christian doctrine of God in comparison with the doctrine of God in other religions. Perhaps our different faiths can enrich one another.

The postmodern context lends itself well to the task of this chapter. This is not to say that prescient religious believers in other historical periods have not been attracted to interreligious dialogue. To recall a few Christians, think of Francis of Assisi traveling to Acre to enter into honest dialogue with the Sultan, or of Thomas Aquinas employing the thought of the Jewish philosopher Maimonides in the development of his theology, or of the early-modern Jesuits like Roberto de Nobili and Matteo Ricci adapting the Christian message to the cultures of India and China. Each of these instances can be named dialogue.

The postmodern period of Western history, however, presents its own reasons for engaging in dialogue. Postmoderns are sensitive to the limitations of their own ways of viewing reality and are oriented toward learning from the other. Entering into conversation with those who are different, who are other, enables individuals and communities to grow in appreciation of what it means to be human and of what it means to be religious. Dialogue partners also increase their self-knowledge specifically as Christians or Muslims or whatever, since the constitutive elements of one's faith become less taken for granted and, instead, they become more precisely and, perhaps, more intimately owned. Finally, new sorts of human community are constituted as new social realities emerge from the various dialogues.

THE NEW MOMENT

When people live in an environment where their particular religion predominates, or when they consider their religion to be superior to others, perhaps even the only authentic religion, interreligious dialogue does not seem significant. It may even be rejected as unacceptable. But when one recognizes, as the Christian tradition has long recognized, that every image or concept of God comes nowhere near being comprehensive of the divine since the divine is always transcendent mystery, one comes to appreciate the value of entering into conversation with devotees of other religions about their religious values and beliefs, of learning about their images and concepts of the divine, and of sharing our own with them in the service of mutual enrichment. Moreover, when communications have advanced to the point of making the planet a global village, and emigration and immigration have resulted in ever increasing numbers of people of different religious persuasions living side by side within the same geographical area, then ignoring or, worse, belittling or dismissing other religions is no longer a viable option.[1] Thus, the present world order is an invitation to interreligious conversation. Hans Küng has recently urged even more serious motivation for interreligious dialogue: "No world peace without peace among religions, no peace among religions without dialogue between the religions, and no dialogue between the religions without accurate knowledge of one another."[2]

While the faithful of any religion should feel quite welcome to participate in the dialogue, I include in the present discussion only those religions which I have been able to observe and learn about by mingling among their adherents. In this way reading is complemented by firsthand observation of religious ritual, together with conversation with those who profess the religion. The partners highlighted here, then, are Hinduism, Judaism, Buddhism, Christianity, and Islam. While I am eager to engage in interreligious dialogue, I also enter the conversation with fear and trepidation. Who am I to presume to say something about the religious traditions of others when it has taken me so many years to learn what little I know of my own religious tradition? So, I do not claim to speak authoritatively of any religion, but only to say that I have read and observed and thought carefully. I stand ready to be corrected as much as correction is needed. In any case, readiness for correction is a necessary part of interreligious dialogue.

TRINITARIAN PRESUPPOSITIONS OF DIALOGUE

Catholic Christians, for their part, can readily enter the dialogue among the religions on the basis of trinitarian doctrine and theology. The Second Vatican Council and subsequent developments endorse conversation on the part of Christians with people of various religious faiths, all in the search for peaceable coexistence, the unity that is desirable for the human race, and a genuine respect for the various ways of communication with the transcendent.

The Second Vatican Council introduced Catholics to a holy reverence for adherents of other religions and for the other religions themselves. Thus, the 1965 *Declaration on Non-Christian Religions* announces that "the Catholic Church rejects nothing of what is true and holy in these religions. She has a high regard for the manner of life and conduct, the precepts and doctrines which, although differing in many ways from her own teaching, nevertheless often reflect a ray of that truth which enlightens everyone."[3]

The *Pastoral Constitution on the Church in the Modern World* is even more explicit. After describing the way in which the indwelling of the Holy Spirit conforms Christians to the image of Christ, the pinnacle of human perfection, the text goes on: "All this holds true not for Christians only but also for all people of good will in whose hearts grace is active invisibly. For since Christ died for all, and since all are in fact called to one and the same destiny, which is divine, we must hold that the Holy Spirit offers to all the possibility of being made partners, in a way known to God, in the paschal mystery."[4]

If anything, these Catholic convictions expressed in the Second Vatican Council have been more strongly affirmed in official Catholic statements in the years since the council. While reflecting on the meaning of the 1986 international day of prayer for peace at Assisi, Pope John Paul II celebrated the radical unity that already exists among all the world's people, no matter how great our religious divisions, because the human race has a common origin in its creation by the living God and a common destiny in the universal divine will to save everyone (I Tim 2:4). In addition, all who seek the true and the good do so because of a universally shared presence of the Holy Spirit. And so John Paul praised the Assisi gathering since it was a "visible expression of the hidden but radical unity which the divine word, 'in whom everything was created, and in whom everything exists' (Col. 1:16; Jn 1:3), has established among the men and women of this world."[5] The pope goes on: "We can indeed maintain that every authentic prayer is called forth by the Holy Spirit, who is mysteriously present in the heart of every person."[6]

In 1997, a little more than a decade after the Assisi day of prayer, the International Theological Commission published a paper entitled "Christianity and the World Religions." The paper concerns itself with the theoretical issue of whether other religions can have salvific value. "[O]ne finds elements of truth, of grace and goodness not only in the hearts of people but also in the rites and customs of peoples, although all must be 'healed, elevated and completed.' . . . Whether the religions as such can have salvific value is a point that remains open."[7]

However the theoretical issue is resolved, an issue addressed in the final chapter of the present work, the International Theological Commission's paper issues a strong practical directive: "Today's Christians, respecting the diversity of religions, must learn to live a form of communion which has its foundation in the love of God for all and which is based on God's respect of human freedom."[8]

THE HOW AND THE WHAT OF DIALOGUE

In 1991, the Roman Catholic Church's Council for Interreligious Dialogue offered two valuable suggestions in service of beneficial dialogue. First, attitudes important for fruitful dialogue are listed. Second, four distinct forms of dialogue are usefully distinguished.

Regarding attitudes, the council writes: "They [the participants] should be neither ingenuous nor overly critical, but open and receptive. Unselfishness and impartiality, acceptance of differences and of possible contradictions, . . . [t]he will to engage together in commitment to the truth and the readiness to allow oneself to be transformed by the encounter are other dispositions required."[9]

Two theologians much involved in dialogue with Eastern religions confirm the necessity of the attitudes highlighted by the council. Raimon Panikkar, a Catholic whose father was Indian and whose mother was Spanish, has long reflected upon the interrelationship that might obtain among the religions. In a recent book he encourages dialogue participants to maintain an "open horizon." At the same time, he counsels against attempting a "global perspective." In his view, each human being is inevitably limited in perspective and is incapable of having or achieving "a global vision of anything."[10] This is a peculiarly postmodern point of view.

Francis X. Clooney, a Jesuit who lived in India for many years and has engaged in extensive research and dialogue on Indian religion and philosophy, offers more details on what such an open horizon might include. The participant in dialogue begins with a "pure desire" to know whatever is to be known in the other's religion as well as in one's own. Then one spends years developing one's competence to read the texts of the other religions comparatively with the texts of one's own religious tradition. This task, Clooney argues, is not only long, but arduous and unpredictable. Finally, the partners who have engaged and become competent in such extended dialogue will need to "defamiliarize" their audiences of familiar, but often quite closed, readings of their own tradition's texts.[11]

Encounter with other religions can enhance and deepen the faith of those who engage in dialogue on the divine. Clooney clarifies: "In our world today, seeing God may also be the goal of learning from another religion, and we may explore Hindu wisdom because we want a deeper, fuller experience of God. We may have seen God before, in our own way in our tradition, but now we want to see God more clearly than before."[12]

On the other hand, dialogue requires great care and a certain level of sophistication, especially when the engagement with another religion moves to the most profound beliefs. Again, Clooney puts it well: "We need to be careful when we go forth to a new spiritual place. Exploring a religious tradition other than our own can be so deeply unsettling that our faith becomes unhinged."[13]

Moving from beneficial attitudes encouraged by the Council for Interreligious Dialogue and supported by Panikkar and Clooney, I turn to four forms of dialogue that are counseled:

1. The dialogue of life, where people strive to live in an open and neighborly spirit, sharing their joys and sorrows, their human problems and preoccupations.
2. The dialogue of action, in which Christians and others collaborate for the integral development and liberation of people.
3. The dialogue of theological exchange, where specialists seek to deepen their understanding of their respective religious heritages and to appreciate each other's spiritual values.
4. The dialogue of religious experience, where persons, rooted in their own religious traditions, share their spiritual riches, for instance with regard to prayer and contemplation, faith, and ways of searching for God or the absolute.[14]

The present chapter deals mainly with the last two of the four forms of dialogue, concentrating specifically on the relationship with the divine that obtains within the five religions. In any case, the first form of dialogue is not to be talked about in a book but must be activated by religious people who find themselves sharing an apartment building or addresses on the same street or who are citizens of the same city or nation.[15] Obviously, in many situations the second form of dialogue is a desirable place to begin, searching for some common ethical principles or precepts that enable different religious communities to cooperate for the common good of a nation or society.[16] In such situations, one might deliberately avoid raising possibly contentious issues such as divergent approaches to the divine. This might be wise at first in order to avoid disputes about complex stances of belief and theological mentalities. But sooner or later problems about determining what the common good entails are likely to arise. Then dialogue about values becomes inevitable, including focus upon the reasons for choices of values. Often the reasons are basic convictions, including ways of relating to God. In any case, in the present context, in which discussion of the divine is the explicit concern, collaboration in the field of action may be a positive outcome of dialogue about experience of and beliefs in the transcendent.

Finally, a word must be said about the final form of dialogue proposed by the council, since the council understands religious experience more broadly than the concept functions in the present work, where religious experience is self-awareness precisely as the awareness of oneself being drawn into the realm of the transcendent (see chapter 3). Religious experience, in this sense, happens within specific religious traditions, and in the midst of worship, action, and personal prayer. But it is a reality distinct from any of these. The importance of maintaining the distinction, in the context of the present discussion, is that attention to religious experience in this strict and precise sense can make an extraordinary contribution to interreligious dialogue, as the next two sections indicate.

RELIGIOUS EXPERIENCE

In a 1975 paper prepared for the Second International Symposium on Belief, Bernard Lonergan clarifies that religious experience underlies all religious rites and prayer forms, doctrines and theologies, ethical norms and community structures as their infrastructure.[17] People may not identify the specific awareness of themselves which underlies these structures. Moreover, the infrastructure can be remarkably diverse in its form. As Lonergan delineates, it can be "universalist, or ecumenist, or 'bottled effervescence,' or alienated by secular or ecclesiastical bureaucracy, or seeking the integration of religious awakening with a fuller development of the second enlightenment, or distorted by human obtuseness, frailty, wickedness."[18]

Employing the precise meaning of religious experience as infrastructure, the meaning developed above in chapter 3, the world religions can enter into a highly fruitful dialogue that can lead to further conversation on the divine. All five religions include those experiences by which their adherents are drawn into the realm of mystery. There are different emphases in the religions, but I suppose these to complement rather than contradict one another. In all five cases, religious experiences that are acknowledged and pursued lead to the commitment of faith; that is their existential quality. In all cases, also, religious experiences, while expressed in doctrines and theologies, are not limited by the latter. On the contrary, the transcending dimension of religious experience invites reflective people of faith to develop their doctrines and revise their theologies in the ongoing historical contexts within which they constitute themselves. Moreover, the mystical quality of religious experience regularly indicates some limitations of doctrinal statements and theological systems.

One avenue of potentially fruitful dialogue would be for committed members of the several religions to share with one another information about their specific religious experiences. It would not be surprising to discover that the infrastructure of each of the religions includes feelings of wonder and awe, longing and love, fear and trust, shame and guilt, joy and contentment. On a visit to Katmandu, Nepal, I spent several hours on several days observing Hindu women and men going about their daily offerings (*puja*). The care with which people performed their rituals to the god Siva or his consort, in any one of her several manifestations, or their son Ganesh, the elephant-headed god, was impressive. Most of the time reverence and awe attended the rituals. Devotion was obvious. In my conversations with them, some Nepali Hindus communicated a sense of the value of mystery in their religious ritual. Others were unable to articulate why they offered their *puja*, except that it was "what we do, what our parents and grandparents did before us." Even in the latter case, profound, if inarticulate, religious experience could be functioning. I discovered a sense of a quite colloquial relationship of Hindus with their gods.

On the same visit to Nepal, I visited Bodnath, a small village outside Katmandu that has become home to several Tibetan Buddhist monasteries. There I sat in the quiet of the meditation halls of several monasteries, relishing mystery in silence. On several occasions I was present when the monks gathered to heighten self-awareness by blowing the long Tibetan horns, alternating the horns with strikes upon large metal disks, and chanting in low-registered, nearly monotone cadences the *sutras*, that is, Buddhist scriptural aphorisms, and other ritual texts.[19] In these settings, I did not observe reverence; sometimes, in fact, I was struck by the nonchalance of the gathered assembly. Instead, the feelings that seemed to be communicated were of equanimity, contentment, joy (as I made eye contact with monks, both in the meditation halls and elsewhere inside the monastic enclosure, warm smiles were spontaneous). Perhaps the nonchalant attitude comes from the Buddhist sense of being in the world but of not taking it too seriously, since this life is fundamentally transitory.

Like Hindus, Jews, it seems, are often quite colloquial in their conversations with Yahweh. The tone of the Psalms indicates as much. At the same time, awe before the great God is equally appropriate, as is the case with Isaiah when Yahweh appoints him to be a prophet (Is 6:1–8). Wonder in the face of the mystery of God characterizes Moses before the burning bush in Exodus 3:2f and when he asks to be shown God's glory (Ex 33:18). Fear and dread before God was an occasional experience of the Israelites while wandering in the desert, particularly after they had failed in their fidelity. Often this self-awareness was followed by sorrow for their sins. Nowhere is the fear of God inspired by the totally demanding love of God more eloquently expressed than in Psalm 139. Trust in Yahweh because he could be counted on suffuses the shepherd themes of Isaiah and Psalm 23. For many Jews today, the most poignant religious experience may be the sense of the transcendent precisely in the empty feeling of God's absence during the Holocaust, or in the aching longing of prayer at the western wall of the Temple, the so-called Wailing Wall.

Christians, too, experience the range of feelings that draw subjects into the realm of the transcendent. Paul experiences wonder and awe (Rom 11:33–36, Eph 3:14), longing (Rom 7:24–25), trust (II Cor 5:6–10, Phil 3:7f), and love (Rom 5:5). Millions of other Christians similarly experience these feelings drawing them into the realm of the transcendent when they relate to the presence of Jesus the Christ in their midst. It is not uncommon for Christians to imagine themselves with Jesus in the historical situations recounted in the Gospels and therewith to experience feelings that, while relating them first to Jesus in his historical humanity, eventually draw them into a sense of communion with the transcendent Three. Something comparable can happen when Christians celebrate sacramental liturgies. Within the event of worship one feels drawn beyond it. For example, William Johnston advises that, for Christians for whom celebration of the Eucharist is central, eucharistic communion is a privileged opportunity for religious experience.[20]

With Islam it is best, perhaps, to start with Muhammed himself. Karen Armstrong writes of the extraordinary experiences that led Muhammed to write the Quran: "Muhammed had had that overpowering apprehension of numinous reality, which the Hebrew prophets had called *kaddosh*, holiness, the terrifying otherness of God."[21] Clearly, this is an experience of awe and fear before the all-demanding God. Subsequently, devout Muslims undergo the several religious experiences that draw subjects into the transcendent when they hear the words of the Quran chanted. Muslims with whom I share conversation and occasional Friday afternoon worship suggest that a faithful Muslim undergoes religious experience simply hearing the Quran in its original Arabic.[22] Other moments that can engender heightened religious experience for Muslims are the performance of the sacred pilgrimage of the *Hajj* and the observance of the fast of Ramadan.

THE RELIGIOUS EXPERIENCE OF LOVE

Being in love in a transcendent way is the primordial religious experience, in which all the others are gathered up. For this reason, I have thus far made no reference to love in the listing of the religious experiences of the five religions, except for a passing reference to Paul (Rom 5:5). I have saved discussion of the religious experience of unlimited love until now. For, along with Bernard Lonergan and Friedrich Heiler, I would propose that transcendent love characterizes each of the great religions.[23]

With Hinduism, there seems to be no doubt. Hinduism proposes three ways or ascents that lead to the divine, otherwise called liberation (*moksha*): the way of knowledge, the way of love, and the way of action. The second, that of love or devotion, is called bhakti. When seeking to define bhakti, a Hindu catechism quotes the author of the *Narada-Sutras* as claiming that bhakti is "an intense love of God:" "A man who loves God has no wants nor sorrows. He neither hates nor joys nor strives with zeal for any ends of his own. For through *bhakti* is he moved to rapture, and through *bhakti* does he attain peace, and is ever happy in spirit."[24]

Later, clarifying *ekanta-bhakti*, the purest form of bhakti, the author speaks of the religious person who "loves God for His own sake," who is "mad after God."[25]

Transcendent love is not so easily identified in Buddhism. Longing for the wisdom of enlightenment might be considered the primary religious experience, although longing here has nothing of the sense of yearning and clinging. For the Buddhist such desire is contrary to the path of enlightenment. Nor is Buddhist compassion for all sentient beings the equivalent of the otherworldly love that is religious experience. For compassion, for all its nobility, is a love turned toward one's fellows in this world, spiritual, sensitive, and vegetative.

Nevertheless, Aloysius Pieris, a Sri Lankan Jesuit long involved in Buddhist-Christian dialogue, devotes the final chapter of his book, *Love Meets Wisdom: A Christian Experience of Buddhism*, to develop the thesis that while Buddhism is a kind of gnosis, it is an enlightenment suffused with love of the transcendent, just as Christianity, which might be characterized primarily as agapic, is a love of God whom the Christian knows (*gnosei*) intimately.[26]

The Jewish experience of transcendent love is well attested in the Hebrew scriptures. Frequently, this is expressed as the love of Yahweh for his people. Think of Psalm 103, which celebrates God's steadfast love. Or Hosea 11:1–4, 8, and passages in Isaiah such as 40:1–2, 43:4, and 49:15–16. The corollary is that the people whom God has chosen to be peculiarly his own love God with their whole being. Thus, the great commandment is expressed in Deuteronomy 6:4–5: "Hear, O Israel, the Lord is our God, the Lord alone. You shall love the Lord your God with all your heart, and with all your soul, and with all your might."[27]

A magnificent expression of the religious experience of love in Judaism is evoked at the beginning of Minchah for Sabbath Eve, the *Yedid Nephesh*:

Beloved of the soul, Compassionate Father, draw Your servant to Your will. Then Your servant will hurry like a hart to bow before Your majesty. To him

Your friendship will be sweeter than the dripping of honeycomb and any taste.
. . . Please be revealed and spread upon me, my Beloved, the shelter of Your
peace. . . . Hashem, show love, for the time has come, and show us grace as in
the days of old.[28]

Love is the primary religious experience of the Christian, for what Jesus
has accomplished is to pour out the Holy Spirit into the hearts of Christians
so that lovingly they can call out to God, "Abba." It is no wonder that
Bernard Lonergan refers repeatedly to Romans 5:5 when he brings up the
love that is at the heart of Christianity.[29] For the Christian, the experience of
being in love in this transcendent way is fully trinitarian. The Christian joins
with his or her brother, Christ, in the power of the Spirit, to find communion
with the living God.

The primary meaning of the word *Islam* is "the act of existential surrender
that each convert was expected to make to al-Lah: a *muslim* was a man or a
woman who has surrendered his or her whole being to the Creator."[30] This
total surrender is achieved in love. One of God's names is He Who loves (*al-
Wadud*), and the committed Muslim surrenders in devotion to God, a God
who is compassionate and merciful. It is a surrender in love. A Muslim commentator has written: "*Din* (Religion) or *Iman* (Belief), according to the
Qor'an, is a state of Islam, i.e., handing over of the person in its totality to
God, being conscious of the Divine Majesty, with utmost love, deep venera-
tion and awe, and conscious of the Divine presence (Qor. 58/7)."[31]

Although religious experience happens within religious traditions and
therefore draws its expressions from the tradition, the experience itself functions as an infrastructure. If adherents of the five religions are willing to enter into conversation about their religious experience, they are likely to discover common experiences underlying their differentiated religious
traditions. Such conversations could well bring people of widely different
traditions to the subjective moment where every devotee is aware of herself
or himself being drawn into the realm of transcendent mystery. Focusing
upon such self-transcending experiences of themselves, religious subjects
can meet in dialogue with others who seem to be so far removed from them
in religious practice, doctrine, and theology, and discover that their religious
experiences take place on the same plane and even have the same infra-
structural content.

DOCTRINES OF THE TRANSCENDENT

The heart of the present chapter is the belief in the divine of each of the five
religious traditions. Any dialogue among religions eventually has to get
around to consideration of what characterizes the transcendent for the reli-

gions in conversation, since that is the guiding reality for every religion's positions on self and society, ethics and nature.

To begin with, the five religions are in agreement that to speak of the transcendent Whole, which grounds the universe we know, is to speak from a position of radical limitation. What human beings can grasp of the transcendent is no more than a glimpse, a recognition that there is something to be grasped, but no ability to grasp it in anything even remotely approaching completeness. In addition, since human expression in any case falls short of what has been grasped, expression of the transcendent is even more inadequate than the passing glimpse. In a major way the glimpse is inexpressible. These limitations of grasp and expression are poignantly highlighted in the Hebrew scriptures in a conversation between Moses and Yahweh. Moses asks Yahweh to show him the divine glory. Yahweh grants the request but with the caution that no one can look upon the face of God. What he grants Moses is a glimpse from behind after God's glory has passed before him (Ex 33:18–23).

If the transcendent is incomprehensible to the human mind and inexpressible in human words, is it not foolish and arrogant to attempt some conception? Such criticism has been leveled often enough. Nevertheless, to plead the limitations of mind and language as reason to avoid every attempt at expression would be, for so many, to pass over persistent questions about the object of the powerful experiences of wonder and awe, longing and love, fear and trust, shame and guilt, joy and contentment that motivate people of every religious stripe. It would be to pretend away the powerful presence of transcendent meaning, which calls out to be mediated at so many turns of human living and in reflection upon living. It would be to ignore a dimension of reality which demands attention, and not just as one more reality among countless others, but as the reality which orders all the others and makes them meaningful in some final sense.

At the same time, the five religions conceive the transcendent reality so differently that it becomes quickly obvious that the move from religious experience of the transcendent to religious conceptualization of the same is mediated in extraordinarily diverse ways. How to evaluate such diversity and dialogue about it is a challenge of enormous proportions to all the religions.

I begin the discussion with a difference between the Western and the Eastern religions that has been suggested by Bede Griffiths, the British Benedictine monk who founded and thereafter lived in a Christian ashram (one Hindu version of a monastery) in India:

> The difference between the Semitic religions (Judaism, Christianity and Islam) and the Oriental religions (Hinduism, Buddhism and Taoism) seems to lie in this; that in the Semitic tradition God is represented as the transcendent Lord of creation, infinitely 'holy,' that is separate from and above nature, and never to be confused with it. But in the Oriental tradition God—or the Absolute, by

whatever word it may be named—is immanent in all creation. The world does not exist apart from God but 'in' God; he dwells in the heart of every creature.[32]

Judaism, Christianity, Islam

Judaism, Christianity, and Islam share a common monotheistic faith. The one God, who revealed the divine self to Abraham of Ur of the Chaldees, grounds the three Western religions. Esteem for the city of Jerusalem by all three faiths stands as a graphic symbolic expression of their common naming of the divine.

The three faiths conceive the one God to be personal. God is not just a life force, but is characterized by qualities which pertain to persons. God interacts as a subject with human subjects. This leads to difficulties for Jews, Christians, and Muslims alike. The infinite, incomprehensible God cannot be a subject with the limitations of human subjects. Otherwise, God ceases to be transcendent. And if God is not transcendent, all kinds of contradictions follow for the relationship of God to the created world. Still, the scriptures of the three monotheistic faiths are replete with anthropomorphic talk about God. It is not easy to conceive of God as personal without attributing human characteristics to God. Thus, God is pictured as walking and talking, becoming angry and relenting, punishing and being moved to pity, and, almost always, God is pictured as being male.

Theologians recognize that ultimately believers must eschew imagination if they are to conceive transcendent personality without contradiction. Gender, physical and emotional movement, deliberation and contingent decision have no place in a conception of God as transcendent. But narrative and ritual and worship, as well as devotion, at least for many, do not fare well when confined by transcendent conceptualization. Thus, for all three faiths there seems to be a built-in, permanent tension. On one hand, God is characterized as transcendently personal. On the other hand, the characterization is inevitably distorted by anthropomorphic attributes. Somehow the provision needs always be in the back of the mind: Although we picture God anthropomorphically, we are aware that God really isn't so.

Christians differ from Jews and Muslims in their belief that God is tri-personal, three divine subjects of one divine communion. Already in the second century, Jews found Christian faith in the three-in-one-God to be intolerable. To them it is crass polytheism. Muslims, too, criticize the Christian conception of God as Trinity. A Muslim's spirituality finds its source entirely in "awareness of the Oneness of God."[33] Thus, the Quran insists that Christian trinitarian faith is idolatry.

Certainly they disbelieve who say: "Allah is Christ the son of Mary." But said Christ: "O Children of Israel! Worship Allah, my Lord and your Lord." Whoever joins other Gods with Allah, Allah will forbid him The Garden, and the Fire will be his abode. There will for the wrong-doers be no one to help (S. 5/72).

They disbelieve who say: Allah is one of three (in a Trinity:) for there is no god except One God (S. 5/73).[34]

The three monotheistic faiths have directed many a polemic against each other on the basis of their concepts of God. And, indeed, it has been no easy struggle for Christians to maintain both monotheism and trinity without collapsing one into the other.[35]

In addition to its trinitarian faith, Christianity is incarnational, another dimension quite contrary to both Judaism and Islam. Christians believe that the transcendent God has chosen to become so involved with humanity as actually to become human in Jesus of Nazareth. Jesus is at once fully human and fully divine, a divine person who has taken on a human nature (as the fifth-century Council of Chalcedon expresses it). Christian incarnational faith is seen as an affront to divine transcendence by both Jews and Muslims. One commentator interprets the Christian-Muslim divide on this issue as a concern about the transcendence of the transcendent God:

> Both religions, of course, accept the primacy of the Divine and the blinding reality of God. But they differ as to whether that Transcendent and Divine Reality can become manifested in the world of becoming and, if so, what constitutes the meaning of manifestation. Islam rejects the incarnation, fixing its gaze upon the Absolute as such, which cannot become incarnated without entering into the domain of relativity. Christianity places its emphasis not on the Absolute as such but on the manifestation of the Absolute as the son or the Truth incarnate.[36]

Nevertheless, for all the mutual antagonism that has marked the monotheistic conceptions of the three faiths, there is much upon which they agree. For all three, the personal God is the creator of the universe, as well as its sustainer and preserver. Nothing creaturely happens apart from God. God is also the liberator or savior of the faithful. Moreover, for the three monotheistic faiths, the faithful whom God saves are not limited to adherents of a particular faith.

The three Western religions also share the conviction that God acts in history. Together with this conviction is the certainty that God acts especially in their particular histories. Thus, the Hebrew Bible is the story of God's action on behalf of the Jewish people. The New Testament, at least partially, tells the story of what God has done in Jesus the Christ to create and give growth to the assembly of the faithful, the church. The Quran is the revelation to Muhammed of God's concern for the people who surrender themselves utterly to God. The historical particularization of divine activity that is enshrined in the scriptures of the three Western religions has led all three to an exclusivity in their relationship with God. Sometimes, as is so painfully evident, it leads them to promote their perceived prerogatives with violence.

Hinduism

Hinduism, too, maintains that God is ultimately incomprehensible to human beings. The incomprehensible God, the ground of all that is, is named Brahman. Brahman is not conceived to be personal or impersonal, but rather beyond both, "the soul of everything."[37] Brahman is immanent in all that exists as the transpersonal or suprapersonal.[38] At the heart of every human being is *atman*, the deepest self, which is basically not different from Brahman.

The one, incomprehensible Brahman has many manifestations.[39] There are the manifestations of Brahman in creation: Brahma, the creating manifestation; Vishnu, the preserving manifestation; and Siva, the destroying manifestation.[40] While Brahma is infrequently worshipped distinctly, Vishnu and Siva are worshipped in countless temples and shrines, along with many other avatars or special descents of Brahman, both gods and goddesses, especially Rama and Krishna, avatars of Vishnu.[41] Thus, while ultimately God is impersonal, God becomes personal in a humanly accessible way in the many avatars, who are not only personal but quite anthropomorphic, or human-animal combinations. Indeed, some of the avatars are contemporary human persons such as the Kumari goddess, who is patroness of Katmandu. In the Hindu conception of the divine, Kumari is the consort of Skanda, who is the adolescent warrior son of Siva and his consort, Parvati.[42]

Hindus claim that the avatars make accessible the multiple aspects of the divine. For this reason none is given definitive priority over the others. In fact, "out of the numerous forms of God conceived in the past by the heart of man and recorded in our scriptures the worshipper is taught to choose one which satisfies his spiritual longing and make that the object of his adoration and love."[43] In this way, all the manifestations of God are intended to assist human beings to relate to the one God. The avatars incarnate all the major qualities of the divine, including directions toward the incomprehensible and inconceivable divine. To give one example, Bede Griffiths writes of Siva: "Thus the God Siva for a Hindu devotee today is a name for the ultimate reality beyond name and form, who is one with the Brahman, the absolute truth and the final good, revealing himself to his devotees as a God of infinite grace and love, and the *lingam* is the sign of the formless deity, God beyond name and form."[44]

Buddhism

Buddhism's approach to God is quite distinct. The Buddhist cosmology includes the many gods of Hinduism, and at least some Buddhists feel quite free to worship these gods.[45] The gods can be helpful in meeting this-worldly needs, such as good health, a suitable marriage, a bountiful harvest. The achievement of enlightenment, however, the great human project, is something which one must pursue and achieve on one's own, or rather, something which happens by utter nonpursuance.[46] For this reason, the gods are not helpful at all in the view of some Buddhists and only secondarily so in the view even of those who venerate the gods. One does not turn to the gods for assistance with the all-important life's work of enlightenment.

Buddhism, then, does not have a conception of God as the Absolute or as Ultimate Reality in the same way that the other four religions do.[47] Yet, Buddhist meditation often has the quality of worship; it appears to be religious devotion. And there are many depictions of bodhisattvas in kneeling poses of adoration or worship.[48] What is the direction of the "worship?" It would seem to be nirvana. Some students of Buddhism suggest that nirvana or the state of total union with the whole is roughly equivalent with what the other four religions name God.[49] It is not a personal God, but, of course, neither is the personal God of the monotheistic faiths simply a human personality writ large. Divine personality utterly transcends human personality. Moreover, like the Hindu notion of God as immanent, Buddhist nirvana is in this world, for what the Buddhist seeks in union is that the utterly transcendent, nirvana, is the wholly immanent, samsara; samsara is nirvana. Once a person has achieved that utterly un-self-conscious communion, she or he is totally gathered up into the whole of the cosmos. Is that the divine?

Donald W. Mitchell cautions that it is not. For while some parallels can be noted between the Emptiness which is the ultimate reality of Buddhist spirituality and that Christian spirituality which conceives of God as a self-emptying Trinity, in the Father's self-emptying love in creation, in Christ's self-emptying love in the ministry of redemption, and in the Holy Spirit's self-emptying love in the sanctification of the world, still God remains uniquely and distinctly Other both in God's inner-trinitarian reality and as well in the divine creative, redemptive, and sanctifying self-emptying activity.[50]

Another possible route to take in dialogue with Buddhism about the divine arises in reference to Pure Land Buddhism. For this branch of Buddhism, the Buddha Amitabha or Amida dwells in a paradise beyond the world characterized by old age, disease, and death. There the Buddha is "the omnipresent power, which is the good in every living being."[51]

Perhaps negotiating these various positions is the conclusion of Bede Griffiths. He claims that

> [p]eople in the East see the whole universe as energy structured by consciousness and coming out of a center that is beyond the energy and the consciousness and is the source of all. That is very near to the Christian idea of the Trinity. The Holy Spirit is that energy which penetrates the whole universe. That

energy is organized by the Word, the wisdom that comes forth from the beginning. Both the energy and the Word come from the primordial mystery that transcends everything.[52]

Relating his point to the specific issue of the divine in various religions, Griffiths continues:

> Vast numbers of people, including some well-meaning but ill-informed Christians, as well as Jews and Muslims, think of God as a monad—one being, one person, a personal God who is organizing the universe. Though that is useful and helpful in many ways, it is only a projection of the mind. Beyond that personal god in every religious tradition, we understand there is a transcendent mystery that probably has no name. It comes out very clearly, of course, in the Hindu tradition. There are the gods and goddesses, but also Brahman. He is the unity beyond all dualities. In Buddhism the sense of unity is similar. There is *nirvana* or *sunyata*: the void which is utterly beyond.[53]

WHY SUCH A VARIETY OF CONCEPTS OF THE TRANSCENDENT?

Having noted that the five religions share feelings that characterize religious experience while, at the same time, their specific conceptualizations of the divine differ so remarkably, it is natural to ask how it is that common experience coexists with such striking conceptual differences. Bernard Lonergan suggests that we conceive of the transcendent addressing human persons in two ways. First, there is "the prior word God speaks to us by flooding our hearts with his love."[54] I have been identifying this prior word as religious experience, spoken within the interiority of the subject. It is the feeling of being drawn beyond oneself and the world at hand into the realm of the transcendent. As a word identifiable with feelings susceptible of a transcendent reach, the range is more intense than broad. Feelings of human subjects are arguably quite similar the world over.

Besides the prior word, the transcendent can be conceived to address human persons in an "outwardly spoken word." This latter is "historically conditioned: its meaning depends upon the human context in which it is uttered, and such contexts vary from place to place and from one generation to another."[55] By this word there are different religious founders and leaders, different scriptures, different formations of community life, moral codes, beliefs, and worship. Lonergan highlights the difference between the two words in the terminology of mediation and immediacy:

> [T]he prior word in its immediacy, though it differs in intensity, though it resonates differently in different temperaments and in different stages of religious development, withdraws man from the diversity of history by moving out of the

world mediated by meaning and towards a world of immediacy in which image and symbol, thought and word, lose their relevance and even disappear.[56]

Lonergan intends that Christians should understand these two words in the trinitarian terms of the two divine missions. The mission or sending of the eternal Logos/Word into human history is the outer word, most especially in the historical divine/human revelation of Jesus of Nazareth in Palestine in the first century of the Common Era. The mission of the Holy Spirit to create communion with human subjects of all times and places is the inner word. The Father, who is the source of the intratrinitarian processions, and thus of the divine missions into the human world, is thus conceived to be the divine mystery which is at once incommunicable in transcendence, despite the missions into the human world, and yet the divine person in whom, by means of the two words, human subjects gain intimate communion with the divine.[57]

From this trinitarian perspective, Christians can relate reverently to those who are devoted to any one of the five religions, and to others as well. Beyond that, Christians can be eager to learn of these other religions. So much may learning of the other religions become valuable that, as Francis X. Clooney envisions, some Christians at least might include the sacred texts of other religions "in the set of Christian theological resources," all the while continuing to read the Bible as normative.[58]

DIALOGUE ABOUT THE DIVINE

Hinduism, Buddhism, Judaism, Christianity, and Islam have developed different conceptualizations of the transcendent. Indeed, Buddhism genuinely avoids any conceptualization of the transcendent as divine. All five religions also hold the conviction that to the human mind the divine is finally incomprehensible and ineffable. To say that the divine is "nothing" in the sense that it is not like anything which is proportionate to the human mind's possibility of comprehension and conceptualization is congenial to all five religious faiths. All can say with the Hindu Upanishad: *Neti, Neti,* that is, *Not this, Not this.* Thus, the religions have to resort to the language of image and metaphor and analogy, recognizing that language about the divine is symbolic. It points toward reality, and is even true in its statements, but it falls far short as finite minds and language must when addressing the infinite. Thus, the divine is not the unknown that is totally beyond the human horizon, but it is the unknown which nevertheless can be approached, and, to this extent, is known.

As people of different faiths meet for conversation, it is well to keep this meaning in mind of the transcendent as the known unknown. First, it keeps one humble about the achievements of her or his own religion and theology.

The truth that our own faith tradition has come to, while it is truth to be affirmed, valued, and celebrated, remains but a partial glimpse. Second, it engenders the openness of respect for and appreciation of the religion of the conversation partner. All five religions represent long and venerable religious traditions. They have received the committed adherence of countless devout and attentive, intelligent, reasonable, and responsible women and men over the centuries. The sense of the divine which the conversation partner brings to the dialogue is as worthy as mine.

At this point it may be helpful to list some factors that are important to prepare for or to accompany dialogue.

1. As a preliminary to actual conversation about the divine, the partners should try to observe first hand important rituals of the other's religion. A non-Christian might attend Catholic Eucharist or a Christian revival meeting. A non-Muslim might approach a mosque, listening to the call to prayer from the minaret, noting the reverence of individuals kneeling with their faces to the floor. Members of other faiths might attend a Jewish Sabbath service in a synagogue; they might even be invited to a Bar Mitzvah or to be guests of a family for Passover. One might visit a Hindu home for the morning *puja* or participate in one of the many Hindu festivals or attend the ceremony of cremation at one of the *ghats* along a sacred river. A non-Buddhist might sit for a time in a Buddhist meditation hall, in silence during meditation or listening to the choral chants. Of course, one can seek even more intense and participatory experiences of religions other than one's own to come to a feeling-toned knowledge of the rituals of the religion. For example, in the United States, a significant component of Buddhist-Catholic dialogue is silent meditation in common by monks of the two religious traditions.[59]

2. From observance of ritual, it is not a huge step to begin conversation about the religious experience motivating the devotion of rituals. As noted above, dialogue about religious experience may well surprise adherents of the different religions that there is something common to all human religious constructions in the infrastructures of the religions. Recognition of common experience can serve as a continual invitation to fruitful dialogue.

3. There is no point shirking the particularity of the five religions. Religious doctrine and action are grounded in those particularities. With Buddhists, Christians, and Muslims, the founder of the religion plays a central role in the formulation of doctrines. With all the faiths, the specific, formative scriptures guide the unfolding of the religion. Moreover, both founders and scriptures are accepted on faith by the adherents of the particular religions. The truth of the founder's witness or of the scriptures cannot be proved or disproved by any of the religions. Nor

can one or another, on these grounds, claim to be superior to the others. What convinces the faithful of the particular religions is twofold. First, there is the long-standing cultural foundation of their religious tradition. People believe what they believe because that is the faith that has functioned in their culture. Second, for those who have arrived at a more reflective faith, there is some way in which they have come to recognize that their religious experience resonates with this founder and/or these scriptures and/or the character of this faith community.

The member of another religion needs to have two lenses at hand as she or he seeks to interpret the religion of the conversation partner. First, there is a need to be fitted with the lens of the other, insofar as that is possible, keeping in mind Panikkar's caution that one cannot simply take on the cultural particularity of others (the impossibility of a global vision) and Clooney's advice to "defamiliarize" oneself and one's audience with what has been taken for granted. One learns the cultural particularities of the rise and ongoing life of the religion. One also learns from the other how the interior resonance of religious experience and the particular sources of that faith work themselves out for the dialogue partner.

Second, as one seeks to dialogue with a person of another faith, one also needs to wear the lens of one's critical affirmations and understandings of one's own particular faith before attempting to sort out actual differences and agreements between the two religions. Both efforts are likely to be the work not only of the lifetime of individuals engaged in dialogue but of generations in the history of the several communities of faith well into the future.

4. Each of the five religious traditions has a long history. Gradually, it developed that there is not simply one way to be a Hindu, Buddhist, Jew, Christian, or Muslim. Within each religion there are, in fact, several, even many, traditions. Often the different ways have led to animosity among the sectarians. At some point in the conversation dialogue partners must acquaint themselves with the sectarian differences that influence the positions being espoused in the dialogue. For example, the christocentrism of an evangelical Christian appears to be quite different from the trinitarian spirituality of a Russian Orthodox Christian. The Jew or Hindu dialoguing with the two could be quite puzzled about the different interpretations of the single Christian faith. So it is with all five religions. Each has its sectarian multiplicity that one ignores at the peril of profound misunderstandings.

5. Although the differences among the five religions in their conceptualization of the divine are major, there need be no hostility. One can be convinced of the truth of one's own faith and still be eager to grow in appreciation of the truth of the other's faith. Given the incomprehensibility

of God, recognized by all five faiths, the two approaches to truth are not incompatible. In any case, dialogue is not for the sake of proselytization but simply to come to some common understanding to the extent that it is possible.

One can still give witness to one's faith, and in this sense evangelize (to use the Christian term) without proselytizing. In fact, the dialogue can hardly be authentic if the partners do not give witness to their faith convictions. Dialogue is not a reductionist enterprise, but a conversation among committed people of religious faith. If, in the process of dialogue, a partner becomes convinced of the truth of a faith other than his or her original faith, such that a need is felt to migrate to the other faith, there is freedom to make such a move, although that is not the purpose of dialogue.

6. Raising the issue of proselytization leads to awareness of one of the hindrances to dialogue, namely, claims to superiority and even exclusive claims to truth. These claims should be aired in a spirit free of proselytization. Thus, Christians should not hide from their conviction that Jesus of Nazareth is the definitive incarnation of God whose mission is to save all humankind from the destruction of sinfulness and for the life of resurrection. Muslims should acknowledge openly that, in their view, Muhammed is the final and greatest prophet of the great Allah, in the lineage of the Hebrew prophets and Jesus, but conveying Allah's further message. Jews will want to be clear that they continue to maintain that they remain in the present as in the past the specially chosen People of God living by a covenant God made with them. Even when adherents put forward the special claims of their respective religions, touting the superiority of a particular religious tradition or seeking to win converts to a religion is not the purpose of dialogue, but rather its purpose is simply honest acknowledgment of one's own faith even as one carries on conversation about all the dimensions of the religious faiths, including their diversity.

Undoubtedly, there is much that the world's religions can achieve by entering into open and honest dialogue with one another. Just as ecumenical dialogue over the last thirty years among Christians who previously were estranged from one another has taught a new appreciation of diversity within the Christian religion, as well as an appreciation of unity, so interreligious dialogue, which has also been developing over the last several decades, will surely yield beneficial results, many of which cannot at this time even be imagined. From the Christian perspective we can be confident as we envision the dialogue to belong to the journey of discipleship along the way of Jesus and as we let the Holy Spirit lead us down new paths.

Thomas Merton celebrated the goal of dialogue at an interreligious conference in India some years ago: "We are already one. But we imagine we are not. And what we have to recover is our original unity. What we have to be is what we are."[60]

NOTES

1. Ewert H. Cousins goes so far as to claim that the world is now in a second axial period. The first, as studied by Karl Jaspers, occurred about 500 B.C.E. and eventuated in "individual consciousness." The second is the presently emerging "global consciousness." See "Interreligious Dialogue: The Spiritual Journey of Our Time," in *Interreligious Dialogue: Voices from a New Frontier*, ed. M. Darrol Bryant and Frank Flinn (New York: Paragon House, 1989), 3–7.

2. Hans Küng, "Christianity and World Religions: Dialogue with Islam," in *Muslims in Dialogue: The Evolution of a Dialogue*, ed. Leonard Swidler (Lewiston, ME: Edwin Mellen Press, 1992), 251. This was a major theme for Küng at a 1989 UNESCO Colloquium and at the 1993 World Parliament of Religions in Chicago. See Hans Küng, "The History, Significance and Method of the Declaration Toward a Global Ethic," in *A Global Ethic: The Declaration of the Parliament of the World's Religions,* ed. Hans Küng and Karl-Josef Kuschel (New York: Continuum, 1993), 45. Thomas Keating argues similarly in "The Search for the Ultimate Mystery," in *Interreligious Dialogue*, ed. Bryant and Flinn, 23.

3. "Declaration on Non-Christian Religions" (*Nostra aetate*), 2 in *The Basic Sixteen Documents Vatican Council II*, gen. ed. Austin Flannery, O.P. (Northport, NY: Costello Publishing, 1996), 570–71. I have taken the liberty to change the language from exclusive to inclusive in texts obviously intending both women and men.

4. "Pastoral Constitution on the Church in the Modern World" (*Gaudium et spes*), in Flannery, *Basic Sixteen Documents*, n. 22 (186). See also n. 92 (279–81).

5. Pope John Paul II, "The Meaning of the Assisi Day of Prayer," *Origins* 16 (15 January 1987): 561, n.3.

6. Pope John Paul II, "Meaning," 563, n. 11.

7. International Theological Commission, "Christianity and the World Religions," *Origins* 27 (14 August 1997): 161, n. 81. A more recent Vatican declaration, *Dominus Iesus*, reiterates that any salvific path which may be provided in other religions nevertheless is effective because of its connection with the uniquely universal salvific activity of Jesus. See *Origins* 30 (14 September 2000): 218, n. 21. Daniel P. Sheridan offers the same view in "Grounded in the Trinity: Suggestions for a Theology of Relationship to Other Religions," *Thomist* 50 (1986): 271.

8. International Theological Commission, "Christianity and the World Religions," 164, n. 102.

9. Pontifical Council for Interreligious Dialogue and Congregation for the Evangelization of Peoples, "Dialogue and Proclamation: Reflections and Orientations on Interreligious Dialogue and the Proclamation of the Gospel of Jesus Christ," *Origins* 21

(4 July 1991): 121, 123–35. The authoritative text appears in Italian and French, as well as English, in the *Bulletin* of the Council 26, no. 2 (1991). See n. 47.

10. Raimon Panikkar, *The Cosmotheandric Experience: Emerging Religious Consciousness*, ed. and intro. by Scott Eastham (Maryknoll, NY: Orbis, 1993), 12–13. If Panikkar and Ewert Cousins (see n. 1 above) were to converse with one another, would they find their views to be complementary or opposed?

11. Francis X. Clooney, S.J., *Theology after Vedanta: An Experiment in Comparative Theology* (Albany: State University of New York Press, 1993), 201–6.

12. Francis X. Clooney, S.J., *Hindu Wisdom for All God's Children* (Maryknoll, NY: Orbis, 1998), 53.

13. Clooney, *Hindu Wisdom*, 79.

14. Pontifical Council for Interreligious Dialogue, "Dialogue and Proclamation," n. 42.

15. Apparently, this sort of living side by side contentedly even with differences thrived in Sarajevo, in what was then the nation of Yugoslavia. Muslims, Roman Catholics, and Serbian Orthodox shared their city, their streets, and even their apartment houses. Unfortunately, the apparent lack of explicit decisions to value the three religious heritages left the inhabitants open to manipulation by tribalists and nationalists who desired so-called ethnic purity and religious exclusivity. The tragic results in Sarajevo are today known to all the world. Thus, Sarajevo provides sad evidence that "dialogue of life" needs to be complemented by the other three dialogues.

16. On the day following the 11 September 2001 attacks by Muslim terrorists upon their targets in the United States, I attended evening prayers at a nearby mosque in Lackawanna, New York. The congregation, mostly of Yemeni origin, welcomed me. Together we pledged to work for a world without terror and violence. Again, shortly after the arrests on 13 September 2002 of six men of Yemeni descent in Lackawanna for participating in an Al-Qaeda sleeper cell, spokespersons of several religious communities met outside the Lackawanna mosque to pledge themselves to stand together against indiscriminate targeting of persons of Middle Eastern descent. This was to counteract any impression that Muslims in general or Yemeni people in general are bent on terrorism. On 30 April 2003 about fifty Christians and Muslims gathered at the Yemeni Social Center in Lackawanna to pray together for peace in the world.

17. Bernard Lonergan, "Prolegomena to the Study of the Emerging Religious Consciousness of Our Time," in *A Third Collection*, ed. Frederick E. Crowe, S.J. (Mahwah, NJ: Paulist, 1985).

18. Lonergan, "Prolegomena," 71. By "the second enlightenment" Lonergan refers to initiatives of many nineteenth- and twentieth-century thinkers to analyze the constitutive role of human consciousness in the making of the world (63–65).

19. See John Renard's description of the feelings associated with Buddhist music-making in *Responses to 101 Questions on Buddhism* (New York: Paulist, 1999), n. 64 (106–7).

20. Johnston, *Being in Love: The Practice of Christian Prayer*, 77–79.

21. Karen Armstrong, *A History of God: The 4000-Year Quest of Judaism, Christianity and Islam* (New York: Ballantine, 1993), 138.

22. Armstrong, *History of God*, 145.

23. Lonergan, *Method in Theology*, 109.

24. D. S. Sarma, *A Primer of Hinduism* (Bombay: Bharatiya Vidya Bhavan, 1989), 60. For further development of the Hindu path of bhakti, see John B. Carman in *The Encyclopedia of World Religion*, ed. Mircea Eliade, vol. 2 (New York: Macmillan, 1987), s.v. bhakti. P. Fallon's essay on "Doctrinal Background of the Bhakti Spirituality" not only stresses the meaning of bhakti as devotional love, and the complicated dimensions of this love within Hindu religion, but also its value as religious experience. See R. DeSmet and J. Neuner, eds., *Religious Hinduism* (Bandra, India: St. Paul Press, 1997), ch. 23.

25. Sarma, *A Primer of Hinduism*, 70, 71.

26. Aloysius Pieris, S.J., *Love Meets Wisdom: A Christian Experience of Buddhism* (Maryknoll, NY: Orbis, 1988). In an interview I had with John Locke, S.J., while I was visiting Nepal, this book was recommended to me for the keenness of its insights. Fr. Locke has spent about three decades studying Buddhism by entering into the experience, and by conversation with Buddhist monks.

27. Relying on the extrabiblical oral Torah of Judaism, Jacob Neusner offers exegeses of the Song of Songs, which describe "the passionate love affair of God and Israel" in *Israel's Love Affair with God: Song of Songs* (Valley Forge, PA: Trinity Press International, 1993).

28. Rabbi Nosson Scherman, trans. and commentary, *Siddur* (Brooklyn: Mesorah Publications, 1985), 341.

29. While Lonergan refers frequently to Romans 5:5 as the classical New Testament statement of the unrestricted love in which Christian subjects experience themselves, he means "love" from several perspectives. For a careful discussion of the several perspectives, see Tad Dunne, "Being in Love," *Method: Journal of Lonergan Studies* 13 (1995): 161–75.

30. Armstrong, *History of God*, 142.

31. Mohammed A. Abou Ridah, "Monotheism in Islam: Interpretations and Social Manifestations," in *The Concept of Monotheism in Islam and Christianity*, ed. Hans Köchler (Vienna: Wilhelm Braumüller, 1982), 46. See also Seyyed Hossein Nasr on the Sufi position that the divine is the object of love in "God," in *Islamic Spirituality: Foundations*, ed. Seyyed Hossein Nasr (New York: Crossroad, 1987), 321.

32. Bede Griffiths, *The Marriage of East and West* (Springfield, IL: Templegate Publishers, 1982), 16.

33. Seyyed Hossein Nasr, "God," in *Islamic Spirituality: Foundations*, 312.

34. *The Holy Qur-an*. English translation of the meanings and commentary, revised and edited by The Presidency of Islamic Researches, IFTA, n.d.

35. See Hermann Häring's helpful essay on the paradox of Christian faith and the misunderstandings which easily follow in "Christian Belief in the Threefold God," in *The Many Faces of the Divine*, ed. Hermann Häring and Johann Baptist Metz, *Concilium* 1995/2, 39–51.

36. Seyyed Hossein Nasr, "Comments on a Few Theological Issues in the Islamic-Christian Dialogue," in *Christian-Muslim Encounters*, ed. Yvonne Yazbeck Haddad and Wadi Zaidan Haddad (Gainesville: University of Florida Press, 1995), 458.

37. Klaus K. Klostermaier, *A Survey of Hinduism* (Albany: State University of New York Press, 1994), 138.

38. See John Brockington, *Hinduism and Christianity* (New York: St. Martin's Press, 1992), 3. Brockington also reminds his readers that on the popular level the supreme deity is named Isvara, who is both personal and an object of devotion (1).

39. Klaus K. Klostermaier explains the relationship between the one God and the many gods of Hinduism in *A Survey of Hinduism*: "Hindu theology has many ways of explaining the unity of Brahman in the diversity of ista-devatas: different psychological needs of people must be satisfied differently, local traditions and specific revelations must be accommodated, the ineffable can only be predicated in—quite literally—thousands of forms. Among the sahasranamas—the litanies of thousand names, which are recited in honour of the great gods—the overlap is considerable: each one would be named creator, preserver, destroyer of the universe, each one would be called Truth and Grace and Deliverance. Each one, in the end, is the same: One" (149–50).

40. Brockington, however, puts little stock in the divine triumvirate. He writes in *Hinduism and Christianity*: "Its only real purpose is to function as another mechanism for the acceptance of essentially competing sects worshipping different deities within the one umbrella of Hinduism" (21).

41. In Mircea Eliade, ed., *The Encyclopedia of Religion*, vol. 2, David Kinsley, s.v. avatara, notes that avatar denotes "'a descent' and suggests the idea of a god coming down from heaven to earth," 14.

42. Gavin Flood summarizes well what can be a confusing combination of avatars in *An Introduction to Hinduism* (Cambridge: Cambridge University Press, 1996), 150–51 and 184–85.

43. Sarma, *Primer of Hinduism*, 64.

44. Griffiths, *Marriage of East and West*, 82.

45. Alice Getty, *The Gods of Northern Buddhism: Their History and Iconography* (New York: Dover Publications, 1988; originally published 1914), esp. xxii and xxvi. Hinayana, the tradition of primitive Buddhism, has almost no use for the gods; Mahayana, a later tradition, is more comfortable with worship of deities. See also the introduction to Buddhism in Sarvepali Radhakrishnan and Charles Moore, eds., *A Sourcebook in Indian Philosophy* (Princeton, NJ: Princeton University Press, 1957), 272–73.

46. In "Kenotic God and Dynamic Sunyata," Masao Abe writes: "Thus, both Christianity and Buddhism talk about freedom, or liberation from sin, death, or karma. In Christianity, however, freedom is the gift of God and is based on the will of God. . . . On the other hand, liberation from karma in Buddhism is not based on any kind of will, divine or human. It is realized through the Great Death of human ego and is based on nothing whatsoever" (in John B. Cobb Jr. and Christopher Ives, eds., *The Emptying God: A Buddhist-Christian Conversation* [Maryknoll, NY: Orbis, 1991], 56).

47. I refer to Masao Abe's essay, noted above, for remarkable clarity on Buddhist conception of God, or lack thereof.

48. Bodhisattavas are humans who have achieved a state of enlightenment that would enable them to enter nirvana. However, in a spirit of generous compassion, they choose to assist others in their journey toward nirvana.

49. See, e.g., Denise Lardner Carmody and John Tully Carmody, *Serene Compassion: A Christian Appreciation of Buddhist Holiness* (New York: Oxford University Press, 1996). "Thus when the Buddhacarita says that Shakyamuni came to know no more alteration, it accords him full divinity. The earth sways in harmony with his

knowledge of his own Buddhahood because it has ventured into the presence of its Lord" (18). Indeed, the Carmodys suggest that the Buddha himself may be looked upon as representing for Buddhists an incarnation of divinity (28). Still, one must distinguish between enlightenment (what Christians might call the holiness achieved finally in heavenly communion with God), which is open to any human, and divinity, which transcends every creature.

50. Donald W. Mitchell, *Spirituality and Emptiness: The Dynamics of Spiritual Life in Buddhism and Christianity* (New York: Paulist, 1991), 28–30 et passim. Compare this view of the Trinity as self-emptying love with that of Hans Urs von Balthasar, as described in the section "God is Triunely Personal: The Analogy of the Cross," found in chapter 6.

51. Tilmann Vetter, "Atheistic and Theistic Tendencies in Buddhism," trans. Henry Jansen, *Studies in Interreligious Dialogue* 6 (1996): 84.

52. John Swindells, ed. *A Human Search: Bede Griffiths Reflects on His Life: An Oral History* (Ligouri, MO: Triumph, 1997), 109.

53. Swindells, *A Human Search*, 110–11.

54. Lonergan, *Method in Theology*, 112.

55. Lonergan, *Method in Theology*, 112.

56. Lonergan, *Method in Theology*, 112.

57. Frederick E. Crowe, S.J., develops this theme in the spirit of Bernard Lonergan in "Son of God, Holy Spirit, and World Religions," in *Appropriating the Lonergan Idea*, ed. Michael Vertin (Washington, DC: Catholic University of America Press, 1989).

58. Francis X. Clooney, *Theology after Vedanta*, 195.

59. See Donald W. Mitchell and James A. Wiseman, O.S.B., eds., *The Gethsemani Encounter: A Dialogue on the Spiritual Life by Buddhist and Christian Monastics* (New York: Continuum, 1997), xv.

60. Thomas Merton, *The Asian Journal* (New York: New Directions, 1973), 308.

10

Jesus: God Incarnate and Savior

If the reader accepts the position proposed in chapter 9 that the Holy Spirit is at work in the adherents of the five world religions under consideration, touching hearts and bringing their devotees into some genuine communication with the divine, and that, as a result, the great religious traditions include important instances of commitment to the truth and the goodness of the transcendent, of the human world, and of nature, then a Christian might readily ask how to understand Jesus as the savior of the world, as Christians commonly profess. Indeed, there are those Christians who claim, in this era of increasing religious dialogue, that Jesus is not the supreme and once-for-all-time effective incarnate Word of God, at least not in any way presently expressible.[1] A major challenge, as expressed by John Hick, is

> new knowledge of the human religious world and of our continuity with that. This raises questions about the theological core of Christianity that emerged out of the ecclesiastical debates and council decisions of the first five centuries: namely, that Jesus of Nazareth was God the Son living a human life. For from this there follows the world-centrality of Christianity as the only religion founded by God in person. It is here that the strain is now being felt. For Christianity's implicit or explicit claim to an unique superiority, as the central focus of God's saving activity on earth, has come to seem increasingly implausible within the new global consciousness of our time.[2]

Not surprisingly, the strongly pluralist direction which some Christian authors are taking in response to the challenge Hick articulates leads others (1) to restate Christian exclusivity, namely, that Jesus is God's final and definitive revelation which must be preached and accepted; or (2) to posit an approach that is inclusive of the other world religions while yet remaining firmly committed to the unique person and role of Jesus.[3] There is much to debate in the ways that various religions and Christian churches and authors stake their claims.[4] In fact, an entire literature has emerged which carries the conversation along.

My concern in this final chapter is to touch down into the conversation about the person and role of Jesus. I ask why Christians claim that Jesus is the savior of all humankind. I also ask what the implications of the person and role of Jesus are for non-Christian religions and how faith in Jesus impacts upon the way in which Christian believers participate in interreligious dialogue. Because the God of Christian faith is triune, it will not do to address the issue of Jesus apart from who Jesus is as the second Person in the Trinity who has become human.[5]

JESUS, GOD INCARNATE

To believe that Jesus is the world's savior is intimately connected with the conviction that somehow Jesus is God incarnate. Belief that Jesus is one of the three in God, namely, the Logos/Word, and that this same one is human as the rest of human beings are, with the one exception that he is without sin, is central to the Christian tradition of faith. What this means, insofar as present understanding has progressed, is the first issue to which I address myself.

The place to begin is the New Testament. The New Testament is the product of those who knew Jesus personally when he lived his historical life in the first half of the first century of the Common Era, or, if the authors of the oral or written tradition that has found its way into the New Testament did not know Jesus personally themselves, they express the faith in Jesus of quite early disciples. Whatever the variations in the stories recounted in the Gospels, the position maintained here is that the stories are fundamentally complementary and faithful enough to the facts that some things can be asserted without doubt about Jesus.[6]

Jesus' Humanity

First, Jesus came across to all he met as quite human. He is known to have mixed comfortably in social settings and to have enjoyed the company of a variety of people, with some of whom he became a close friend. He could be compassionate and helpful, but he could also be uncompromisingly challenging. He functioned for a time as an itinerant preacher; indeed, it was his message, along with some dramatic healings, which attracted his first followers. Finally, we may draw attention to the religious faith of Jesus as an observant Jew and his devout relationship to Yahweh. In short, no one doubted Jesus' humanity or his religious devotion.

The New Testament is also clear in its language about the ways in which Jesus is religiously set apart in his extraordinary role vis-à-vis Yahweh. Often enough he is said to refer to himself obliquely as son of man, which can simply refer to his lot as a human being, but the phrase is also used as a title with apocalyptic overtones reminiscent, for example, of the Book of Daniel, chapter 7, where one like a son of man is foreseen to come on the clouds of heaven at the end time.

A good indication of early believers' growing conviction about the distinctive role of Jesus is the use of titles in the Acts of the Apostles. The one crucified by the political and religious leaders with the support of a variety of ordinary folks is called by followers of the new way of faith, "Lord and Messiah" (Acts 2:36), "Holy and Righteous One" (Acts 3:14), "Author of life" (Acts 3:15), "prophet" (Acts 3:23), "Leader and Savior" (Acts 5:31). These titles recognize Jesus' extraordinary role in close relationship with Yahweh.

Jesus' Divinity

Among the above titles applied in the New Testament to Jesus, two begin, at least, to lead beyond an extraordinary, but nevertheless human, role. They refer to the divinity of their bearer: "Lord," which is the name Jews used to refer to Yahweh, whose revealed name they dared not speak; and "Author of life," since no one else is the author of life but God. John's Gospel is especially strong in its naming of Jesus as God in the prologue (Jn 1:1) and in the confession of Thomas, "My Lord and my God" (Jn 20:28).[7]

Besides titles, there are further indications in the New Testament that his early followers discerned something divine in Jesus. In the Gospels, when Jesus forgives sins, all recognize that only God can forgive sins (Mk 2:7). When he commands a lake storm to subside, his disciples are moved to ask: "Who then is this, that even the wind and the sea obey him?" (Mk 4:41). The implication is significant.

Jesus' unique relationship with the Father in John's Gospel also merits mention. Thus, in love God gives his only Son (Jn 3:16). Jesus asserts that "before Abraham was, I am" (Jn 8:58). He claims that he and the Father are one (Jn 10:30). Nor are the several places in which Jesus and the Spirit are named closely along with the Father to be ignored (Jn 14:16–17, 26; 15:26; 16:7–11, 13–15). There is no mistaking the Johannine community's high Christology.

The Letter to the Hebrews also uses high language of Jesus and seems to be explicit in naming Jesus God (Heb 1:8). The cumulative effect of these and other New Testament references is to point in the direction of a divine character combining with the human character of Jesus.

Divine-Human Savior

Chapters 4 and 5 of this study have already attended to the struggle of the early church as it proceeded toward affirmation of its belief in the triune God. Intimately a part of this struggle is the person of Jesus and the church's effort to maintain its belief both in his humanity and in his divinity. In fact, at the heart of the struggle toward trinitarian faith and toward faith in Jesus as both divine and human is the work of salvation or redemption or atonement, which his followers believed was the purpose of Jesus' entry into human history. For the conviction was—and it continues to hold among many, perhaps most, Christians today—that Jesus is savior and that he is so precisely because he is at once human and divine. Here I reprise briefly the struggle of the early church.

The Arian controversy began as a cosmological concern but then became a soteriological concern, that is, a concern about Jesus as savior. Arius claimed that Jesus could not possibly be divine in the way that Yahweh, or as Christians now named him, the Father, is divine. There was no question that the Logos/Word of God preexisted all the rest of creation, including every human being and that it was this preexistent Logos who became human in Jesus of Nazareth. But, for Arius, and a host of followers for centuries thereafter, the Logos could not possibly be divine. It had to be a creature of God. Otherwise, there would be an offense to the conviction that there can be only one God and that this God unequivocally surpasses the created universe. So, Arianism claimed, although the Logos was with God to mediate the world's creation, there was an earlier "time" when the Logos was not.

The problem with his theological reflection for Arius's combatants was that if the Word become human was not divine in every sense that the term, divine, is to be taken, then the Word could not be savior. For precisely what human beings need to be saved from is their sins, and sin, in its precise meaning, is a rejection of the sovereignty and norms of God. No one other than God could release human beings from the bondage of their sinfulness. If Jesus, the incarnate Word, was but a creature of God, albeit a highly superior one, he could not save humankind from its sin, no matter to what extent he cooperated with God.

Christians were sure that it is precisely from its sin that Jesus has freed humankind. They knew that Jesus had to be God to do that. At the same time, Christians of the early centuries believed that God was one, and they had no difficulty naming this God Yahweh, whom Jesus addressed as Father, and whom he instructed his followers to address as Father. They also knew that Jesus the savior was somehow God. The problem became one of maintaining the oneness of God while yet recognizing distinction between the Father and Jesus the savior. A sizeable group of bishops gathered at the behest of Emperor Constantine at his summer home in Nicea in June of the year 325

C.E. to resolve the problem. After some struggle, they agreed upon the term *homoousios* to designate the identity of the divinity of the Father and his Word/Son, who became human in Jesus of Nazareth.

A problematic word then and now, *homoousios* designates that the Son is God as the Father is God. What makes them distinct is that the Father is not the Son. Eventually, with the help of the Cappadocian theologians later in the fourth century, the distinction of the Father and the Son, and also the Holy Spirit, who by this time had come into greater focus as well, was determined to be on the basis of their relations of origin. Moreover, a commonly accepted terminology was worked out, so that while the three in God were said to be identical in their *ousia* (which the Latins, since Tertullian, named *substantia*; the contemporary English translation of the Nicene-Constantinopolitan Creed adopts the term *being*), they were said to be each a distinct *hypostasis* (an equally problematic term, for which the Latins had already been using the term *persona* and which is commonly translated into English as *person*).

No less important to fourth- and fifth-century theological development was the human stature of Jesus. On the one hand, only God can save humanity from its sinfulness, and thus, if Jesus is truly Savior, he must truly be God. On the other hand, divine wisdom has chosen to save humanity through the very historical suffering and death of the same Jesus. This led Christian believers to the conviction that the Savior had to be human in every way that all other women and men are human, with the one exception noted in Hebrews 4:15, namely, that Jesus was without sin. The significance of the full humanity of Jesus has been famously expressed by Gregory Nazianzen: "For [whatever human characteristics] he has not assumed he has not healed."[8]

Granted, then, that Jesus is somehow human and somehow divine, how can these two infinitely different modes of being be understood to coexist with one another in the same reality? Is there any acceptable human way of stating this belief? After puzzling for more than five decades, with not a little rancor exhibited among many sincerely seeking to say something that might lend clarity, the Council of Chalcedon, in the year 451 C.E., came up with several propositions that represent as close to a social (in this case, ecclesial) conviction as one is likely to get.

The gist of Christian tradition on the identity of Jesus since Chalcedon's statement is that the Word/Son of God who is the second person of the Trinity took on humanity shortly before the beginning of what is today often named the Common Era. This divine person, while remaining entirely the same divine person as from all eternity, became the human being Jesus of Nazareth. Thus, the divine person who is the second person of the Trinity, from that moment on possessed both a fully divine way of being, a divine nature, and a fully human way of being, a human nature. Each nature exists distinct in itself and distinct from the other; they do not become mixed up and are not to be confused with one another. But the substratum of both natures is the divine person who is the second person of the Trinity.

Metaphysics of Jesus

Because the terminology of Chalcedon, *person* and *nature*, can easily lead to misunderstanding, further clarification is needed. This was provided in the metaphysically informed theology of Thomas Aquinas.[9] Basically, this theology is an effort to think things through more systematically. Aquinas's reflection on the identity of the Word incarnate begins with what makes a thing to be a thing. Everything that exists as a distinct being is what can be named an actual existent.[10] The actuality by which it exists is a fundamental principle of each thing's reality. This is how the divine person functions in the Word incarnate. It is the existent actuality without which Jesus would be neither divine nor human. Besides actual existence, everything that exists has to be informed by a particular way of being; it has to have a form. If actual existents were uninformed, then there would be no distinction among birds and bees and flowers and trees, not only generically but also specifically. So, with Christ Jesus. The one divine actual existent is divine by his divine form or nature and human by his human form or nature.

Since normally actuality brings into existence only one form, it is reasonable to ask how the originally divine person can assume a human form without losing the divine form. Here we must plead that God who is the supreme actual existent, the creator of every other actual existent, has the power to assume a lesser form alongside his greater one. Not only that, but it makes eminent sense for God to do this if it brings an even fuller meaning to the universe God created than was present before the Word became flesh. In so creating a divine incarnation, God, of course, undergoes no change within the divine reality, including the person of the Word, for God cannot change. God already is infinite actuality. Change takes place in the limited order of created reality, the universe of changing being. What changes is that in Christ Jesus there is a new human reality whose ground, whose existent actuality, is the unchanging divine Word.

Psychology of Jesus

All who read the New Testament in faith and participate in Christian life and spirituality are confident that God is personal. Jesus, who is God incarnate, is a someone who relates to other someones by interpersonal relations. Thus, metaphysical clarity is not sufficient. The clarity of psychology is important too. We need to speak in psychological terms of the person and natures that make up the divine Word who is Jesus of Nazareth. This can be accomplished relatively easily by transposing the terminology of person and natures that has been expressed in the metaphysical terms of the principles of existent actuality and form. In Christ Jesus there is one conscious subject, the divine person of the Word, who is conscious in two distinct, unmixed and unconfused, subjectivities, one divine, the other human. In an essay on the question, Bernard Lonergan writes that "the person of Christ is an identity that eternally is subject of divine consciousness and in time became subject of a human consciousness."[11]

Through a divine subjectivity the divine Word knows itself as subject and knows all that is; through a human subjectivity the divine Word experiences himself as subject and experiences the data that come through his five senses and through his inner psychological state. Since a divine subjectivity does not move from experience to understanding to judgment to decision, but simply knows and understands all that exists or could exist and loves it insofar as it is good, all this in one infinite, eternal act, the Word through the divine subjectivity is simply God in the second person.

Since a human subjectivity moves from experience to understanding to judgment to decision, the divine Word—through the first-century, Palestinian, Jewish, male subjectivity which it assumed—only gradually came to know his world and who he was and what he was about and to make appropriate decisions. The self or subject he experienced is divine, since there is no other self for him to have experienced; his existent actuality is the divine. On the other hand, recalling that experience is one thing and knowledge another, by his human consciousness alone Jesus could not know himself to be God.

By the supernatural gift of the grace of union, Jesus may well have gradually come to know himself to be God, to be a human being without sin, and to be on a mission to save the world from its sinfulness.[12] If Jesus did not in some sense know these things about himself and his mission, how could he intelligently, reasonably, and responsibly mediate God's saving work? Jesus' knowledge is something very remotely akin to the sense of being drawn into the realm of the transcendent that we ordinary mortals experience. But what is so very incipient in us was advanced in Jesus. Nevertheless, how to express or transpose his self-knowledge in human words and gestures in his time and place demanded of Jesus a lifelong process of prayer, thought, decision, and action.

Other Religions and the Incarnation

Let me bring this section to a close by asking how the Christian belief that Jesus is at once God and human sits with adherents of the other four religions. For Jews and Muslims alike, Christian belief is a scandal. The reason is that just as the Trinity is taken to be an intolerable tritheistic distortion of monotheism, so the doctrine of the incarnation is a heinous reduction of the blinding transcendence of God. For Hindus, on the other hand, for whom Brahman, the divine in its transcendent being, becomes accessible to human beings in a multiplicity of anthropomorphic avatars, incarnation is readily comprehensible; the difficulty would rather be the Christian conviction that there is only one divine incarnation in all of human history.

For Buddhists, the situation is somewhat more complicated. While some Buddhists respect the values espoused by Jesus and recognize in him a somewhat kindred spirit on the way to nirvana, others estimate that the supposedly divine Jesus seems to be a puny figure in comparison with the great Buddha, who after all never claimed to be more than human.[13] These Buddhists observe Jesus rejected, tortured, and humiliated, without any of the dignity that shines forth in the Buddha, who sits serenely unmoved by the vagaries of life, totally gathered up into enlightenment. Obviously, then, the dialogue about Jesus, the divine-human being who is savior, must be conducted variously with those whose religious faith is formed by the other religious traditions.

JESUS, SAVIOR

Mention has been made several times of the Christian conviction that God became human in Christ Jesus in order to save humankind from its sinfulness. It has also been noted that human evil is sin insofar as it is a rejection of the order or intelligibility or law that God communicates to the human race either in the act of creation or by special revelation. Now we must seek to understand more precisely just what there is about sin that only God is sufficient to offer the needed salvation.

The second chapter of this book claims that human beings function at their best when they pursue truth and goodness wherever it is to be found. Here it can be added that the pursuit is not simply an enterprise for human beings as individuals. A wise and loving society is desirable, one in which the needs of all are met, one in which all can develop according to their full potential.

Sin

Bernard Lonergan suggests that we conceive human beings to be incarnate spirits motivated by four fundamental desires: for God, goodness, happiness, and immortality.[14] Even if one does not accept that the four desires are at the heart of every human being, it is likely that anyone who has some vision of society as a community of individuals banded together for the sake of truth and goodness is likely to agree that phenomenological observation shows something to be out of order, both communally and individually. We do not have to be Christian to agree with St. Paul that we human beings too often do what we know we shouldn't and fail to do what we know we should (Rom 7:19). One need not be a Buddhist to agree that suffering is all too often caused by greed, ignorance, and hatred. No need to be a Jew to recognize that following the Decalogue leads to order in one's personal life and in society, and that failure to live by the Decalogue is to take the path toward chaos.

What every human being can observe is that ways destructive of the human spirit and society, rather than constructive ways, are commonly chosen. What is worse, we human beings seem caught in a cycle of destruction from which we are unable to free ourselves. Lonergan describes the sad human state as an "incapacity for sustained development."[15] Christian theology refers to original sin, which is understood as the inherited incapacity endemic in all human beings individually and in all societies. Eventually, each one chooses the destructiveness that is evil by personal choice (actual sin), but the incapacity precedes anyone's actual choices. It is a weight borne by humanity.

Using the word *sin* to describe the incapacity renders a further dimension of the reality. It is a claim that the all-too-frequent human movement away from the true and the good and from wisdom and love is so serious as to be a rejection by the creature made in God's image and likeness of the God who creates human beings. This is so whether the referent is the incapacity with which human beings seem to be born or the actual, specific choice of evil. As such, the incapacity is indicative of alienation from God; the evil choices are actual affronts to God. It is the conviction of Christians that the chasm which sin has opened between humanity as a collectivity (a "concrete universal," to use Lonergan's term) and God is so wide and deep that human beings are powerless to close the gap or bridge it. Only God, the omnipotent creator, can liberate humanity from its sinfulness.

The Divine Trinity and Evil

Since God is infinitely wise, good, and loving, we human beings can be confident that such liberation is available. From the Christian perspective we are convinced that the liberation has fundamentally occurred. Even more, beyond liberation from sin, human individuals and the societies which they form are invited to share communion with the divine Three, incipiently in this life and, beyond anything we can possibly imagine, in the life of resurrection with Christ Jesus after death and in the end time of cosmic glorification.

When we ask how God saves or liberates humankind from its sinfulness, our first answer must be that it happens in the same way that the triune God does anything outside its own mutual self-communication. When God creates, it is the one God creating, with the Father acting as the one from whom the Word confers the ordered reality of created being, while the Holy Spirit confers the love of the triune God for God's creatures. So when the triune God redeems the human creation, which has to some extent (that is to say, finitely) chosen disorder rather than intelligibility and love, it is the Father acting as the one from whom and within whom the Word restores order (or intelligibility) in the empowering Holy Spirit.

It is Christian revelation that in saving humanity God acts within human history through the Word incarnate, thus appearing as a historically existing human being, while the Holy Spirit is also active but without the kind of visibility that characterizes the Word. Why did God choose to become visibly present in the midst of humanity in the incarnation of the Word? Thomas Aquinas addresses this question in his *Summa theologiae*.[16] He asks whether the human suffering of Christ somehow brings about the salvation of humankind from its sinfulness. His answer is, as we expect, that it does. He develops his answer by distinguishing carefully between two ways in which causes bring about their effects. Some causes are "principal"; others are "instrumental." The former are primary, the latter secondary.[17]

The entire Godhead, the Trinity, acting specifically through the proper role of each of the three persons, is the principal and primary cause of liberation from sin, for only God has the capability to effect liberation. The Word acts in this causality according to its proper way of being God, namely, as the affirmation of the love of God who is in love. The Spirit acts as the love of the Lover that is affirmed by the Word.[18] In the case of redemption, the Word affirms that God's saving love for humanity effectively restores the order of the universe and, indeed, enhances it by raising it to a higher, supernatural level in which it actually shares in the life and truth and love of the divine community. Simultaneously (to use a very time-laden term for an eternal act), the Spirit communicates the divine saving love to the spirits of people of every time and place who are receptive. The Father's will to save, the Word's affirmation, and the Spirit's love, by their absolute, divine effectiveness create a redeemed universe.

The Human Jesus Redeems

From the causality of the Word as divine we move to the divine Word as human. For mediating the divine, principal, and primary causality in the work of redeeming humanity is the instrumental, secondary causality of the Word become human.

If, by faith, we accept as fact that the second person of the Trinity has entered into the human condition in Jesus of Nazareth, then implicitly we accept that God has chosen to deal personally and intimately with the human world (and as well the wider sensitive, biological, and physical-chemical universe of which humanity is the pinnacle) on the level of humanity, namely, by means of human instrumentality. The witness of the New Testament and the long Christian tradition is abundant that Christ in his humanity, that is, in his ministry and dying and rising, has liberated humanity from sinfulness. This belief has never been taken for granted but has always been explicitly affirmed from the beginning and throughout the tradition.

The New Testament and the Christian tradition are also unequivocal in the conviction that it is God who reconciles humanity to divine friendship by means of the humanity of Christ and the empowerment of the Holy Spirit. It is this twofold divine-human causality that Aquinas seeks to sort out with his distinction between principal and instrumental causes. Lonergan offers a clarification of why God adopts this twofold causality in effecting the liberation of humanity. He theorizes that God the creator of the universe always exercises his principal or transcendent causality in the ordinary development of the universe by letting limited, created things interact with one another according to their own powers. After all, that seems to be the point of creating the universe: to allow other beings the opportunity to participate in Being. These limited causes are always secondary, since God remains the primary and principal cause creating, sustaining, and ordering the world. Thus, the limited, created causes are also instrumental of the principal divine cause. When it comes to the problem of evil introduced into the world by sin, God is simply allowing human beings, who are secondary, free causes, to exercise the freedom with which they have been endowed. To be free is fundamentally a good thing. Similarly, when God acts to redeem humans from the sins which they stupidly and selfishly commit by abusing the good of freedom, once more God acts through secondary, instrumental causes, chiefly the incarnate Word.[19]

A most difficult question remains. Why would God choose the gruesome event of execution by crucifixion to be the centerpiece of Christ's saving work? How do the malevolence of his accusers, the treachery of his betrayer, the complicity of his executioners, the fickleness of his followers, the derision of the passers-by, the enormous humiliation of the entire event relate usefully to the mediation of divine reconciliation? Can the torture and agony of a derided, humiliated victim mediate the loving, redemptive power of God? Over the centuries Christians have puzzled over these questions and have come up with various answers. Two answers that have enjoyed great currency have to do with punishment for sin and restoration of divine honor.[20]

The Manner of Redemption

The argument of the punishment theory is that the sinful destructiveness of humanity is deserving of eternal separation from God, which is the ultimate punishment. This is the meaning of hell. But if the sinless Son of God should take on, in a dramatic instance, the punishment of sin which is the vast destructiveness that has resulted in human society, that extraordinary act would be sufficient to overcome the sinfulness of all humanity, and reconciliation between God and humankind would be effected.

The argument of the restoration theory is that God's honor is profoundly offended by a recalcitrant, ungrateful humanity that gives itself over to sinfulness. If this otherwise hopeless situation is to be reversed, God's honor must be duly restored. No human being caught in enslavement to sin is capable of bringing about divine justice. Jesus the Christ is capable because he is at once the all-powerful God and a human being free of enslavement to sin. Jesus' suffering on behalf of sinful humanity restores justice by giving due honor to God through his obedient acceptance of the event of the cross.

Many Christians are no longer comfortable with either theory of redemption. The New Testament is not about punishment or the restoration of justice. It is about generous forgiveness that does not count the cost. Jesus tells his followers to love their enemies, turn the other cheek, pattern their lives after that of their heavenly Father who bestows the sun and the rainfall equally upon the just and the unjust (Mt 5:38–39, 44–48; 6:14–15). Jesus counsels Peter to forgive without keeping count (Mt 18:22), and the parables of forgiveness in Luke 15 have nothing to do with justice or punishment.

There is another time-honored theory, however, that can be rehabilitated to bring about some understanding of redemption in terms of forgiveness. It builds upon the doctrine that the cross is Jesus' victory over the enslaving forces of sin, with all its bitter results. The most tangible of the results of sin, although not the most serious, is the certainty of death, which phenomenologically is the end of every human being's short and uneven life, a life in which suffering abounds for many and often the least guilty are the greatest victims. Indeed, it is noteworthy that death is first reported in the Bible not as a natural phenomenon, but as the hateful act of Cain's murder of his brother, Abel; thus, as a result of sin (Gen 4:8). Thus, Jesus' humiliating and painful death is a graphic acceptance of all that is most terrible in life. Instead of being overcome by the worst that life entails, however, Jesus overcomes an unjust and hideous death together with its sinful source and continues on to a life beyond pain and injustice, as well as the limitations of space and time, a life of *human* communion with the divine Three, a life which is named resurrection.

Bernard Lonergan articulates this theory. He calls it the law of the cross because, in the manner of scientific laws that illuminate the intelligible relations among quite diverse data, the theory brings together so many of the diverse symbolic ways in which the New Testament expresses the faith of the early church in the saving life, death, and resurrection of Jesus.[21] On the cross one human being, Jesus, took unto himself evil in one of its most heinous and complex forms. He accepted torture and death willingly because he knew that to do so was of God and was accomplishing God's saving work, even if in his human mind he was not sure just how. This is the meaning of his prayer in the Garden of Gethsemane and of Matthew's quotation of Psalm 22 ("My God, my God, why have you forsaken me?"[Mt 27:46]). Throughout the events of his passion Jesus was never overcome in the slightest by bitterness, hatred, resentment, or a longing for revenge toward his accusers, execution-ers, or fickle disciples. His thoughts were of forgiveness (Lk 23:34). It can be said that he continued to put his trust in God, even as he did not know just how he would manage the suffering. He continued to love God and love his enemies.

In these attitudes of his suffering and dying, Jesus in his sinless humanity, which was grounded in the divine person of the Word, was taking all evil to himself. More by far than every other human being whose situation is to live in the midst of sinfulness and to be afflicted by it themselves, Jesus' sinless closeness to God made him quite clear, in his human mind, about the horror of sin. As a result, he felt keenly the sinful dimensions of the malevolence of his accusers and executioners, the complicity of the soldiers who were just doing their duty, the cowardice of the disciples, the sorrow of his mother, Mary, and the others standing faithfully by the cross (the sorrow of Mary and the other bystanders was, of course, not sin, but pain caused by the sinful deeds of others). By taking this evil to himself Jesus broke it down, dispersed it, and transformed it into a greater goodness which is his love, that is, the love of God the Word in his human nature. What seemed to be more pow-erful (conspiracy, betrayal, false accusation, ridicule, violence, execution) turns out to be literally nothing compared to the power of divine love medi-ated in the humanity of Jesus.[22]

What Jesus accomplishes as the Word of God become human is to estab-lish a reversal of the spiraling disorder sin introduced into the human world and to bring about a restoration of the order of creation. But Jesus' accom-plishment goes beyond a restoration of order. In addition, it mediates a new opportunity for all human beings everywhere to enjoy more than the good-ness of creation. The new opportunity is to enter into friendship with the di-vine community, incipiently in the present temporal life and after death in the eternal life of heaven. Both moments of the new opportunity, named in the New Testament "the kingdom of God," are a share in the resurrection of Jesus. They are effected through the mediation of the humanity of the Word as the Holy Spirit communicates to human persons the power of love and life which Jesus brought to bear upon the human world in his historical passage from life through death to resurrection.

Finally, we might ask whether the world should not be quite different from the way it actually is if human sinfulness has been overcome. One might ex-pect so. Alas, not much seems to have changed because of the efforts of Je-sus. But if we return to Aquinas's theory that God acts in the created universe by means of the secondary causes which he created, allowing them full exercise of their causality, then the process by which the world and its human participants appropriate the saving work of Christ is likely to be a very long haul. Human beings must be persuaded freely to appropriate the salvation effected in Christ. God does not force himself upon anyone. On the other hand, with its history of violence toward perceived enemies (in the Crusades, the Inquisition, pogroms of Jewish communities, Protestant-Catholic mutual destruction in the Thirty Years' War, and so on), the history of Christianity is a stunning witness to the failure of the Christian church to make its own the meaning of Christ's cross.

THE UNIVERSALITY OF JESUS' SAVING WORK

With infinite wisdom and love God creates the human world with an intelligible order. Sin is a major, although finite, distortion of that order. With infinite wisdom and love, but by means of finite human mediation, the incarnate Word (by his own instrumental causality) and the Holy Spirit (by enabling the instrumental causality of countless human persons) restore and immeasurably enhance world order. Each of these activities is on a basic or fundamental level, which is to say that it enables in a general way what happens in each historical instance of action and reception. In this sense, creation, sin, and redemption have a universal effectiveness. The effectiveness is universal because no creature remains unaffected. In the case of creation and redemption, universal effectiveness is more easily understood because the divine Trinity is the principal historical agent. In the case of sin, which is not a divine activity—although it is permitted by God insofar as God wills the good of freedom and thus permits its abuse even as God directs freedom to the good—the reason why every human being is affected, and through humanity every creature, is not clear. Phenomenologically, there can be little, if any, doubt. But philosophical or theological reasons are not readily forthcoming.

In all three cases, namely, of creation, of sin, and of redemption, human beings are major players, for human beings are incarnate spirits. It is in the realm of spirit that active intelligence seeks and gains progressively greater understanding and knowledge of the universe and of its creator, and thus gains some control over secondary causes that are its equal or less. Human beings can act within and upon creation intelligently, reasonably, and responsibly, or otherwise. When deliberate irresponsibility is at work, original sin becomes actuated by human individuals and societies.

Human beings can also act out of religious conversion, out of the state of being in love in an unrestricted way, and then they are allowing themselves to be influenced by the redemptive act of Christ and the Spirit. The participation of religiously converted persons in the redemptive activity of God may be witting or unwitting. Indeed, does any human being or group of human beings, including the Christian church, actually grasp redemptive effectiveness except from partial, very partial, perspectives? Redemption is immanent in historical process. Since God acts in the created universe by means of secondary, instrumental causes, the fundamental effectiveness of redemption is achieved gradually within the developing process of world historical order.[23]

The full flowering of the redemption of humankind must await some future time. As much as all other individuals, Christians have only partially made their own the redemptive work God has accomplished in Christ and the Spirit. The same is true of the church, or the Christian religion in general. They, too, have only partially appropriated what God is working within redeemed creation. This accounts for Christianity's stunning failure to live out the law of the cross. Can we even go so far as to say that Christianity has gone no farther than the other religions to incarnate historically what God wills and is doing for the good order of the world? An examination of Christian history can lead to just such a conclusion and to the further conclusion that in some areas Christianity lags behind other religions.

DOES JESUS' ROLE DIMINISH OTHER RELIGIONS AND THEIR ADHERENTS?

The Second Vatican Council affirms the importance for world historical order of the world's religions other than Christianity, and even of people of no religion who nevertheless genuinely seek truth and goodness.[24] On the other hand, Christians do not doubt that the world has been redeemed once and for all in the living, dying, and rising of Jesus, the incarnate Word. How are we to correlate these two seemingly divergent positions?

Open-minded study of Hinduism and Buddhism, Judaism and Islam by Christians reveals that these religions have discovered dimensions of the transcendent in the areas of theology of God, ethics, formation of society, and physical nature that we must judge to be true and good. Christian acknowledgment of such achievements is nearly as old as Christianity. For second-century Christian thinkers such as Justin Martyr and Irenaeus of Lyons, such achievements were considered to be a *preparatio evangelica*, a preparation for the full revelation of the Gospel.

That is one way to interpret what is true and good outside the Christian religion. Another way is to value other religions as participants along with Christianity in the historical process of divine revelation, all in the direction of the full coming of God's kingdom. In this way each of the religious traditions can be appreciated for its distinctive contribution. Thus it can be affirmed that in some instances God's saving wisdom and love are discovered without historical reference to Christ, although, as stated above, such instances nevertheless participate in the absolutely universal effectiveness of Christ's saving death and resurrection. Perhaps this is a cosmic view somewhat akin to the teleological theology of Teilhard de Chardin. How everything will come together in the future no human being is able to predict.

I do not think that it is helpful to name people of other religious faiths "anonymous Christians" whose doctrine or worship or ethics or community life are favorably comparable to the Christian view of the whole. It would certainly be an important part of interreligious dialogue to alert these others to similarities between themselves and Christians. But to label them anonymously Christian seems to belittle their own religious experience and convictions and to lose sight of the reality that to be Christian is to commit oneself to Christ Jesus quite explicitly.

CAN CHRISTIANS PARTICIPATE HONESTLY IN INTERRELIGIOUS DIALOGUE?

It is Christian faith that Jesus Christ, the divine Person, has mediated through his historical and resurrected humanity the divine restoration and enhancement of the created order of the world of which humans are a part. This is a definitive achievement because it has been enacted by God and because it has changed once and for all the actual world order. As the world order laden with the burden of sin is real, so the world order liberated by God's gracious action is real. Thus, there are not several "real" world orders dependent upon or according to the multiple perspectives of different religious traditions. Jesus, and Jesus alone, is the savior of the world. The world extends to every human person who has ever lived, who lives now, and who will live. So, too, does redemption.

It is not faithful to divine revelation, however, to forget, as has so often happened in the Christian tradition in the past, that it is God who saves the world through the mediation of the humanity of Christ. God includes the Father from whom all that God is and does takes its start and God includes the Holy Spirit who proceeds from the Father through the Son. The Father directs all the work of the divine Trinity in the universe. The Holy Spirit unobtrusively works divine love within human spirits individually and socially, bringing Christ's work to bear within world order as it historically unfolds. The Holy Spirit is not at work only within persons baptized into Christ Jesus, but within persons of all religious persuasions and none.

In an infinitely profound way the action of the transcendent God cannot be narrowed to the confines of the finite human mind.[25] It makes sense that through the power of the Holy Spirit Jesus' redemptive life, death, and resurrection is effective beyond the knowledge and understanding of every human being.[26] Of all people, Christians should be cognizant, for we have been jolted into recognition often enough in our history, of how limited is our individual and social (including ecclesial!) appropriation of the saving work of God.

Christians as much as anyone can learn from genuine interreligious dialogue of God's truth and love as it is present and handed on in other religious traditions. What is needed on our part, as on the part of all, is to be open to love and truth. We can count on God's revelation to surprise us.

NOTES

1. Two contemporary authors who are frequently singled out for their espousal of this view are John Hick and Paul Knitter. Both have written extensively. For present purposes one book of each might be singled out: John Hick, *The Metaphor of God Incarnate: Christology in a Pluralistic Age* (Louisville, KY: Westminster John Knox, 1993); Paul Knitter, *No Other Name? A Critical Survey of Christian Attitudes toward the World Religions* (Maryknoll, NY: Orbis, 1985). For an assessment of the shortcomings of this approach, see Gregory H. Carruthers, S.J., *The Uniqueness of Jesus Christ in the Theocentric Model of the Christian Theology of World Religions: An Elaboration and Evaluation of the Position of John Hick* (Lanham, MD: University Press of America, 1990).

2. Hick, *Metaphor of God Incarnate*, 7.

3. A blunt but cogently articulate proponent of an exclusive claim, but with a nod to inclusivity, is Carl Braaten in *No Other Gospel! Christianity among the World's Religions* (Minneapolis: Fortress, 1992). Jacques Dupuis takes the approach that Jesus' salvific role is constitutive and relational. By constitutive he means that Jesus is "the privileged channel through which God has chosen to share the divine life with human beings." By relational he means that a "reciprocal relationship . . . exists between the path that is in Jesus Christ and the various paths to salvation proposed by the religious traditions to their members." See Jacques Dupuis, S.J., *Toward a Christian Theology of Religious Pluralism* (Maryknoll, NY: Orbis, 1999), 305. Gavin D'Costa, *The Meeting of Religions and the Trinity* (Maryknoll, NY: Orbis, 2000), offers yet another approach by which a Christian might enter into interreligious dialogue and prayer, namely, expecting that Christian faith itself may well be enriched by learning of and from the other, although just what the enrichment may be cannot be determined a priori. Although appreciating that to enter into dialogue is to take a risk of infidelity (including idolatry) if a misstep is taken, the Christian church, nevertheless, can and must engage the other religions on the strictly theological grounds that the triune God is communicating itself in them too. See especially part II of *The Meeting.* D'Costa's arguments and mine overlap in their appreciation of the importance of trinitarian theology and the absolute salvific role of Jesus.

4. In *The Diversity of Religions: A Christian Perspective*, J. A. Dinoia, O.P., recommends a rethinking of Christian theology of religions which is neither simply exclusivist nor inclusivist nor pluralist (Washington: Catholic University of America Press, 1992). From Dinoia's perspective, "one could affirm that Christianity supersedes

other religions as ways of salvation" (77), but other religions might be found to be superior to Christianity in other ways.

5. With minor variations, the first two sections of this chapter are a summation of the theology of Bernard Lonergan on the person and work of Jesus Christ. See *The Ontological and Psychological Constitution of Christ*, transcription by Michael G. Shields. Vol. 7 of *Collected Works of Bernard Lonergan* (Toronto: University of Toronto Press, 2001). See "The Redemption," in *Theological and Philosophical Papers 1958–1964* and "Mission and the Spirit," and "Healing and Creating in History," in *A Third Collection: Papers by Bernard J. F. Lonergan, S.J.*

6. See chapter 3, the section titled "Biblical Witness," and chapter 4, the section "Belief in the God as Triune."

7. Both texts cited in this paragraph, as well as Hebrews 1:8–9, are referenced in Raymond Brown, *An Introduction to New Testament Christology*, as New Testament passages that clearly refer to Jesus as God (185–89).

8. Gregory Nazianzen, Letter 101, in *Christology and the Later Fathers*, ed. Edward Hardy and Cyril Richardson (Philadelphia: Westminster, 1959), 218. For further patristic references see the Second Vatican Council's "Decree on the Missionary Activity of the Church" (*Ad gentes*) 3, footnote 4, in Flannery, *Basic Sixteen Documents*, 454–55.

9. Thomas Aquinas, *Summa theologiae*, III, q. 2. Helpful in understanding the metaphysical terminology employed on this topic is Appendix 2, "Technical Terminology," by R. J. Hennessey, O.P., in vol. 48 of *Summa theologiae*, Latin/English edition (New York: McGraw Hill, 1976).

10. This is the contemporary translation of individual being or "subsistens distinctum" which W. Norris Clarke, S.J., proposes and develops in his *Person and Being*, The Aquinas Lecture, 1993 (Milwaukee: Marquette University Press, 1993), 29.

11. Lonergan, "Christology Today: Methodological Reflections," 91.

12. Edward Schillebeeckx discusses affirmatively, although with great nuance, Jesus' sense of his death as salvific in *Jesus: An Experiment in Christology* (New York: Crossroad, 1979), 307–12.

13. See Pieris, *Love Meets Wisdom*, 87. Because of the Buddha's nobility, Pieris specifies the Buddhist-Christian tension: "To put it more precisely, the crux of the problem is whether it is Jesus or Gautama who is unique in the sense of being the exclusive medium of salvation for all" (131).

14. Bernard Lonergan, S.J., *De Verbo Incarnato Supplementum*, 1963–1964, transcription by Michael G. Shields, S.J. (1988), 11 and also in article 35 of the same text, 23.

15. The comment appears in the chapter in *Insight* on the demand of the human spirit for ethical behavior, even as the human spirit is frustrated in its response to the demand (653).

16. Thomas Aquinas, *Summa theologiae*, III, q. 48, a. 6.

17. See chapter 8 of this work on primary and secondary causality.

18. I assume the understanding of the divine Trinity articulated in the psychological analogy in chapter 6.

19. See *Insight*, 743–51, for the philosophical background of this theology.

20. Two recent studies that examine the theories of redemption as punishment and restoration of justice, together with other theories, are Vernon White, *Atonement*

and Incarnation: An Essay in Universalism and Particularity (Cambridge: Cambridge University, 1991), and Michael Winter, *The Atonement* (Collegeville, MN: Liturgical Press, 1995).

21. For a reflection on Lonergan's theory of the law of the cross parallel to that presented in these pages, see William P. Loewe, "Lonergan and the Law of the Cross," *Anglican Theological Review* 59 (1977): 162–74.

22. The scholastic theory is that evil is a lack of good, a *privatio boni*. Good is something. Evil is a lack of something that ought to be. In this sense, evil can be said to be "literally nothing."

23. A major category of Lonergan's metaphysics of being, explanatory of how redemption emerges within the development of world historical order, is that of emergent probability. See *Insight*, 144–51, 476–84, and passim. See also Lonergan's "Healing and Creating in History," in *A Third Collection*.

24. For a survey of relevant conciliar texts, besides those mentioned in this and the preceding chapter, see Jacques Dupuis, S.J., *Jesus Christ at the Encounter of World Religions* (Maryknoll, NY: Orbis, 1991), 136–40.

25. J. A. Dinoia, O.P., maintains that "[t]he providential roles or divinely willed missions of other religions might include the function of teaching some truths to the Christian community." See *The Diversity of Religions*, 92.

26. As mentioned in the preceding chapter, the International Theological Commission leaves open for reflection and discussion how non-Christian religions are salvific, in some relationship to the redemptive work of Jesus. See "Christianity and the World Religions," Origins 27 (1997): 152 (n. 8), 159 (n. 63), 161 (n. 84).

Index

About the Author

Peter Drilling is professor of systematic theology and pastoral studies and chair of the Pastoral Studies Department at Christ the King Seminary in East Aurora, New York. Some of his published works include a book on the relation of the doctrine of the triune God to several aspects of Christian ministry, *Trinity and Ministry* (1991), and a 1993 article studying how a trinitarian ecclesiology came to be adopted in the documents of the Second Vatican Council.